Dismantling a Nation
The Transition to Corporate Rule in Canada

Second Edition

Stephen McBride and John Shields

Fernwood Publishing
Halifax

Editing: Robert G. Clarke and Brenda Conroy
Design and production: Brenda Conroy and Beverley Rach
Cover collage: Richard Slye

Printed and bound in Canada.
A publication of Fernwood Publishing.

Fernwood Publishing
Box 9409, Station A
Halifax, Nova Scotia
B3K 5S3

Canadian Cataloguing in Publication Data

McBride, Stephen

Dismantling a nation.

      Includes bibliographical references and index.
      ISBN 1-895686-81-4

1. Canada -- Politics and government -- 1984–1993. * 2. Canada -- Politics and government -- 1993– * 3. Canada -- Economic policy -- 1945-* I. Shields, John, 1954– II. Title.

FC630.M27 1997   971.064`7   C97-950035-4
F1034.2M33 1997

This book is dedicated to
Monica and the late Fred McBride and Flo and Harold Keeton
Jessie and the late Jack Shields and Jean and John Neuert.

Contents

Preface to Second Edition

Many people have provided encouragement and support to us in undertaking the revision and updating of the first edition of this book. In particular we would like to thank our publisher, Errol Sharpe, and Greg Albo, who provided detailed suggestions for the reorganization of chapters to make the book more useful for a student audience. The text was improved through comments received from Bill Carroll, Bryan Evans, and the interventions of Robert Clarke, Brenda Conroy, and Beverley Rach.

Stephen McBride would like to acknowledge financial support from SSHRC for a project on labour markets—some of that research is alluded to here. As well the BC Work Study program made possible the helpful research assistance of Elinor Delgatty and Maggie Lam. Linda Wong proved a research assistant of great diligence and insight and her contributions are gratefully acknowledged. In the Department of Political Science at Simon Fraser University a number of colleagues—in particular Andrew Heard, Michael Howlett, and Paddy Smith—answered queries on their areas of specialization, and all colleagues and staff in the department have created a most supportive environment for research and writing. The computer and word processing skills of Maggie Nicolson meant that a very tight final deadline was actually met.

John Shields would like to thank the International Social Sciences Institute, and in particular Professor Ged Martin at the University of Edinburgh, Scotland, for sponsoring him as a visiting associate during the summer of 1996. It was there that his contributions to the second edition of this book were begun. John would also like to acknowledge the continued support of a number of colleagues and friends, including Mike Burke, Janet Lum, Diane Granfield, Gerda Kaegi, Colin Mooers, Bob Russell, Larry Stickland, and Len Wallace. The Chair of the Department of Politics, Carla Cassidy, and the Dean of Arts, Errol Aspevig, are owed a special debt of thanks for their key roles in nurturing a research-friendly environment at Ryerson.

Last but not least, none of this would have been accomplished without the active support of our families. To Jan, Emily, Morna, Shona, Hawley, and Raya, thanks.

Stephen McBride   *John Shields*
North Vancouver   *Toronto*

Introduction

Publication of the first edition of *Dismantling a Nation* coincided with the 1993 federal election; the appearance of the second edition comes on the heels of another national electoral contest. In 1993 the government passed from the hands of the Progressive Conservative Party to those of the Liberal Party amid hopes of a change in political direction from the neo-liberalism pursued by the Mulroney Conservatives. Such hopes were to be dashed as the Chrétien government moved to implement a neo-liberal agenda with greater vigour than its predecessor—a process recorded in some detail in the following pages. Despite this record and continued evidence of public opposition to neo-liberal values, the result of the 1997 election was another Liberal government, albeit with a substantially reduced majority and only 38 percent of the popular vote.

On the political left, the New Democratic Party, with 11 percent of votes cast, was able to regain official party status in the House of Commons and achieved a significant electoral breakthough in Atlantic Canada. However, the chief opposition to the Liberals will come from the right. The western-based Reform Party became the official opposition with increased seats (none of them to the east of Manitoba) but with a static share of the popular vote—19 percent. The Progressive Conservatives re-established their presence as a recognized political party in Parliament, with 19 percent of the vote but with fewer seats than any of the other parties. The Bloc Québécois, the exclusively Québec-based separatist party, declined in its level of popular support from the last election but was still able to secure 38 percent of the Québec vote and the majority of the seats in that province.

Parliament has become more politically and regionally fragmented as a result of the 1997 election. The bulk of the popular vote, 76 percent, and over two-thirds of the seats (235 out of 301) went to parties with explicitly neo-liberal platforms—the Liberal, Reform and Progressive Conservative parties. But while the bulk of Canadian voters may have cast their national ballots for parties that have embraced neo-liberal ideology, this is not necessarily a reflection of broad-based ideological agreement with neo-liberal policies. Rather, it may be the result of the complex matrix of contemporary electoral politics, dominated as it is by media images, content-less campaigning, and negative voting. When mass public attitudes have been probed, they reveal strong support for a wide array of social policies, public health care, and government action on job creation over neo-liberal deficit fighting and tax cuts (Salutin 1997:12). Yet such attitudes find little expression in the electoral process.

The focus of this book is upon the effects of neo-liberal policies on the Canadian state, nation, and society. It addresses the various crises that are part of Canadian politics—the crisis of "permanent recession," which has gripped Canada since the early 1980s; the crisis of national disunity and its potential to splinter the state; and the crisis of political sovereignty and the very survival of the state in the face of globalizing pressures. Neo-liberalism is depicted as part response, part creator of these crises.

Our central argument is that the neo-liberal agenda threatens the continued existence of Canada. There is ample evidence to suggest that Canada in 1997, a decade and a half into the neo-liberal revolution, is far more fragile as a nation than it was in 1984. Québec separatism has become a more powerful and threatening force, the federal parliament is more regionally fragmented and cantankerous, we are economically and culturally more closely integrated into a continental order dominated by the United States, and, at a societal level, there are heightened levels of polarization, exclusion, and alienation. While not the root cause of all of these problems (for example, the Québec question and regional divisions have deep and long-standing causes that pre-date the hegemony of neo-liberalism), neo-liberalism has served, as we shall see, to amplify such divisions and tensions. Because it plays into pre-existing divisions and assaults the role of the state—the fundamental building block of Canada's political nationality—neo-liberalism plays a more destructive role in the continued national existence of Canada than the ideology has tended to play in other countries.

The corrosive force of neo-liberalism has been insufficiently acknowledged in the debates about the future of the Canadian state. Our intention is to go beyond rhetorical arguments and to document, through careful analysis of its theory and practice, how neo-liberalism undermines the conditions necessary for Canada's continued existence.

The first edition of *Dismantling a Nation* largely chronicled the Mulroney Conservative Government's tenure in Ottawa between 1984 and 1993. In the current edition we extend our analysis to cover the first Liberal government of Jean Chrétien (1993–1997). The Mulroney government's policies were driven by an ideological predisposition for neo-liberal economics, free trade, minimal state involvement in the economy and society, and social policy retrenchment. In the first edition we referred to this combination of policy preferences as "neo-conservatism." We received a fair amount of commentary on our usage of the term neo-conservative, much of it suggesting that "neo-liberalism" was more descriptively appropriate as it places emphasis on the central component of the ideological direction—its neo-classical (liberal) economic orientation. We decided to adopt the neo-liberal designation as a more useful description of the political agenda that has been dominant in Canadian national politics since the early 1980s—an ideological direction that can be equally applied to the tenures of Progressive Conservative and Liberal governments.

Ironically, while the Liberals were the national political party that oversaw and administered the construction of the Canadian welfare state, they have proven to be most effective and efficient architects of its dismantling. While in opposition the Liberals were harsh critics of the Conservatives for their one-sided focus on fiscal restraint to the neglect of social, environmental, cultural, and employment policy. But upon assuming office the Liberals became even more committed to deficit reduction, cutting much further and faster than their Conservative predecessors. The chief victims of budget cuts have been fiscal transfers to the provinces for social welfare, health, and post-secondary education, the federal (un)employment insurance program, and the federal public service (see Swimmer 1997; Evans and Shields forthcoming).

Indications are that the re-elected Liberals will stay the course on deficit elimination and then turn to the task of reducing the total government debt load and issuing tax breaks (McCarthy 1997:A1–A2). A return to an activist federal state and a renewed social policy focus seems quite unlikely despite the fact that economic growth has failed to reduce the unemployment level below 9 percent, where it has been for nearly seven years; income inequality has increased; and there has been a dramatic rise in child poverty rates (see for example Naiman 1997:ch. 5; Clarke 1997:124–27).

The subtitle of the first edition of *Dismantling a Nation* was *Canada and the New World Order*. This gave emphasis to the important changes in capitalism under which neo-liberal political agendas are being played out. Globalization has been the catch phrase used to depict the growing internationalization of capitalism, which poses a threat to national governance: Globalization is about "the worldwide wave of liberalization of trade, investment and capital flows and the consequent growing importance of these flows and of international competition in the world economy" (International Labour Organization 1996:1). The process of the internationalization of capitalism has fostered "deep-seated economic and social changes" that have helped to erode "the social contract—the predominant understandings about core economic and social relationships—that was built during the postwar era" (Banting, Hoberg and Simeon 1997:4). The power of capital has been strengthened by threats to relocate if its demands for enhanced flexibility with regard to taxes, state regulation, and labour-market policies are not met by policy-makers. The neo-liberal political agenda has both shaped and been advanced by globalization.

Neo-liberal policies implemented by all the major states have facilitated the internationalization of capitalism since the 1980s. In turn this has contributed to strengthening supporters of neo-liberalism who argue that "there is no alternative." We have subtitled the current edition of this book *The Transition to*

Corporate Rule in Canada. The new subtitle highlights the class dimension to the political power shift that neo-liberalism entails—a dimension frequently ignored in both popular and scholarly accounts of these developments in political economy. Fundamentally, neo-liberalism is about shifting decision-making power to the marketplace and establishing a government policy environment that is driven by corporate priorities. In these ways neo-liberalism represents the move to corporate dominance in Canada.

In Chapter 1 we look first at the role of the Canadian state and its historic statist legacy. Next we examine the ascent of neo-liberalism as a political and economic doctrine. Its rise can be traced to external political developments in countries such as the United States and Britain. Although its proponents have sought to modify the ideology to fit Canadian conditions, neo-liberalism remains fundamentally incompatible with the basic principles of the Canadian polity— particularly the well-established traditions of public enterprise and collective social provision.

Chapter 2 turns to consider the growth and rationale for the development of an interventionist state in Canada. Special consideriation is given to the difficulty of creating the Keynesian welfare state given Canada's federal political structure and the trade dependence of its economy. Nonetheless, a Canadian version of a Keynesian-based welfare-state structure was gradually constructed. Without exaggerating the depth of Canada's attachment to the Keynesian regime, we stress that developments in Canada contrasted significantly with those in the United States and profoundly contributed to national integration. Finally outlined is the crisis of the welfare state, caused by both domestic and global forces, which created a political opening for neo-liberalism's rise.

The dismantling of the post-war economic order is addressed in Chapter 3. The neo-liberal policies of the Mulroney and Chrétien governments as they relate to macroeconomic policy (especially deficit reduction), privatization and deregulation, industrial relations, and regional development are considered. In Chapter 4 the attack on the Keynesian social order is examined. Here federal support to social policies, health care, unemployment insurance, and cultural policies are scrutinized. A consistent pattern of state retrenchment aimed at attacking the Canadian Keynesian welfare state is observed. The foundations of post-war Canadian order have been eroded considerably under Mulroney and Chrétien; the process of dismantling the state has only been slowed by the lack of broad-based public attachment to neo-liberal values and the institutional restraints of federalism. The extent to which these constraints are themselves eroding is considered in the concluding part of the chapter.

In Chapter 5 the constitutional crisis of Canadian federalism receives attention. We focus on the Mulroney years and the implication of neo-liberal ideology in some of the proposals for constitutional reform, including the Meech Lake Accord, the post-Meech process, and the Charlottetown Accord. Never the driving force behind the constitutional agenda, neo-liberals nevertheless sought to use constitutional openings to institutionalize their opposition to the redistributive state.The defeat of the Charlottetown Accord in October 1992 had the effect of temporarily preserving the constitutional status quo.

The victory of the anti-Québec sovereignty forces by only the narrowest of margins in the June 1995 vote should have given federalists reason to pause. Neo-liberalism's reduction of the role of the state had, over time, made the federal government increasingly less relevant to Québecers, especially in the realms of social and employment policies. This played a part in accounting for the weakness of the federalist vote. However, Ottawa's post-referendum response has been to weaken the federal state still further by devolving policy responsibilities to the provinces. This movement to "flexible federalism" also served to accomplish the neo-liberal goal of weakening national standards and policy capacity. Radical decentralization of political power in Canada is at least partially driven by the neo-liberal preference for weak government. But it gives Québecers, and for that matter everyone else, fewer positive reasons for belonging to the political community known as Canada. These issues are the concern of Chapter 6.

In Chapter 7 we explore the role which the Canadian state has played in the historical interplay between the forces of nationalism and continentalism leading up to the free-trade agreements. The ideology of comparative advantage (free trade), an integral component of neo-liberalism, is examined and the position of Canada in the new global order is considered. A world of regionally-based trading blocks engaged in intensified competition, creating higher levels of instability and increased risk of economic crises, appears to have been the end product of globalization and its ideological counterpart, neo-liberalism.

The most fundamental assault on the Canadian polity and the Keynesian state system is represented by continental free-trade agreements—the Free Trade Agreement (FTA) and the North American Free Trade Agreement (NAFTA). The implications of these agreements are clear: the logic of a continental market brings extreme pressures to harmonize the Canadian system with our more powerful neighbour to the south. This result is attractive to Canadian neo-liberals, because strong resistance to their legislative "reforms" could well be bypassed if enough people see the shift in policy direction as being induced by the "natural" forces of the market rather than as the result of government initiatives. In Chapter 8 we examine the provisions of FTA and NAFTA on such matters as the resolution of trade disputes and the future disposition of Canadian natural resources like water and energy. In light of the growing link with Washington, we examine the implications for Canadian sovereignty and the paradox of the neo-liberals' anti-statism combined with their simultaneous need of a strong state for market-enhancing purposes.

At the time of writing, the Organization for Economic Development and Cooperation (OEDC) is secretly negotiating a Multilateral Agreement on Investment (MAI). If approved, it will represent a broad corporate charter of rights and freedoms that goes beyond even the provisions of NAFTA: "Any government program requiring foreign capital to invest in local communities—through job-creation quotas, living-wage requirements, or community re-investment—would be deemed "discriminatory." Many grants and loans that "favour" small businesses would also be banned. Other outlawed actions would include any attempt to keep foreign investors out of certain sectors, such as utilities; regulations designed to hinder job flight to low-wage countries; and sanctions against corporations with unethical ties. Under MAI, many of the South African anti-apartheid boycotts would have been illegal. To top off the coup, corporations will have the power to sue local governments for any failure to comply, and disputes will be resolved through binding arbitration" (Klein 1997:44).

This is a clear attempt at decimating the policy capacity of nation-states and ensuring that popular democracy will not be able to subvert the will and self-interest of corporate decision-makers. This agreement, once in place, will truly consolidate the transition to corporate rule. Challenges to these developments are most evident so far in the extraparliamentary arena—from the country's great wealth of social action organizations working from the grassroots—the "organizations of dissent" (see Carroll 1997)—and an increasing social-unionism orientation (Russell 1997) in the activities of organized labour.

Chapter 1

The Canadian State
and the Neo-Liberal Revolution

The conventional wisdom is that the "golden age" of the nation-state is over. The nation-state, which dominated the political stage for several centuries, is held to be losing power and capacity as a result of "globalization." We do not subscribe to the view that this process is an inevitable product of uncontrollable structural forces or that it need render the nation-state irrelevant. Nevertheless, as a description of trends over the past couple of decades, the thesis of the eroding capacity of nation-states has considerable validity. Globalization itself pre-dates but seems to have been stimulated by the economic crisis of "permanent recession," which struck most of the world's economies in the mid-1970s and from which they have not emerged. The era of permanent recession has seen momentous changes in world politics:

> The collapse of the communist regimes between Istria and Vladivostok not only produced an enormous zone of political uncertainty, instability, chaos and civil war, but also destroyed the international system that had stabilized international relations for some forty years. It also revealed the precariousness of the domestic political systems that had essentially rested on that stability. The tensions of troubled economies undermined the political systems of liberal-democracy, parliamentary or presidential, which had functioned so well in the developed capitalist countries since the Second World War. They also undermined whatever political systems operated in the Third World. The basic units of politics themselves, the territorial, sovereign and independent "nation-states," including the oldest and stablest, found themselves pulled apart by the forces of a supranational or transnational economy, and by the intranational forces of secessionist regions and ethnic groups. . . . The future of politics was obscure, but its crisis at the end of the Short Twentieth Century was patent. (Hobsbawm 1995:10–11)

The impact of this general crisis on multi-lingual or multi-ethnic federations has been profound. In the last decade two of them—Yugoslavia and the

U.S.S.R.—have disintegrated amid conditions of civil war or political chaos. In Canada, to which it was once predicted the twentieth century would belong, there is real doubt that the country will survive long into the twenty-first century. And, many would argue that, even if it does, it will be in a dramatically changed form.

Most analyses of Canada's present crisis and uncertain future emphasize the linguistic, regional, cultural, and national tensions associated with the federal system and, in particular, the place of Québec in Canada. These are clearly central issues and this book will certainly recognize their importance. The emphasis of our analysis, however, will be on the impact in Canada of the more general crisis that the world has experienced; permanent recession, and the dominant political response to it: neo-liberalism.

By neo-liberalism we mean the theoretical and practical rejection of the active state that had emerged in the Keynesian post-war era, and its replacement by *laissez-faire* free-market doctrines and practices.[1] We recognize that neo-liberalism may come in a number of variants, depending, in part, on political party and national context. However, its essential features seem to lie in its determination to reduce the state and to rely increasingly on market mechanisms and individual rather than collective approaches to economic and social problems. The driving force behind the neo-liberal revolution has been the corporate sector. Neo-liberalism provides the perfect ideological vehicle for a transition from a society based on democratic political decision-making to one where many issues are outside politics and are settled by the undemocratic rule of the marketplace. Here, we are concerned principally with the effects of neo-liberal ideology on the existence and future prospects of the Canadian state.

Our central argument is that neo-liberalism has a more corrosive effect on the continued existence of Canada than it does on most other countries and that its impact has been insufficiently recognized in Canadian debates about the crisis of national unity. The pursuit of market-centred approaches to the resolution of economic problems has reinforced the disintegrative tendencies emanating from regional, cultural, and national tensions. Thus, while neo-liberal policies are not solely responsible for Canada's crisis of Confederation, the politics of neo-liberalism have worked to magnify pre-existing cleavages. The fragile foundation of the Canadian union is a consequence of the country's binational origins, its highly regionalized nature, and its location near to, close association with, and economic dependence upon the United States. The neo-liberal agenda of the federal Progressive Conservative government of 1984–1993, of its Liberal successor and of a number of provincial governments of various party labels has served to undermine the uneasy basis for national unity.

During the 1970s and 1980s there were vigorous debates about the role played by the state in capitalist society. Much of the discussion focused around two major activities: facilitating capital accumulation and ensuring the legitimation of the system (see, for example, O'Connor 1973). However, in Canada's case, the state has also been instrumental in the very creation and survival of the nation itself, and Philip Resnick argued that, at least for English Canada, the state pre-dated the development of a Canadian nationality and was the major instrument for fostering its growth (1990:207). Although not unrelated to accumulation and legitimation, an additional and distinctive role of the state is the creation and defence of national sovereignty itself (Resnick 1990:116).[2] The uncertainty surrounding national survival (or maintenance of sovereignty) is, in our view, tightly linked to the state's strategy for facilitating capital accumulation in the period of permanent recession—a strategy that has relied on market mechanisms rather than state involvement—and on its failure, in the same period, to perform legitimation activities adequately.

The notion that the state has been central to Canada's political existence extends far beyond the debates just cited, concerning the nature of the state in capitalist society. From a different theoretical perspective Donald Smiley (1967) argued that Canada was a uniquely *political* nationality. The state has always had a special role to play in the development of Canada. Alexander Brady once observed, "The role of the state in the economic life of Canada is really the modern history of Canada" (quoted in Brooks and Stritch 1991:28).

There have been a number of explanations for the relatively activist Canadian state. One line of thought is that an interventionist state was necessary to preserve an independent nation to the north of the forty-ninth parallel. The creation in the early twentieth century of the Radio Broadcasting Corporation (which would later become the CBC) and Trans-Canada Airlines (later Air Canada), for instance, was part of a project "to reinforce national unity in the face of American entrepreneurship" (Appel Molot 1990:508). George Grant (1965) saw the unrestricted marketplace and the encouragement of closer ties to the United States as fostering an extreme individualism that undermined a more distinctive Canadian culture rooted in a greater respect for order and community values. The threat of "America" is a theme that partially explains the act of Confederation itself. Similarly, others have argued that Confederation and the ensuing major commitment to the use of the state for the purposes of public policy could best be explained in terms of "defensive expansionism"—the need to protect the North West from the expansionary aims of U.S. interests (Aitken 1967). Some of these accounts place an emphasis on the building of a distinctive political community in a hostile environment; Canada was forged in spite of great geographical obstacles; it was a triumph of human will over nature (Simeon and Robinson 1990:47). All of these explanations for an activist government are rooted in the Canadian state's role in establishing sovereignty.

A more decidedly economic explanation of the Canadian statist tradition can be found in the staples theory favoured by one of the major schools of thought within Canadian political economy. Harold Innis maintained that Canada was not created as a reaction to U.S. expansionism but was a natural outgrowth of the territory's trade in natural resources. Canada was made because of its geography, not in spite of it. This trade in primary products placed special demands on the state—demands linked to the process of capital accumulation. Because of the large amounts of money necessary to develop transportation networks to bring Canadian staple products to foreign markets, and the reality of the shortage of private capital, the state was the only agency that could help build and finance such infrastructural megaprojects (Innis 1975:400). An interventionist Canadian government was thus necessary to stimulate growth and create a viable "national" market "through the development of 'infrastructure'—railways, canals and, later, roads and electric power" (Simeon and Robinson 1990:47). In a study done for the Rowell-Sirois Report, J.A. Corry explained the "special" role for the state in the nineteenth century in a new society like Canada, in comparison to that in old Europe.

> In a new country, the state is saddled with positive duties of helping people to help themselves. Even though its ultimate function is only that of a referee, it must turn in and help to build the playing field before the game can begin. Thus it has been easy to get agreement on a considerable range of state action in the name of national development. . . . Laissez faire philosophy, as interpreted in this country, has never objected to the principle of state promotion of national development. . . .
>
> This kind of grandfatherly paternalism which distributes sweetmeats and is sparing of restraint has been a striking feature of Canadian government since Confederation. Subject to this qualification, laissez faire was long regarded as the appropriate political maxim. . . . The belief in a self-reliant individualism was strong enough to postpone any serious attempt at state regulation until the twentieth century and to prevent any significant development of social services other than education, until after the Great War. . . .
>
> While we have always made much bolder use of state assistance in industry, England went much further than we in providing services. (1939:3–6)

Corry's point—that in this earlier period the role of the Canadian state was strictly limited to the active nurturing of private capital accumulation—is of prime importance. In that era the state adhered to a doctrinaire *laissez-faire* approach to social policy. Canada may have been born with a "public enterprise culture," as Herschel Hardin (1974) describes it, but it was not initiated for altruistic reasons. A tradition of active state involvement owed its existence much more to the logic of crass class politics than it did to "romantic notions of the public purpose" (Gonick 1987:284).

The development of the Canadian state's role in society and economy can be described as a series of national policies (Fowke 1967:237–58). The first National Policy (1879–1930), initiated by John A. Macdonald and the Conserva- '

tive Party and taken up as well by successive administrations, was centred around building a national economy. The policy consisted of three major planks: first, the building of a trans-Canada railway, with the aid of massive government subsidies, to link the new economy on an east–west axis; second, a policy of high tariff walls to encourage industrialization; and last, encouragement and state sponsorship of high levels of immigration both to populate the West and to provide the labour for the new manufacturing enterprises in Central Canada. The involvement of the state in the task of nation-building fits neatly under its accumulation activities as well as its role in establishing political sovereignty.

The second national policy was forged, in large measure, in response to social disruptions expressed by Western farmers and the industrial and resource proletariat during the 1920s and 1930s. It took shape during the Second World War and was consolidated afterwards under the guidance of the federal government, which used its spending power and Keynes' rationale for an interventionist state to engineer a welfare state and to maintain economic management designed to achieve full employment. In terms of federal–provincial relations, this was the era of shared-cost programs and "cooperative federalism." These initiatives were a "response to the instability and inequities inherent in the operation of a market economy" (Leslie 1987:5).

The state can be viewed as the major arena where the regulation of class struggle under market capitalism occurs. Federal states are also concerned with territorial politics (conflicts between communities). Federal capitalist states are thus systems "regulating the conflicts and struggles of community and class" (Hueglin 1990:1). In the period of the second national policy the focus on both class and regional accommodation in Canada became prominent. Social class pressures from below were addressed through the development of the Keynesian welfare state. In terms of federalism, the social and political pressures of uneven economic growth became increasingly difficult to resist by the early twentieth century and were further accelerated by the Depression of the 1930s. The state eventually responded by developing a set of regional development programs and by regional transfer grants from more to less wealthy provinces, guided by the principle of equalization (Norrie, Simeon and Krasnick 1986:99).

In all Western countries the desire to contain class conflict provided an important motive for enlarging the role played by the state. In Canada the reality of federalism and regional inequality provided another. Consequently, in the period of the second national policy, building the sovereignty of the Canadian state came to be addressed increasingly through legitimation measures such as social policy and regional development initiatives. Although the role of the Canadian state in facilitating capital accumulation remained predominant, the balance between legitimation and accumulation was redrawn, to the greater benefit of the former. By the 1970s the statist tendencies in Canada's political economy were well-entrenched. In many respects they had become the defining characteristic of national identity.[3]

The implications of a more statist orientation to Canadian development, particularly with respect to questions of social and regional development, are important:

> Choosing closer economic integration with the United States has always meant choosing the American power and value systems as well. Those values have represented pure classical liberalism—what in the 1980s came to be called 'neo-conservative' economics, in which the marketplace is virtually the only arbiter of social values, the power of big business is unrestricted, and the values of extreme individualism are paramount. Choosing a more independent economic course for Canada has always meant not only emphasizing trade links outside North America and government strategies to diversify the economy beyond resource exports, but also embracing communitarian values to partially offset those of the predominantly economic liberalism. The Canadian soul has wanted a more peaceful and ordered society and has shown a greater willingness to use government and public institutions to compensate for the economic or social shortcomings of pure capitalism. (Laxer 1989:3)[4]

Neo-liberalism, of course, challenges precisely these features of the "Canadian formula."

Neo-Liberalism: Outlining the Doctrine

The first elected neo-liberal (or neo-conservative) regimes were in Great Britain and the United States. In Canada, piecemeal movement towards a neo-liberal policy agenda was first evident in the mid-1970s, but it was only in 1984, with the landslide victory of the federal Progressive Conservative Party led by Brian Mulroney, that a systematic shift in this direction occurred at the national level. Despite an election platform indication that a change of course was planned, the Liberal government elected in 1993 under Jean Chrétien has been firmly neo-liberal in its policies.

Neo-liberal doctrine proposes an "alternative to the logic of the post-war 'consensus' on economic and social policy" (Leys 1980:43). It is founded upon the belief that "the clock can be turned back and the dynamic of the market place restored" (Palmer 1980:41). To some degree, the social rights and benefits developed under the welfare state have been in a "constant flux, expanding in some periods and contracting in others" (Banting 1982:171). But the neo-liberal assault on the Keynesian welfare state is of a rather different nature than the "normal" policy flux that characterized the past. In the past governments might "restrain" social services during recessionary periods; these cuts were carried out with the intention that they were "temporary" and would be restored with the economic recovery. It was a policy, in short, emphasizing a continuity with past commitments to services. What is new is not "quantitative" cutbacks of resources for social services but rather the "qualitative" attacks on them. It is in these "qualitative" policy shifts that the distinctively ideological character of neo-liberalism is made clear (Gough 1980:7).

Modern neo-liberalism sees socialism embodied in almost all forms of collectivism, statism, and rationalism: "The trend toward centralization of power in the state and the use of that power to reorganize and plan social life in a systematic, self-conscious way." From the neo-liberal perspective, Keynesian liberalism, social democracy, and communism are but variations of the same phenomenon; some are simply "more benign than others" (Himmelstein 1983:18).

The core ideological thrust of neo-liberalism is *laissez-faire* economic doctrine. In the hands of conservative politicians this is often combined with the values of social traditionalism. However, the addition of such values does not seem to be a necessary element in neo-liberalism *per se* and different social values may serve as a point of differentiation between politicians or political parties that share an attachment to market economic doctrines.

The rediscovery of classical liberalism resulted from developments in modern economic theory and its application to political questions. Monetarism, supply-side economics and public choice theory were particularly important in the revival movement and supply both policy advice and ideological sustenance. We will consider each briefly.

Monetarist economics centres on the role of money in the economy and contends that government actions designed to stimulate or contract the economy will have little effect unless the money supply is altered (Buchholz 1989:227). Thus, inflation is produced by a sustained growth of the supply of money above the rate of growth of national output, and recessions and unemployment are induced by "unanticipated reductions of money growth" (Meltzer 1981:44). As a technical doctrine that addresses itself to the relationship between public expenditures and their financing, monetarism postulates that deficit financing has negative inflationary consequences, although it does not declare whether the way to eliminate public deficits is through raising taxes or cutting expenditures (Hoover and Plant 1989:156).[5]

Budget deficits are inflationary, according to monetarists, because if deficits are financed by printing money, prices will rise. This is because, as the quantity theory of money asserts, there will be more dollars chasing fewer goods. If the deficit is financed through borrowing, banks create new deposits, resulting in a de facto rise in the money supply. Either way, from the monetarist perspective, inflation is the result, and this causes industry to be less competitive, which in turn generates unemployment (McBride 1991:178).

Monetarists use the same rationale to attack Keynesian attempts to manage the economy. For them, government spending geared towards easing or preventing recessions only leads to inflationary pressures. This is because:

Government securities sold to finance a deficit during a recession represent additions to the private and public debt that the economy normally generates. Thus, when the economy moves back to a full-employment level of activity, they argue, the money supply must be increased in order to support the extra debt. With a larger money supply the price level will be forced up as full employment is approached. (Fusfeld 1990:157)

Job creation generated in such a manner is only temporary and comes at the cost of inducing inflation, which produces the conditions for another round of economic destabilization. Government attempts to produce stability in the economy are consequently doomed to failure (Donner and Peters 1979:13). Unemployment, from this perspective, is not a problem governments can solve, whereas controlling inflation through the sound management of the money supply is achievable.

Aside from carefully controlling the printing of money and resisting government debt generation, the state can undertake another policy initiative in its battle to control inflation. High interest rates serve an important function here, because they keep the value of money strong and constrain the involuntary growth of the money supply by making credit expensive.[6]

For its part, supply-side economics, as the name suggests, focuses upon supply and production rather than on consumption. It is essentially a reaction against Keynesian "demand management" economics:

Keynesianism is demand sided . . . and neglects or ignores the supply side of the economy. It stresses the manipulation of the components of aggregate demand to regulate the economy and assumes that whatever the level of such government stimulated demand, the supply to meet this will be forthcoming without producing serious economic problems. Supply-siders, however, challenge these assumptions. They argue that subsequent growth in the size of the government intervention in the economy will produce inflationary pressure, but also a moribund and inflexible supply position. They are particularly concerned with the conditions of labour supply in this context. . . . In general terms however the idea is to put strong downward pressure on the input costs of production, i.e. to increase the cost of competitiveness of the economy. (Thompson 1986:82)

A major plank in supply-side thinking is the rediscovery of Say's law of the market. The French businessman-intellectual Jean-Baptiste Say (1776–1832) argued that it was goods that in the end financed other goods. Businesses engaged in healthy levels of production and selling are naturally going to be in a position to buy more. Thus production rather than consumption is the key to economic progress. Supply-side economics shifted the focus from the Keynesian emphasis on economic equilibrium to the unabashed pursuit of economic growth through producer-oriented incentives (Bartlett 1982:1). As Say maintained: "The encouragement of mere consumption is no benefit to commerce; for the difficulty lies in supplying the means, not in stimulating the desire of consumption; and we have seen that production alone furnishes those means. Thus, it is the aim of good government to stimulate production, of bad government to encourage consumption" (quoted in Bartlett 1982:1). Say's law suggests that supply creates its own demand, and that in the longer term supply and demand are equalized if the market is allowed to operate freely. States need to centre their attention on creating conditions that facilitate aggregate production and supply. This necessitates flexibility in the price system (including the price of labour) so that conditions of equalization between supply and demand can be quickly realized (Thompson 1986:84–86; Gonick 1987:118).

Price flexibility is one of the key elements in the supply-side equation. It is a logic that forces government to direct its attention "towards the taxation and income maintenance side of budgetary policy" (Thompson 1986:86):

> The supply-side image of the economy is that of a great spring, held down by the weight of high marginal taxes and excessive spending. Take away the taxes that discourage risk taking and expansion, roll back the government spending that absorbs labor and resources that ought to be available to the private sector, and the inherent dynamism in the spring will manifest itself (Heilbroner and Thurow 1986:104).

For supply-siders tax cuts can operate as a "magical weapon." Like Keynesians, supply-siders maintain that cutting taxes can increase employment levels, but for opposing reasons. Tax cuts to the poor and middle classes are not necessary to stimulate consumer demand because it is supply that drives the economy. Rather, cuts in taxes should be directed towards the wealthy and business to induce savings and investments (Sherman 1983:157). It makes a critical difference where tax cuts are directed. Tax cuts that only increase spending (that is, cuts directed at the lower and middle classes) are negative because they have the effect of driving up demand without helping to increase the supply of goods; the result is inflation. Likewise, attempts by government to stimulate the economy through increases in state spending have similar negative effects. Supply again is not affected by such moves, and the increase in spending must be financed either through government borrowing, which "crowds out" private sector borrowers and increases interest rates, or by printing more money. Either way, inflation is the end result (Bartlett 1982:6).

In addition to a policy agenda favouring generous tax relief to capital, supply-siders are concerned with labour-market policy and welfare benefits. They consider that generous social benefits produce disincentives to work and that trade unions create monopolies of labour, forcing up the price of wages. Likewise, unions work to undermine the tendency of the price of labour to drop during periods of unemployment and recession. This undermines the role of depression as a necessary force in restoring the balance between the price and supply of labour (Chernomas 1983:133). Similarly, they argue, welfare measures such as unemployment insurance insulate individuals from market forces, often encouraging them to pursue leisure over work, which shrinks the size of labour markets, driving up the price of labour.

Thus it is argued that by creating an extensive welfare state, the government seduces people into becoming its dependent clients. According to this logic, supplying welfare payments creates welfare claims; unemployment insurance induces unemployment; financial aid to single mothers prompts single women to have children; and subsidizing medical care manufactures more sickness (Marchak 1988:190). Neo-liberals wish to dismantle the current welfare state (a system based to a degree upon universal benefits and increasing standards of provision) and replace it with a system of "disciplinary state policies based on minimalist, means-tested and discretionary benefits subject to cash limits, rationing and queuing" (Keane 1988:9). If there is to be a welfare role for the state it should be a residual one in which social spending becomes public expenditure of "last resort" (Galipeau and Johnson 1990:10).

Tactically, neo-liberals recognize the importance of attacking the universality of social programs. This is because:

> When the welfare state's clientele included the entire population, rather than narrowly targeted problem groups, the likelihood of a middle class backlash [against the welfare state] is significantly reduced. In other words, universalism in social policy manufactures its own universal political constituency, which in turn helps maintain a basic sense of social solidarity and shared responsibility. (Esping Andersen 1983:30–31)

Because universalism grants all members of the citizen body the same rights and treatment, it undermines "both the stigmatizing nature of poor relief and . . . the self-reliance mechanism of private insurance" (Esping-Andersen 1983:30). For neo-liberal values to triumph and for the welfare state to be successfully rolled back, the notions of social citizenship must be subverted. This logic helps explain the Mulroney government's assault on universality in Canada.

Thus, according to supply-siders, unions and social legislation operate to distort the natural price flexibility of the marketplace, resulting in higher levels of unemployment and wage-based inflationary pressures. Consequently, government policy should be directed towards eliminating these sources of inflexibility.

Kenneth Hoover and Raymond Plant argue that in practice monetarism and supply-side economics complement one another.

> The monetarist claims that demand management by central government is inflationary and is the major cause of unemployment. The cure for inflation is sound monetary policy whereby government borrowing is reduced progressively to zero. This can be done by raising taxes or cutting expenditure and in its narrow form is agnostic about these. The supply-sider holds that the causes of unemployment are due to lack of output, but unlike Keynes they do not look to a government stimulation of demand to increase output, but rather a reduction of taxation and regulation. It is the view of conservative capitalists that a combination of these policies is more likely to increase growth and cure poverty than state-contrived means to do the same. Most conservative monetarists hold to the supply-side doctrines . . . and therefore reject the theoretical option, held open within monetarist theory, to reduce budget deficits by raising taxation, because of what they see as the negative incentive effects which would follow from this. Hence a combination of monetarism and supply-side economics leads naturally to a critique of public expenditure and the principles and values which have underlain its growth since the Second World War. (Hoover and Plant 1989:33)

Neo-liberal economic doctrine represents a synthesis of what has come to be known as the "new neoclassical economics." New neoclassical economics is informed by a monetarist critique of Keynesian policies, "but it moves away from the monetarist preoccupation with the money supply to concentrate on the relationship between unemployment, inflation, expectations, and the 'supply side' of the economy" (Fusfeld 1990:179). It contends that there is a natural rate of unemployment at which the level of inflation rests at zero. If governments make artificial attempts to reduce unemployment below the natural rate by fiscal and monetary policies in an attempt to increase aggregate demand, the result will be a series of inflationary pressures that undo any short-term gains.

The notion of "rational expectations" is important to this theory; it maintains that people quickly learn, as governments stimulate the economy and drive up aggregate demand, that inflation is the result. Eventually, instead of a reduction of unemployment followed by inflation and then a movement of unemployment back to its natural level, "The time sequence is compressed until, after several experiences, the intermediate steps are eliminated. The economy responds immediately to increased aggregate demand with inflation, while unemployment is unaffected" (Fusfeld 1990:180).

The policies that flow from the new neoclassical economics are pro business. On the supply side of the economy, this approach offers business tax cuts and reductions in state regulation aimed at reducing costs of production, more tax credits to those with means to stimulate investment, and negative inducements to those outside the labour force to enter it. Such inducements include reducing or eliminating alleged disincentives to work such as welfare and unemployment benefits. The assumption is that, left alone, the economy operates at full employment. Unemployment results from the voluntary actions of workers who are simply waiting for jobs at higher wage rates (Fusfeld 1990:180–81). Decisions not to work are encouraged by the existence of social benefits and unemployment insurance.

The neo-liberal foundations of Canadian governments' economic and social strategy since 1984 are evident. The strategy is marked by: 1) encouraging market forces through a free-trade agreement with the United States and weakening social services and unions, which have operated as market barriers; 2) targeting deficit reduction and inflation rather than employment generation as the primary government objective (the primary means of deficit reduction and shrinking the state have been through gradually dismantling social programs); 3) restructuring taxes to make them more beneficial to capital; and 4) directly attacking the Canadian statist tradition through privatization initiatives and deregulation.

The basic rationale behind neo-liberal economic theory has also been extended to the analysis of politics in the shape of "public choice" theory. The main thrust of its logic has been summarized by Todd Buchholz: "If businessmen are self-interested, why not assume that government officials are 'political entrepreneurs'? What do they maximize? Their power and their ability to gain votes" (1989:243). Public choice theorists maintain that both politicians and bureaucrats are rational actors: politicians seek to maximize votes (and thus make promises to the electorate that state budgets cannot properly fulfill); and bureaucrats seek to increase the size and the power of their departments or programs (and thus increase their status and income) (King 1987:11). Human nature is selfish, and thus government officials must also be seen as fundamentally self-interested (Friedman 1989:99).

Milton Friedman contends that the widespread perception that the government is geared to satisfying the "public interest" is fallacious. Government, in this view, is seen, incorrectly, as operating by principles that do not hold for private sector business. In reality, however, the arena of politics is, like the private sector, an imperfect marketplace. In the political marketplace there is a great incentive and benefit for special interests to push their own policy agenda at the cost of the interests of the public at large: "The benefits are concentrated; the costs are diffused; and you have therefore a bias in the political marketplace which leads to ever greater expansion in the scope of government and ultimately to control over the individual" (quoted in Thompson 1986:69).

Neo-liberals have tended to identify the rise of interest-group politics with the overpoliticization of the mass public. A Trilateral Commission report, *The Crisis of Democracy*, first expressed concerns about "excessive democracy." The report maintained that the political system was being "overloaded with participants and demands." Such demand overload was being fed by an "adversary culture" cultivated by the media and liberal and social democratic intellectuals (Crozier, Huntington and Watanuki 1975:6–7, 12). Neo-liberals have often dubbed this adversarial force the "new class," which, they claim, is the major force behind the construction of the welfare state.[7] While welfare state policies were nominally constructed to aid the poor, according to neo-liberals, "They actually enriched and empowered the 'social engineers' who designed them and the army of bureaucrats and professionals who staffed them" (Ehrenreich 1987:167).[8]

Hence, public choice theory operates to delegitimize the notion of a "public" sector and feeds into populist disparagement of "big government" and "bureaucracy." For these theorists, democratic government has come to mean that the state is being forced to correct the problems confronting differing interest groups within society; government overload is the inevitable end result as demands come to exceed governmental ability to deliver. The economic consequence of political-demand overload is inflation, and the political result is ungovernability.

Public choice advocates express this point by contending that Keynesian economics have led to what they term "democracy in deficit." This has occurred because the Keynesian paradigm licensed politicians to spend without regard for budgetary deficits and long-term ability to repay these debts. Keynesianism, in effect, destroyed any effective constraints on the public purse. This was possible because Keynesian "free"-spending policies became mixed with "democratic" pressures on politicians to deliver more and better services to their constituencies, which inevitably led to the crisis of "democracy in deficit" (Buchanan and Wagner 1977:4–19).

Neo-liberals are thus critical of the form that modern mass democracy has taken, and they wish to restore the values of individualism and liberty that they believe serve as the pillars of a truly free society. Like classical liberals they are concerned with the dangers of arbitrary and oppressive majority rule and the tendency for majority rule to become the rule of its agents. They define "legitimate" political action as a "legal democracy" (Held 1987:247), which requires above all that the rule of law be upheld. The public and private realms must be clearly demarcated by law so that individual liberties and choices are protected. Consequently, for neo-liberals, government intervention in the private sphere must be minimized: "Citizens can enjoy liberty only if the power of the state is circumscribed by law; that is, circumscribed by rules which specify limits on the scope of state action—limits based upon the rights of individuals to develop their own views and tastes, to pursue their own ends and to fulfill their own talents and gifts" (Held 1987:249). Government intervention in society is only warranted "to enforce general rules, rules which broadly protect 'life, liberty and estate'" (Held 1987:250).

This is a restatement of classical liberalism's view that the chief threat to liberty comes from those who wield political power. The theory is blind to the effects of concentration of economic power in a supposedly free market. Indeed, a major assumption of neo-liberalism is that there is a direct relationship between democracy and capitalism, with the existence of a capitalist marketplace being an essential precondition for both economic and political freedom. For neo-liberals, freedom becomes defined as the freedom to compete. Keynesians and social democrats, however, have used the state for the pursuit of "welfare and equality rather than freedom" (Friedman 1982:5). Neo-liberals emphasize the distinction between the traditional civil and political rights that they regard as legitimate and the more recent social and economic rights that they see as driven only by people's desires, wants and needs. Thus, this category of rights should not be placed on the same plane as the more traditional civil and political liberties.

Neo-liberalism represents an assault upon the underlying logic of welfare state capitalism and on the mass-based democracy from which the welfare state emerged. It seeks to undo the norms surrounding mass-based democracy and the Keynesian welfare state by challenging a politics guided by the values of equality and based on the ability of groups to influence economic and social policy. Instead, neo-liberals promote the value of free-market individualism. Consequently, public institutions should be structured in a way that enhances the values of individual freedom. The state must be constrained in its spending and in its monopoly of power. "Constitutional government" becomes extremely important because it provides an avenue by which governmental activity can be limited (King 1987:12). Frederich August von Hayek contends that free government is always constitutional government, which limits the state's ability to act (1960:177–78). Governments must be circumscribed in their ability to interfere with the marketplace and thus maximize the ability of individuals to enjoy property.[9]

While democracy cannot be eliminated, it is possible, according to the new right, to "depoliticize the economy." Cy Gonick's observations about the position of monetarists is also true of the thinking of neo-liberals generally.

> Monetarists have a problem with unlimited democracy; their solution is to simply limit the powers of government and release the forces of the market. But they also have a problem with social justice. Like nature itself, the market order knows neither justice nor injustice. Free individuals put up with the costs of the market order if they want its benefits. Social obligation, the idea of solidarity between self and community, has no place in the monetarist logic. (1987:130)

In the neo-liberal view, of course, the "road to serfdom" is being designed by welfare state architects. Keynesians and social democrats closely link welfare and liberty; neo-liberals seek to break this association. The welfare state's function as dispenser of social justice requires that state officials distribute material resources on the basis of what it believes people should receive (Held 1987:250). Neo-liberals wish to depoliticize resource allocation, and they hope this can be achieved by freeing up the marketplace. For them the free-market system best perpetuates liberty and justice because it does not predetermine results but preserves "consumer sovereignty." Free-market capitalism promotes individual freedom and responsibility, the two foundational values for neo-liberalism (Shields 1990:158). Constitutionally this can be more easily achieved by entrenching property rights and by placing other limits on the state's ability to act independently.

In its neo-conservative variant, economic liberalism is combined with social traditionalism and expresses concern for, and plays upon, the popular values of morality, the work ethic, law and order, the preservation of the family and church, and the denunciation of feminism, homosexuality, sexual permissiveness, and drugs.[10] Clearly other variants of neo-liberalism do not share these social values and restrict their emphasis to economic individualism, the superiority of the market when compared to the public sector and so forth. However, a consequence of all forms of neo-liberalism, and in the view of neo-conservatives a desirable consequence, is an assault upon feminism—pushing women back into traditional roles in the family. According to neo-conservatives, the existence of the welfare state is undermining the conventional role of the family. A primary function of the family should be to provide a considerable amount of the health, welfare, and education of individuals; but these responsibilities have increasingly been shifted to the state (King 1987:17). Patricia Marchak clearly outlines the neo-conservative policy solution to this problem:

> If social services are removed from the public sector, private individuals will have to perform them. Someone must care for the children, the handicapped, and the elderly when no profit-making business can be made of them. Women are being urged to "return to the home." The new right argument is that they never wanted to leave it; they did so only because the high taxes levied to pay for social services obliged them to find paid employment. (1991:100)

A strong family is necessary to ensure that individuals do not become too dependent upon the state. In this way a male-dominated household comes to be linked to a free-market economy.

The Free Economy and the Strong State?
While classical liberal economics calls for a minimalist state presence, it requires a state strong enough to protect and promote market liberalism. In some countries this has permitted the association of neo-liberalism and nationalism. President Reagan in the United States and Prime Minister Thatcher in Britain, for example, were strong proponents of national discipline and a strong defence. They contended that the state had become too entangled in the economy and society and, as a result, had lost its effectiveness and authority. A reduction in the scope

of the state's activities would restrict its role but enhance its power. A strong state was seen as essential to defend property rights against the power of the trade unions and other special interests. Under their direction the coercive powers of the state would be enhanced, domestically to maintain law and order and externally to combat communism and other foreign threats (Gamble 1988:30, 36; also see Shields 1990; Hall and Jacques 1983), as well as to protect foreign investments. Reagan was a strong nationalist who wished to restore U.S. imperial hegemony irrespective of cost (Kuttner 1991:81). Similarly, Thatcher invested heavily in attempts to revive some of the grandeur of British colonialism (witness the Falklands War). The use of the state to promote civil obedience and patriotism was a major component of the New Right's bid for popular support.

In Canada, using the state simultaneously to promote patriotism and maintain federal state authority, while implementing a neo-liberal agenda, involves insurmountable contradictions. Canadian nationalism has always contained an anti-American element. This is because the major threat to Canada's existence has been consistently posed by its much larger southern neighbour, and Canadians have often defined themselves in relationship to the United States by stressing difference: "a Canadian is not an American." In Canada nation-building and an active state involvement in the economy have gone hand in hand. This was "natural" given the country's size and its staples-based economy. The state was necessary to maintain east–west linkages against powerful continentalist north–south pulls. The English Canadian identity has come to be closely tied to central government projects like the national railway, the CBC and, more recently, regional and social security programs. Indeed, as we noted earlier, in English Canada the state pre-dates the very development of a nation. All this contrasts with American championing of free enterprise and the free market—values that are also central to neo-liberalism, as we have seen. The difficulty in trying to associate neo-liberalism with Canadian nationalism is that the doctrines are in opposition to one another. Thus, neo-liberals favour policies such as continental free trade and closer links with the United States, deregulation and privatization, and dismantling the social programs that have served as ingredients of Canada's national identity.

The two nations question adds a further complicating factor to Canadian nationalism. This was especially true for the Mulroney Conservatives. In contrast to Trudeau's pan-Canadian vision, Mulroney played to Québec nationalist sentiments and forged a winning electoral coalition composed of Western Canadian regionalists (especially free enterprise Albertans) and Québec nationalist forces (including a strong component of Parti Québécois supporters). Part of the appeal for these interests was the Conservatives' promise to decentralize political power in Canadian federalism. Given the need to retain the support of Québec nationalists, and his own visceral pro-Americanism, Mulroney had to play down appeals to Canadian nationalism. The nationalist card so useful to the U.S. and British neo-liberals and neo-conservatives has thus been less available

to their Canadian counterparts.[11] This is because neo-liberalism is about dismantling the building blocks used in constructing Canada's uniquely *political*
nationality.

Notes
1. In the first edition of this book we used the term "neo-conservatism" to describe the
    market-based, anti-state strategies typified by the examples of Thatcher and Reagan
    internationally and that of Mulroney at home. However, similar policies are pursued
    by governments, Liberal and social democratic, that would reject the neo-conserva-
    tive label, but nevertheless buy into the logic of dismantling the state and unleashing
    market forces. In any event, as a number of commentators on the first edition have
    noted, neo-liberalism is a more accurate description of the return to classical liberal
    doctrines that was embodied in various "New Right" governments of the 1980s but
    that is also reflected in the doctrines and practices of their opponents. In this edition,
    therefore, we have used the term "neo-liberal" to depict the apparently hegemonic
    "common sense" of the 1990s and reserve "neo-conservatism" for that variant of the
    dominant paradigm in which the values of social conservatism were coupled with
    those of economic liberalism.
2. It should be obvious that here we are using categories such as accumulation,
    legitimation, and sovereignty to descriptively analyze state activity rather than to
    explain why the state acts in a certain manner, as some functionalist theories of the
    state may have attempted to do. In this regard we follow the advice of Ian Gough, who
    argues that while "we must reject any functionalist explanation of the [welfare] state,
    it is still useful to delineate the functions of the state, so long as they are used to
    indicate tendencies at work within the capitalist state" (1981:51).
3. For a recent version of this argument see Gwyn 1995:ch. 1.
4. In this quotation "Canadian soul" may be taken, at least in our interpretation, as a
    metaphor for a particular configuration of political economy, class forces, political
    culture, and institutional arrangements that made statism desirable, necessary, and
    possible.
5. Monetarist doctrine can, theoretically, come into conflict with the supply-side
    components of neo-liberal economics if the supply-siders advocate cutting taxes to
    encourage production without seriously addressing the question of the deficit. It was
    on just such questions that the Reagan administration ran into criticism from
    monetarist-oriented conservative groupings (Heilbroner and Thurow 1986:122).
6. Critics argue that monetarist policies that promote high interest rates tend to benefit
    the wealthier while disproportionately hurting the less well-off. This is because high
    interest rates support and expand the value of money, which aids the affluent and
    especially creditors. Additionally, high interest rates increase the cost of financing
    the public debt. This leads to public money being transferred from government
    coffers, that is, state revenues, to debt holders. The debt is owed primarily to the
    affluent while government revenues are raised out of the pockets of the general
    public, thus making such transfers inherently regressive (McBride 1991:191–92).
7. The "new class" is sometimes referred to as the "university-government-media
    complex." The use of this term by neo-liberals is revealing of the location of the
    groups that they view as responsible for promoting the "adversary culture." These are
    class forces, the neo-liberals argue, which are armed with the dangerous weapon of

the liberal and social democratic ideology of economic planning and social reform (Grosscup 1982:40–41; Kristol 1978:ch. 2). According to the neo-liberal position, the new class has waged an ideological war that has produced the political crisis of demand overload.

8.   The image of the poor as pawns of the new class is revealed in the following excerpt from the neo-liberal journal *The National Review:*

> The 'poor' must be understood in a special sense, as potential clients for the redistributive ministrations of the New Class, the middlemen of social justice. Analytically, 'the poor,' as a concept, legitimizes the power-grab of the New Class middlemen in the same sense as 'the proletariat' legitimizes the power-grab of the Leninists. (quoted in Ehrenreich 1987:167)

9.   To such arguments critics respond:

> It might well be argued that the market prevents the tyranny of majorities by institutionalizing, through the system of property rights and ownership, the tyranny of minorities—private property owners. Private property ownership is central to the market system and is thus the basis for success and power; this means that those weakly placed in the distribution of property are less well favoured. (King 1987:106)

10.   According to neo-conservatives, the humanistic value system of the new class was reflected in governmental policies and cultural trends in the post-war period and served to infect society, contributing to a "process of social breakdown and moral decay" (Himmelstein 1983:16). Part of the appeal of neo-conservatism is directed at "those who are disenchanted with modern life, anguished by its complexities, and dizzy from its rapid pace." In this regard, neo-conservatism directs society "to a better yesterday to comfort those frightened by the present" (Galipeau and Johnson 1990:6). It is an appeal to a more ordered and traditional social structure. Neo-conservatism's attempts to legitimate its policies are partly based on an espousal of these conservative social values. Neo-conservatism combines the liberal value of possessive individualism with a social conservatism in an effort to construct a strong defence of property rights against the attacks of "welfarist" politics. The liberal and conservative blend of ideology is contradictory in theory, but in practice these ideological tensions within neo-conservatism have caused little difficulty for new right politicians (King 1987:27). In fact the surface tensions displayed by the crosscurrents of ideas that make up the totality of neo-conservative thought do contain an internal unity. Desmond King sets forth the relationship in this way:

> Liberalism is the source of new right economic and political theories and policy objectives; conservatism provides a set of residual claims to cover the consequences of pursuing liberal policies. For example, the liberal objective of reducing public welfare provision implies a traditional role for women and the family; conservatism provides an ideology justifying such outcomes from public policy. (1987:25)

11.   The Reform Party offers a version of neo-conservatism complete with English Canadian national chauvinism (see Dobbin 1991).

Chapter 2

The Post-War Canadian State

Constructing the Keynesian Welfare State

At the ideological level neo-liberalism was a response to the perceived crisis of Keynesianism in the 1970s. At the level of social forces the attack on Keynesianism was carried by the corporate sector. The defenders of Keynesian arrangements in economic and social policy included labour and various popular sector organizations. The battle over the continuation of the Keynesian welfare state therefore represents a breach in the tacit class compromise of the post-war era. Establishing those arrangements had been a victory for labour and social action groups; dismantling them represented a victory for corporate interests and an important ingredient in the transition to corporate rule in Canada. Here we provide an outline of the Canadian state and its activities in the Keynesian era. In subsequent chapters we record the dismantling of these arrangements.

The adoption of Keynesianism by most Western countries in the post-war world was a response to the deep interwar economic crisis, the challenge of an ideological competitor in the shape of the Soviet Union, whose performance in the Second World War lent it enormous prestige in working-class circles, and the pressure from below for full employment, labour rights and economic security. Another factor was the experience of the Second World War: it seemed that an active state was quite capable of organizing not only a military victory but the economic activity that made it possible—a practical refutation of classical economic doctrines. The seminal experience was probably that of the Great Depression.

The Great Depression was a profound crisis that shook capitalism to its roots. Internationally it generated a political crisis as well. Capitalist nations, attempting to adjust to the new circumstances and end the crisis, engaged in wide-ranging political experiments, varying from fascism to social democracy. The period's legacy would be the emergence of the modern welfare state in the advanced capitalist nations.

In the aftermath of the Great Depression and the Second World War the classical *laissez-faire* doctrine of minimal state intervention was laid to rest in most Western countries—temporarily as we now can see. In Canada there was a marked change in the approach to social policy. Furthermore, the state's role in actually managing and regulating the economy was enhanced.

There was a general fear in the Western world that capitalism would drift back into deep economic crisis if reforms were not made. Even supporters of the capitalist system believed that, "without state intervention and regulation in the economy, the market simply would not survive" (Savage and Robins 1990b:3).

Thus it was deemed essential that capitalism be humanized and that the state provide a shield to protect the people from "the insecurities and hardships of an unrestrained market economy" (Piven and Cloward 1982:ix). Both economic and political stability were viewed as essential for economic growth to be maintained. This required the integration of the working class into the system. The growing power of the working class had been demonstrated by the rapidly increasing unionization and militancy of labour in the late 1930s and the 1940s. As well, in many countries, governments had committed themselves to giving labour a greater place in the sun in return for pledges of cooperation during the war.

In his book *The General Theory of Employment, Interest and Money* (1936) John Maynard Keynes provided the theoretical justification for state intervention within modern capitalism, and his views became widely accepted. Classical economics had rested on the belief that there existed "natural built-in equilibrating forces which ensured that a capitalistic economy would generate continuing prosperity and a high-level of employment." Economic downturns might occur, but they would trigger reactions that would set the equilibrium right. The Depression of the 1930s, however, undermined the belief in the existence of such equilibrating forces. Keynes set forth a major challenge to the classical paradigm by denying "the very existence of the self-equilibrating forces of the capitalist economy" (Buchanan and Wagner 1977:25):

> There is nothing akin to the "well-functioning market" which will produce optimally preferred results, no matter how well embedded in legal and institutional structure. Indeed, the central thrust of the Keynesian message is precisely to deny the existence of such an underlying ideal. "The economy," in the Keynesian paradigm, is afloat without a rudder, and its own internal forces, if left to themselves, are as likely to ground the system on the rocks of deep depression as they are to steer it toward the narrow channels of prosperity. . . . The overall direction of the economy by governmental or political control becomes almost morally imperative. (Buchanan and Wagner 1977:28)

Under the influence of Keynesianism, the capitalist state came to embrace a "legitimation" mandate based on the provision of material benefits to subordinate classes. Keynesianism was able to steer the capitalist state clear of both "the political shoals of conservative *laissez-faire*" and the massive state ownership that socialism would bring (Wolfe 1985:128).

The genius of Keynes was his ability to devise a technical solution to the crisis of capitalism, one that sanctioned a measured degree of government intervention while maintaining market dominance. The key to the "Keynesian solution" was the use of countercyclical fiscal measures to produce high and stable levels of both income and employment. Keynes shifted the focus of economic analysis towards the need for economic stability as the basis for generating necessary levels of aggregate demand in the capitalist economy and away from the "concern over the organization of production and supply."

By placing aggregate demand at the centre of its economic program Keynesianism was able to sketch a middle path for capitalist economic recovery, a path that sidestepped both the conservatives' concern with providing optimal conditions to encourage savings and the socialists' demand for the public ownership of the means of production. The ideological debate and struggle around the role of the state in the economy and society were consequently placed on the back burner (Wolfe 1985:128). Keynesian economics could compel capitalism to function better without at the same time upsetting the "underlying social relationships" of the system: "To a significant extent the particular appeal of the new Keynesian policies was to be found in the sense of 'changeless change' which they actually embodied" (Russell 1987:3).

Keynes's policy prescriptions not only provided credence for the active use of the state in fiscal policy matters; they also contained a vital social component. The development of an extensive network of social policies could be justified on the grounds that they contributed to high levels of aggregate demand: "This spending was legitimated, not as charity, but as 'automatic stabilizers' built into the economy to sustain aggregate demand in periods of cyclical downturns" (Wolfe 1985:128).

By the 1960s the responsibilities of government, throughout the Western world, were decidedly Keynesian: "full employment; a high rate of economic growth; reasonable stability of prices; a viable balance of payments; and an equitable distribution of rising incomes." In short, the state had come to be responsible for ensuring a measure of "equity, efficiency, stability, and growth" (Stewart 1991:92). Keynesianism helped to complete the logic of what is sometimes termed the Fordist regime of accumulation, the major elements of which have been characterized "as the era of the dominance of mass production (economies of scale, assembly-line production, detailed division of labour, separation of execution and control at the level of the workplace), balanced by high levels of mass consumption maintained by institutional supports which include Keynesian demand policies, and an accord between business and labour" (MacDonald 1991:182).

During the twentieth century, state involvement in the areas of education, health, social security, and the economy in general mushroomed in all the advanced capitalist nations. The greatest state expansion occurred in the period from the 1940s to the early 1970s under the aegis of Keynesianism; thus it is this timeframe that deserves the label "the golden age of the welfare state" (Gough 1981:1). There is no single statistic that can adequately and accurately measure the extent and impact of state involvement in the economy and society of modern capitalism, but one that is commonly utilized is government spending as a portion of Gross Domestic Product (GDP). In the Canadian instance, government's share of the GDP increased from 15.7 percent to 26.4 percent between 1920 and 1950, and by 1984 it had reached 46.5 percent (Banting 1986b:2; Bakker 1990:429, Table 2.1). This pattern of state expansion was not exclusive to Canada but represented part of a trend common to all Western democracies. In comparative terms, in fact, Canada falls into the lower third of developed nations with regard to levels of social spending (Canada 1985a, vol. 2:554). Comparatively speaking, while Canada enjoys a long statist tradition, it remains a welfare state laggard, although in the context of North America its social welfare status is "advanced."

Canada's adoption of Keynesianism was complicated by the federal system and the way it had evolved between 1867 and the 1930s. The authors of Confederation had intended a centralized federal system:

> The division of powers in the (BNA) gave the federal government control of the great apparatus of development—the massive capital equipment which formed the bones of the economy, from canals and railroads to lighthouses and harbours. With it went the two sovereign functions of government—defence and currency. Thus the full armed power of the state was centralized [with the obvious lesson of the American civil war in mind] and what is more important in peacetime, the control of banking, credit, currency and bankruptcy, in fact of the whole range of relationships central to the formation of capital was given to the Dominion.
>
> The rigid exclusion of the provinces from this field and the use of the power of disallowance to protect the sanctity of contract in the years before 1890 show how important this step was. Its effect was to exclude the provinces from interfering with the direction, control and operation of the economy. (Mallory 1954:25)

By the 1930s Canada's federation had become considerably decentralized. The causes of these developments lie in the complex interaction of social forces; institutional developments, including judicial reinterpretation of the British North America Act; and a dominant ideology that leaned increasingly to *laissez-faire* economics once the nation-building stage of Canada's economic and political history was judged complete (by the 1920s). The constitutional preference of that ideology, then as now, was for a weak state accomplished through decentralization.

Without putting explanatory weight entirely on judicial decisions, for these were reflections of social and ideological developments, the constitutional reinterpretation of the Judicial Committee of the Privy Council had, by the 1930s, produced an impasse. Jurisdiction had increasingly devolved to the provinces. The power of taxation, and hence fiscal capacity, rested predominantly with Ottawa. Thus one level of government had the authority to act in the social and economic areas where the impact of the Great Depression seemed to call for action, but that level of government lacked the fiscal capacity. The other level of government had the fiscal capacity but lacked the jurisdiction. The fact that political elites at both levels were ideologically opposed to government intervention on the scale necessary indicates that this was not entirely a constitutional problem. As the desperation of the Depression increased and the example of Roosevelt's New Deal resonated in Canada, along with the threatening spectre of communism and fascism in Europe, the constitutional impasse created a genuine obstacle to social reform, additional to that caused by the ideological blinkers of the governing class.

The ultimate resolution of this impasse by 1945 depended only partly on formal constitutional amendment, such as the transfer of unemployment insurance to the federal level in 1940. More important was the use of Ottawa's spending power in the post-war period to engineer shared-cost programs, meeting national conditions or standards, in areas of provincial jurisdiction. This system became known as cooperative federalism and it was under this label that the Canadian version of the post-war Keynesian welfare state was created. This development was made possible by the popular determination not to return to the conditions of the Great Depression, Ottawa's post-war prestige, and the legitimation afforded an active role for national governments by the Keynesian paradigm.

The impact, in Canada, of the provision of these benefits had profound effects, including providing an ingredient of Canada's national identity. Gradually Canadian citizenship came to mean more than simply having a formal set of "negative" constitutional rights such as "life, liberty and security of the person." It meant an assortment of more "positive" social welfare rights that "you are entitled to simply because you are a Canadian" (Rae 1991:i).

> Over time, the idea of a Canadian citizenship has evolved and broadened. Today, a national system of health care, an array of income support programs, free public and secondary education and affordable post-secondary education are claims that all Canadians make on their governments. Taken together, these programs represent and symbolize Canadians' sense of themselves as members of a community where solidarity and mutual responsibility are fundamental social norms. (Ontario Ministry of Intergovernmental Affairs 1991:2)

The Keynesian consensus, in its attempt to produce a stable and efficient capitalism, pursued universal social programs and other policies embodying principles of mild redistributive justice, and this helped to promote "a sense of common social citizenship" (Doern and Purchase 1991b:9). The bonds of modern citizenship have come to be "anchored in the social contract" (Ontario Ministry of Intergovernmental Affairs 1991:12), which, according to David Cameron, provided an "expression of the common interest and the sense of shared purpose that underlie a society and hold it together" (Simeon and Janigan 1991:36).

The Keynesian Welfare State in Canada
The social contract constructed in Canada after the Second World War rested upon four pillars. First, the state respected the key interests of capital: investment decision-making power was left in the hands of private enterprise. In exchange the state made three major concessions to labour that, together, constitute the post-war welfare state. It made commitments to pursue policies ensuring high, stable levels of employment and incomes. For individuals unable to participate fully in the labour market, the state would provide assistance, thus sanctioning the various aspects of the social welfare state. Last, the state made an "explicit commitment . . . to recognize and support the democratic rights of trade unions to bargain collectively to improve wages and living standards of their members and, in some instances, to participate directly in the determination of public policies" (Wolfe 1984:47). We will briefly outline each of these building blocks to set the scene for our account, in the remainder of the book, of the impact of neo-liberalism. One component of the post-war package, foreign trade, is dealt with separately in Chapter 7.

Full Employment
The Canadian version of full employment Keynesianism (cf. Campbell 1987:ch. 2) was launched by the 1945 White Paper on Employment and Income. It stopped short of promising *full* employment, preferring, instead, the phrase "high and stable levels of employment" (Canada, Department of Reconstruction, 1945). The focus was on the demand-side of the economy, leaving the supply-side to the private sector—an example of "bastard Keynesianism" in practice. The possibilities inherent in Keynes's discussion of the "socialization of investment" were ignored and the government's role was essentially limited to aggregate demand management by way of fiscal and monetary policy.

Doubts have been expressed about the strength of the commitment to full employment in Canada. For much of the post-war period unemployment, though low, exceeded levels in other Western countries (see McBride 1992:ch. 2), and some commentators have drawn attention to the passivity of fiscal policy in this period. Budgets, for example, tended to be passive rather than countercyclical. Policy goals were not limited to those favoured by the Keynesians, and the priority of various goals was contested rather than the subject of a consensus. Full employment certainly does not seem to have been the primary goal of government:

The economy experienced a few brief periods of "full" employment, but there were far more jumps than declines in the level of unemployment. In thirteen years in the post-war period [1945–1975], government economic policy was unsuccessful in preventing a substantial rise in the level of unemployment. In six other years, government policy did not encourage a fall in the level of unemployment. In the remaining years, a low level of unemployment was the result of healthy economic conditions. (Campbell 1987:191)

As well as suspicions that attachment to full employment on the part of state and business elites was less than whole-hearted, there were technical criticisms of Keynesianism that tended to attribute the blame for continuing unemployment to the Keynesian paradigm itself. It could be argued that the Canadian version of Keynesianism tended to focus on one type of unemployment—that caused by deficiencies in aggregate demand. Canadian unemployment rates in the 1950s and 1960s ranged from around 3 percent to over 7 percent. As it was argued that not all of this unemployment was of the demand deficient variety, aggregate demand measures derived from Keynes were unlikely to deal with it. Other more active measures focused on the supply-side of the economy, would be necessary.

Further modifications were suggested by the concerns about the allegedly inflationary effects of high employment levels. At or close to full-employment levels of aggregate demand, the argument ran, the balance of power in collective bargaining shifted towards the trade unions. If business, as was likely under conditions of high demand, granted wage demands that exceeded productivity increases, then inflation would result. These criticisms were to become more prominent in the 1970s before being swamped by the general rejection of Keynesianism that the triumph of neo-liberalism represented.

The view that the Keynesian era in Canada was not as Keynesian as it might have been certainly has some validity. From the perspective of the 1990s such criticisms help explain why neo-liberalism was able to sweep away the commitment to full employment with such apparent ease after 1975. Doubts about Keynesianism had deep roots and its adoption and practice was hardly institutionalized.

Nonetheless, such accounts do miss something. The notion that the adoption of Keynesianism may have been more rhetorical than real was not apparent to observers at the time. The terms of economic policy discourse had changed dramatically since the 1930s. Accepting the concept that maintaining full employment was an essential function of government changed the terms of political debate and the practice of politics itself. Moreover, during this period the Canadian state was operating in an international economic environment shaped by Keynesianism and in which many nations' policies did implement the paradigm. This had real implications in Canada as well and the depiction of a Canadian Keynesian era is not entirely a misnomer.

A *Social Safety Net*

The Canadian version of the Keynesian welfare state was constructed piecemeal and gradually. The Second World War provided a stimulus and saw the creation of some programs, but the process as a whole continued for years, culminating with the reform and expansion of the unemployment insurance system in 1971. The process had various origins: the demands of ordinary citizens for a better future—demands that under wartime full-employment conditions became more vocal and insistent; the realization of the elite that suitable plans for post-war society were an important motivating force in prosecuting the war; and the intellectual influences of Keynes's economic theories and the Beveridge Report on post-war reconstruction and social policy in Britain (Guest 1987).

Canada's own version of the Beveridge Report, Leonard Marsh's *Report on Social Security in Canada*, appeared in March 1943. It recommended full-employment policies, supplementary programs for occupational training, comprehensive systems for social and medical insurance (covering unemployment, sickness, maternity, disability, old age, and health), family or children's allowances, and general welfare assistance for those who, should the full-employment policies fail, had exhausted unemployment insurance benefits or were not covered by them (Guest 1987:212–13). The immediate policy impact of the Marsh report was modest: Canada's implementation of the report's recommendations proved tepid and unenthusiastic. As we have seen, this applied to the principle of full employment itself (McBride 1992; Campbell 1987, 1991).

Despite these important caveats, a version of Keynesianism was officially adopted in Ottawa; henceforth policy discourse took place in Keynesian terms and full employment was a legitimate goal of economic policy. In these respects Canada differed from its neighbour to the south, where the official reception of Keynesian ideas and policy goals was considerably cooler and occurred later.[1] The same point can be made about the creation of a welfare state in the two countries. Canada was not in the vanguard internationally, but the gradual piecemeal extension of programs did result in a more comprehensive social network than found in the United States, and the role of the state in promoting economic stabilization and social welfare arguably became an important element of political and national integration in Canada.

The federal government set up an unemployment insurance system in 1940 after a constitutional amendment had established federal jurisdiction in the area. Whether the delay in introducing unemployment insurance (UI) was attributable to the constitutional problem (see Pal 1988:151–52) or whether this served as a useful excuse for inaction (Struthers 1983:209–10) need not detain us here. The initial scheme was a cautious, actuarially sound system of insurance, which initially covered only 42 percent of the workforce (see Pal 1988:38–41 for a summary). From 1941 to 1971 the scheme's coverage was steadily expanded and the qualifying criteria were eased. The Unemployment Insurance Act of 1971 significantly expanded coverage (to around 96 percent of the workforce),

Figure 2.1
The Public Income Security System

Income Security Technique	Recipients	Federal	Provincial
Demogrant	Elderly	Old age security	
	Families with children	Family allowances	Québec family allowances
Social insurance	Retired, disabled survivors	Canada Pension Plan	Québec Pension Plan
	Unemployed	Unemployment insurance	
	Injured workers		Workers' Compensation
Social assistance	Needy persons		Social assistance
Income supplementation	Elderly	Guaranteed income supplement	Various provincial supplements and tax credits
	Families with children	Child tax credit	Saskatechewan, Manitoba, and Québec supplement plans

Source: Banting 1987:8.

introduced more generous income-maintenance provisions, relaxed entrance requirements and increased their sensitivity to regional disparities in unemployment, and offered coverage for maternity leave. By the early 1970s the UI system had undergone significant liberalization and was considerably different from the truncated system available in the United States.

In 1945 the federal government introduced a universal family allowance system. Its stated purposes were to contribute to the well-being of all Canadian children (indicative of determination to leave the Depression era behind) and to the maintenance of post-war purchasing power should the anticipated slump occur (Guest 1985:128–33). The legislation was passed unanimously on its second reading in the House of Commons—a sure indication that a version of Keynesianism, however qualified, had attained hegemonic status in post-war Canada.

Other elements of social security included the Canada Assistance Plan (a cost-shared federal–provincial program providing welfare and social assistance services); old age pensions; a variety of job creation and training programs that expanded considerably in the late 1960s and early 1970s; and a number of regional development programs to encourage economic diversification in disadvantaged regions. Most of these programs were implemented or extended gradually over the course of the post-war decades. The 1960s stand out as a particularly active period in the construction of the Canadian welfare state.

Health care is primarily a provincial responsibility, but through its spending power Ottawa gradually acquired a significant role in shaping the health care system. The end result is that health care in Canada is publicly organized and universally available, with around 90 percent of hospital and doctors' costs paid by provincially-administered plans. The federal Medical Care Act (1966) established five criteria that provincial health programs must meet to qualify for funding: universality, comprehensiveness, portability, accessibility, and public administration. The Established Programs Financing Act (1977) seemed to establish a long-term federal funding commitment for the health area, and the Canada Health Act (1984), as well as reiterating the principles of the 1966 legislation, permitted the federal government to withhold funding from provinces that implemented direct user costs—a device that had emerged as the main challenge to the universality principle. The contrast between Canada's cheaper, universally accessible health care system and the costly U.S. system, under which coverage varies dramatically with individual income and wealth, is a frequent object of commentary in Canada, and the Canadian health care system is a source of national pride.

Thus, in the years following the Second World War the Canadian state established for itself an active profile in social policy to match its traditional role in economic development. Its adoption of a version of Keynesian economic theory was followed by the development of stabilization policies that contributed to full employment. Together these activities involved a significant modification of market forces and the individualist values associated with them. Collective provision of social benefits and collective (in the sense of state) management of the economy became features of Canadian political life and society to an extent that clearly differentiated this country from the United States. In comparing Canadian and U.S. social policy, Robert Kudrle and Theodore Marmor argued that Canadian social programs were

> usually . . . more advanced in terms of program development, coverage and benefits. . . . In every policy area it appears that the general public

> as well as elite opinion . . . [is] more supportive of state action in Canada
> than in the United States. This support appears to underlie not just the
> typically earlier enactment of policy in Canada but also subsequent
> changes . . . (and expansion). (1981:110-18).

It is precisely this situation, of course, that Canadian neo-liberals have set about
changing.

Canadian social policy in the post-war period also had a decidedly regional
dimension as befitted a federal society. The new social welfare measures
approved by the central government "would not only benefit individuals, but also
would help protect the regional communities" from the ravages of poverty and
unemployment. The Keynesian policies of providing minimal levels of social
and economic security were viewed as "economically advantageous and fair" in
the peripheral provinces (Simeon and Robinson 1990:134). Initially the Keynesian
social and economic management policies designed for national development
were viewed as containing within them an inherent regional development
component. However, by the 1950s, as part of the Canadian state's commitment
to greater fairness and equity, more explicit policies were designed to address the
persistent problems of regional economic disparities (Norrie, Simeon and
Krasnick 1986:281). These included equalization payments to "have-not" provinces and targeted regional development programs. The goal was to ensure "a
more equitable distribution of the national benefits of the economic union"
(Simeon and Robinson 1990:134) and thus alleviate some of the tensions that
arose from the geographic disparities and discrimination stemming from uneven
national development. The Canadian social contract was expanded in this period
to include a territorial equity provision. In this respect Canadian social and
economic policy was "intended to foster east–west interregional links in order to
offset or lessen north–south pressures" (Doern and Purchase 1991b:9). The
Keynesian welfare state in Canada was thus designed to meet the challenge of
regulating not only class struggles but also territorial ones.

Rights for Labour
The Keynesian era commenced with P.C. 1003, an order-in-council establishing
a new legislative environment for industrial relations that is often, but inaccu-
rately, regarded simply as a Canadian imitation of the U.S. Wagner Act. Like the
Wagner Act it included acceptance of trade unionism and collective bargaining
as a right, provided there was evidence of a certain level of worker support, and
the establishment of an enforcement machinery (Woods 1973:64–70; 86–92).
However, Canada's post-war legislation also contained provisions for compulsory conciliation and mediation before strikes could occur, banned strikes during
the duration of collective agreements, and placed a number of other restrictions
on the way unions could operate. These provisions built upon earlier Canadian
labour legislation such as the Industrial Disputes Investigation Act, and en-

trenched a corporatist dimension into the post-war industrial relations system (see McBride 1996a).

The growing acceptance of Keynesian theories did something to reconcile Canada's political and economic establishments to an enhanced role for trade unions. In the Keynesian paradigm unions could play a positive role in sustaining levels of aggregate demand. More importantly, unprecedented working-class pressure, both industrial and political, produced the concessions that are represented in the 1944 order-in-council and in post-war legislation (Panitch and Swartz 1988:16–20). Cold-War coercion against radical unions and unionists also played a role in ushering in the new system.

The legal framework that did emerge was not an unqualified victory for labour. It was characterized by elaborate certification procedures, legally-enforceable contracts, no-strike provisions for the duration of contracts, and liability of trade unions and their members if illegal strikes occurred. On the other hand, the legislation did guarantee the right to organize and to bargain collectively; it forced employers to recognize unions once certain conditions were met, defined unfair labour practices, and provided remedies under the law for violations.

Although the balance of class power had shifted in labour's favour during the Second World War, the unions had still lacked sufficient power to force the employers into recognition and bargaining unassisted by the state. The price of state assistance was regulation and the continuation of the compulsory conciliation and "work stoppage delay" features of earlier legislation (McBride 1983:508–9). The cumulative effect of the restrictions was to curtail severely labour's right to strike (Woods 1973:93).

Most labour relations fell under provincial jurisdiction. However, a Canada-wide system of collective bargaining existed because most provinces adopted legislation patterned after P.C. 1003. A significant change to this situation only came with the development of special provisions for public sector collective bargaining in the 1960s and early 1970s.

Growing differences in policy towards public service labour relations tended to undermine the existence of the national industrial relations system that developed in the immediate post-war years. The economic crisis of the 1970s and the displacement of Keynesianism first by post-Keynesianism and, later, by monetarism was reflected in attacks upon the collective bargaining rights of unions generally, and of public sector unions in particular. The "post-war consensus" had, perhaps, been particularly fragile concerning the rights of unions, which, however moderately they might conduct themselves, represent a challenge to the rights of property owners.

The Crisis of the Canadian Keynesian State
In the Keynesian era the emphasis was upon building a social consensus that would outline the acceptable boundaries within which political contests were to

be waged. Broadly speaking, there were two versions of the consensus: one that "talked about the 'mixed' (i.e., still overwhelmingly private-enterprise) economy;" and another that stressed the social democratic elements, emphasizing to a much greater degree the state sector, welfare, and planning (Leys 1980:49). The mixed-economy version predominated in Canada, although it still resembled the social democratic version enough to differentiate the country from its southern neighbour.

In political terms, the consensus meant that the major political parties and forces accepted the Keynesian welfare state and Keynesianism was adopted as the new "common sense." On questions of policy and style of government there was a substantial degree of cross-party agreement. Political opposition and conflict over the extent of welfare provision did occur; but within mainstream politics it was unquestioned that the state should play a central role in welfare provision and be active in economic regulation (Savage and Robins 1990b:2–3). By the mid-1970s the Western world had entered a period of profound change. While the term "crisis" has been overworked, it is difficult not to use it in describing the current economic and political conjuncture in the West. Antonio Gramsci's assessment of his country's situation in the 1920s is relevant to our own: "The crisis consists precisely in the fact that the old is dying and the new cannot be born; in this interregnum a great variety of morbid symptoms appear" (Gramsci 1971:276).

The long economic boom that had begun in the expansionary climate of post-Second World War reconstruction was brought to an abrupt end in the early 1970s, signaled by, but not solely due to, the 1973 Arab oil embargo and the subsequent dramatic increase in oil prices by the Organization of Petroleum Exporting Countries (OPEC). This event was the first shock wave of an economic earthquake that rocked the international economy. One indicator of the changing times, some have argued, was the decline of profits.[2] Another was capital flight, as multinational corporations rapidly shifted their manufacturing investments to the newly industrializing centres of the Third World where cheap pools of labour could be readily found. A process of deindustrialization, "a widespread, systematic disinvestment in the nation's basic productive capacity" (Bluestone and Harrison 1982:6), was set in motion in the industrial core. The traditional smokestack industries—steel-making and other heavy manufacturing—rapidly declined, causing unemployment in the industrial belts and a transformation of the structure of employment. In Canada, employment in goods-producing industries fell from 34.8 percent of the labour force in 1951 to 26.7 percent in 1981, a pattern replicated in most other OECD nations (Economic Council of Canada 1984b:157, Table 11–5).

The global jockeying of investment and production was paralleled by a technological revolution as corporations attempted to modernize their enterprises, thus lowering labour costs and boosting profits. The impact of technological change on employment opportunities alone was vividly illustrated by the

Economic Council of Canada.

> Throughout the 1971–79 period, advances in technology made it
> possible to produce the 1979 level of output with 8 percent fewer jobs
> in the commercial sector of the economy than would have been required
> under 1971 conditions. This represented a labour saving of approxi-
> mately 630,000 jobs. As expected, the impact of technology varies from
> one industry to another. Only in seven of the thirty-nine industries did
> the introduction of new technology call for additional labour skills. In
> all others, labour saving ranged from 37 percent of total employment in
> knitting mills to 1 percent in the construction industry. (1984a:75)

During the 1950s and 1960s unemployment in OECD countries stood at about
3 percent—a level generally regarded as full employment. This scenario changed
dramatically during the 1970s. In Canada the ever-expanding army of unemployed caused the federal government to officially abandon this full-employment definition in 1972 along with its policy commitments to maintain full
employment (Gonick 1987:24–25; also see McBride 1992). The official unemployment figures steadily advanced from 3.6 percent in 1950 to 5.9 percent in
1970, finally peaking in 1983 at 11.9 percent (Marr and Paterson 1980:427, Table
13:3; Ruggeri 1987:322, Table 3). For the OECD area as a whole the problem
worsened but remained less serious than in Canada as the unemployment rate
climbed from an average of 3.5 percent in 1973 to 5.5 percent in 1975 to 8.4
percent in 1983 (Gonick 1987:341).

Increased unemployment was initially accompanied by upwardly spiraling
prices. Economic assumptions concerning a trade-off between unemployment
and inflation were turned on their head as a new phenomenon, "stagflation," the
coexistence of economic recession and high inflation, made its appearance.
Inflation rates rose steadily during the 1970s, reaching double-digit figures and
easing only after 1982 (see, for example, Ruggeri 1987:297, Table 3).

The twin evils of recession and inflation stimulated the revival of the neo-
liberal policy paradigm. Proponents pointed to the apparent inability of
Keynesianism to explain or counter inflationary pressures. Similarly
Keynesianism's lack of concern about government deficits and the public debt
became a major plank in the neo-liberal platform. According to the Royal
Commission on the Economic Union and Development Prospects for Canada
(the Macdonald Commission): "In the past, economists who subscribed to
Keynesian views on demand management usually argued that the size of the
deficit was not a matter for concern. The important point was 'to balance the
economy' rather than 'to balance the budget'" (Canada 1985a, vol. 2:294). But
for most economists the perceived failure of Keynesian policy to correct
economic difficulties served to undermine its logic concerning deficits. Management of the public purse soon became a heated topic of policy debate; public

deficits were cited as a major factor in the economic decline.

During the 1950s and 1960s, periods of deficits had been followed by surpluses, which limited the growth of government debt. After 1974 government revenue shortfalls rapidly increased. Public debt consequently "increased not only in absolute value but as a proportion of the country's gross national expenditure" (Economic Council of Canada 1984a:35). The fiscal crisis generated by the public debt problem led many to question the legitimacy of the Keynesian welfare state (Resnick 1989:105)—even though the debt burdens currently experienced by the state are in no small measure a consequence of neo-liberal economic policy itself—a point to which we will return in a later chapter (see also Workman 1996).

The social welfare state also came to be seen as creating economic blockages. Citizens utilizing democratic institutions are able to challenge the market distribution of power and income by insisting that a measure of equity be introduced, thus subverting pure market outcomes. The welfare state is "an embodiment of concepts of sharing which subordinates market results . . . to citizenship concerns and community values" (Canada 1985a, vol. 1:45).

To some extent, of course, the welfare state does operate as a restraining agent on private profit and accumulation, which together serve as the basis for the expansion of the capitalist system. The reason for this is not because welfare policies attempt to redistribute wealth to any significant extent. Leo Panitch has referred to welfare's redistributive effects as "socialism in one class" (cited in Leys 1980:52) because the transfers are largely "from younger, employed workers, to retired, unemployed workers, workers' widows and one-parent families." However, the welfare state can act to constrain profit levels by introducing barriers to the free-market mechanism. Prior to the welfare state, the reserve army of labour under free-market conditions served to undermine labour's demands; whereas the welfare state's existence has placed labour in a stronger position than otherwise (Gough 1981:14).

However, the problems that the workings of the welfare state present to capital should not be exaggerated. Social welfare provisions allow for the creation of a much more secure, healthy, and educated labour force: "A comprehensive system of income security may therefore help improve productivity, transform bad jobs into good ones, and hence boost economic growth" (Esping-Andersen 1983:32). However, the existence of "the welfare state has made the exploitation of labour more complicated and less predictable." To some extent the welfare state fortifies the power of labour against capital: "While the reasons for struggle remain unchanged, the means of struggle increased for the workers" (Offe 1984b:151–52).

Such perceptions may explain the withdrawal of support for the Keynesian welfare state by the capitalist class. Russell has observed that the welfare state, once "portrayed as an important adjunct to Keynesian economic policy," is now "depicted as a destabilizing influence that has indeed given rise to a new set of economic problems" (1991b:489). The driving force behind this redefinition has been the corporate sector speaking through its own peak organization—the Business Council on National Issues—and through business-funded think-tanks like the Fraser Institute and C.D. Howe Institute.

The phenomenon of globalization has become a popular explanation of the changes in the economic setting that began in the 1970s. Globalization is characterized by three major features: the first is the creation of larger markets—the nation-state can no longer satisfy the needs of multinational corporations, so big business is demanding larger trading areas; second, in this new environment capital, especially financial capital, has become increasingly mobile; and third, there has been greater global specialization of production. Globalization, the class forces that benefit from it, and the revival of neo-liberalism stand in symbiotic relationship.

Once trade and investment barriers are dismantled, nations must alter their institutions radically to "accommodate the dramatic changes in world trade" (Drache and Gertler 1991b:xi-xii). Increasingly, capital's perception is that there is too much government hindering the globalization process, and this has led to an assault on the powers of the nation-state: "The erosion of national power is often analyzed in terms of a transition from Fordism, a regime of production and accumulation based on national-domestic markets, to a post-Fordist regime driven less by domestic demand than by international trade and competitiveness" (Johnson, McBride and Smith 1994:2). It is often argued that globalization/post-Fordism has introduced problems of such scope and scale that it becomes extremely difficult for nationally-based political institutions to deal with them: "Keynesian fiscal and monetary policy is rendered largely ineffective in open global financial markets" (Simeon 1991:47–48, 49). Or, as Thomas Courchene argues, "This situation poses major concerns for national welfare states since they were . . . geared to national production machines" (quoted in Simeon and Janigan 1991:39). In short, it is argued, the foundations and support system for the post-war social contract have been undermined.

As we have noted previously we are skeptical about the inevitability of such processes. Rather they seem to us to be the product of political and ideological struggle as much as they are of structural forces. But there is no doubting the impact of these changes.

With the advent of economic crisis and global capital restructuring, the Keynesian consensus unraveled and its institutions were questioned. Even the quintessential Keynesian economist, Paul Samuelson, was forced to conclude that "our last consensus was wrong" and would have to be replaced by a "new one" (1983:19). The economic crisis has generated political strains. The 1979 Task Force on Canadian Unity, *A Future Together: Observations and Recommendations*, lamented: "The rather rough-and-ready consensus which once ensured the reasonably effective governing of the country is at the point of breaking down" (quoted in Marchak 1981:171). This view was echoed by the

Macdonald Commission, which reported: "Clearly, in recent years, political consensus on social policy has given way to more active ideological debate and uncertainty" (Canada 1985a, vol. 2:578). This reshaping of political priorities occurred in the context of a fiscal crisis of the state, and it brought the issue of governmental restraint to the forefront of the political agenda.

Notes
1. See Ginsburg (1983) for an account of disputes over the full-employment commitment in the post-war United States.
2. According to Gonick, profit rates for business in the advanced capitalist economies plummeted by 50 to 60 percent between the 1960s and 1980s (1987:341–42; see also Heap 1980/81; O'Connor 1986).

Chapter 3

Dismantling the Post-War Economic Order

A version of Keynesianism was officially adopted in Ottawa by 1945; thereafter policy discourse took place in Keynesian terms and full employment was a legitimate goal of economic policy. In these respects Canada differed from its neighbour to the south, where the official reception of Keynesian ideas and policy goals was considerably cooler and occurred later. The same point has been made about the creation of a welfare state in the two countries. Canada was not in the vanguard internationally, but the gradual piecemeal extension of programs did result in a more comprehensive social network than found in the United States, and the role of the state in promoting economic stabilization and social welfare became an important element of political and national integration in Canada.

Macroeconomic Policy in the Neo-Liberal Era
Macroeconomic policy includes fiscal and monetary policies as well as the occasional use of other instruments, such as comprehensive wage and price controls. Monetary policy consists of the state's efforts to control or influence variables such as money supply, interest rates, and exchange rates. Fiscal policy pertains to the state's powers of taxation and spending, and the balance between them, expressed in budget deficits (or surpluses). While fiscal and monetary policy are constant activities, the use of comprehensive wage controls has been much more limited. The degree of state interventionism that is involved in a society-wide system of wage controls renders it, in theoretical terms, an unattractive option for neo-liberals. The proper conduct of fiscal and monetary policy has been at the centre of the debate between the neo-liberals and their opponents. Indeed, neo-liberals consider that interventions such as wage controls are quite unnecessary if the state follows proper fiscal and monetary policies.

A considerable part of the neo-liberal agenda is focused on fiscal policy and can be summed up in four distinct, though related, issues: the size of government as expressed by its spending (measured either in absolute terms or, more usefully, as a percentage of GDP); the balance between revenues and expenditures (expressed in recent times by the budget deficit and the accumulated public debt to which annual deficits contribute); the taxation system; and the priorities in government spending. By the mid-1970s neo-liberals were arguing that government was too large, deficits were unacceptable, the tax system was in need of reform, and spending priorities were in need of reallocation. Their ideas soon found expression in government pronouncements but, in fiscal policy at least, received considerable reinforcement with the election of a Progressive Conservative government under Brian Mulroney in 1984. Despite a 1993 election campaign that promised a different approach, the Liberal government of Jean Chrétien followed through with a neo-liberal fiscal agenda even more vigorously than its predecessor.

After 1984, as Table 3.1 shows, there was a slight reduction in federal expenditures (as a percentage of GDP) until the recession of the early 1990s. Table 3.1 also indicates the gradual and limited impact of neo-liberalism in that the size of the federal state was greater in the early 1990s than it had been in the 1970s and early 1980s. To some extent, however, the total expenditure figure understates matters. If program expenditures are considered in isolation from debt-servicing costs, the impact is more striking. In the recession of the early 1980s, spending on programs climbed to 19.4 percent of GDP. In the 1990s recession this item accounted a peak of 17.8 percent of GDP before subsiding again to under 17 percent—where it is projected to remain through the rest of the 1990s. Indeed, according to the Liberals' *Budget Plan* (Martin 1996) program expenditures will shrink to a mere 12 percent of GDP by 1998/99.

Table 3.1
Federal Budgetary Expenditures as a Percentage of GDP

	Total Exp.	Prog Exp.	Public Debt
1980–81	20.1	16.7	3.4
1981–82	21.0	16.8	4.2
1982–83	23.6	19.1	2.5
1983–84	23.8	19.4	4.5
1984–85	24.6	17.9	5.0
1985–86	23.3	17.8	5.3
1986–87	23.1	17.5	5.3
1987–88	22.8	16.5	5.3
1988–89	22.1	16.0	5.5
1989–90	22.0	16.0	6.0
1990–91	22.6	16.2	6.4
1991–92	23.1	17.0	6.0
1992–93	23.4	17.8	5.6
1993–94	22.2	16.8	5.3
1994–95	21.8	16.3	5.5

Source: Public Accounts (various years); Budget Papers. Figures for 1994–95 are estimates.

In the midst of the 1990s recession, a former minister of finance was pleased to point out that the government's operating balance—the difference between program spending and revenues—showed a significant surplus of $12.5 billion in 1990–91: "Of this improvement, two-thirds is due to program expenditure restraint, the remaining one-third results from revenue increases. . . . But rapidly rising debt servicing costs absorbed much of this improvement in the operating balance, hampering deficit reduction efforts" (Wilson 1991:86). Another way of putting this was that by the 1990s Canadians were receiving fewer services relative to their tax payments. In terms of neo-liberal objectives the reduction of *program* expenditures was a major success—the 1990–91 level (as a percentage of GDP) was significantly below the average levels in the 1970s, and thus the federal state's impact on society was correspondingly smaller. And, on current projections, this will shrink even more dramatically by the end of the decade. Nevertheless, in the cause of further deficit reduction, successive governments have maintained that further spending cuts are necessary.

Neo-liberal governments are ideologically committed to expenditure restraint and deficit reduction. It will be useful to elaborate this point by considering briefly the realities and myths surrounding the deficit. Much evidence suggests that deficits and rising public debt have nothing to do with profligate expenditures by government. Rather, these phenomena are the product of foregone tax revenues, high interest rates, and recessions that are largely the product of neo-liberal economic policies. Rather than originating in the Keynesian era, these problems flourished after the monetarist economic theories favoured by neo-liberal politicians took root.

We have already noted the restraint exercised in federal expenditures and particularly in program expenditures. On the revenue side, restraint of a sort has also been prominent. In 1975 revenues amounted to 18.5 percent of GDP (down from 19.7 percent in the previous year). Since then this proportion has never been equaled, notwithstanding public perceptions of an increased tax load. In 1990–91, after several years of increases, it was estimated to be 17.8 percent. The Conservative government acknowledged that revenue shortfalls were a major contributor to the deficit, and it restored revenue yields to levels comparable to or slightly above the 1970s average (Wilson 1991:85).

The Chrétien government continued to hold revenues beneath 17 percent of GDP and program spending was projected to decline to 12 percent of GDP by 1998–99 (Martin 1996). The government's primary focus, both rhetorically and in reality, was on the expenditure side of the ledger. According to the *Budget Plan* 1995, the ratio of expenditure reductions to tax revenue increases was projected to increase from 4.4:1 in 1995/96 to 8.3:1 in 1997/98. The imbalance in successive governments' treatment of expenditures and revenues led some observers to depict the deficit as a "Trojan horse" for a somewhat different agenda: reduction of the state's role (Doern, Maslove and Prince 1988:28).

A number of writers have drawn attention to the scope and impact, in terms of equity, of the loopholes, tax breaks, and tax expenditures that led to the shortfall in revenues after 1975 (Maslove 1981; McQuaig 1987; Ternowetsky 1987; Wolfe 1985). The size of revenues foregone as a result of these devices is hard to estimate, but the sums involved considerably exceeded the annual deficit in the early 1980s (Canada 1985b:4–7). Not all of these tax breaks are targeted at corporations or the wealthy, but this does seem to have been the general pattern (Blais and Vaillancourt 1986; Maslove 1981:233–41).

In a 1994 report the National Council of Welfare recommended eliminating a select number of tax expenditures that would yield the federal, provincial and territorial governments approximately $10 billion a year in additional revenues without any general increase in taxes. The council argued that these revenues could be split, half going towards reducing federal, provincial and territorial deficits and half used to enhance social programs. This estimated amount would be just enough to allow the federal minister of finance to realize his deficit reduction goals for the next fiscal year (National Council of Welfare 1994).

Apart from revenue shortfall the main cause of increased deficits has been high real interest rates resulting from monetary policy—a case advanced most comprehensively by Harold Chorney (1988) and Linda McQuaig (1995). Noting that, as a result of monetary policy choices, real interest rates (nominal interest rates minus the inflation rate) were at historically high levels throughout the 1980s, Chorney pointed out that much of the burden of servicing the debt is self-inflicted, and that "the steady increase in the ratio of debt to GNP from 1975 to the present coincides with the reintroduction of monetarist policies by the Bank of Canada" (Chorney 1988:45).

Canadian monetary policy has reflected monetarist principles since the Bank of Canada's conversion to "monetary gradualism" in 1975. Monetarism is unambiguous in stating that inflation is the chief economic problem that governments should be concerned with and that Keynesian attempts to achieve full employment were inflationary and, in any case, doomed to failure. Monetarist analysis suggests that there is a natural rate of unemployment (though what this level is at any particular point in time is hard to determine). If policy-makers concentrate their efforts on controlling inflation and, preferably, reduce it to zero, unemployment will settle at its natural level. Nothing else can or should be done. In practical terms, monetarists advocate controlling the supply of money, primarily through rationing credit by way of high interest rates and by reducing government spending and deficits. In discussing fiscal policy we have already noted some of the consequences of the high interest rate policy.

It is worth emphasizing just how high Canadian interest rates have been in real terms. Table 3.2 provides the basic information.

Table 3.2
Nominal and Real Interest Rates

Year	Inflation Rate	Prime Business Loans Nominal	Prime Business Loans Real	Long Term Gov't Bond Yield Nominal	Long Term Gov't Bond Yield Real
1971	2.9	6.48	3.58	6.95	4.05
1972	4.7	6.00	1.3	7.23	2.53
1973	7.8	7.65	-0.15	7.56	-0.24
1974	10.8	10.75	-0.05	8.9	-1.90
1975	10.8	9.42	-1.38	9.04	1.76
1976	7.5	10.04	2.54	9.18	1.68
1977	8.0	8.5	0.5	8.70	0.7
1978	9.0	9.69	0.69	9.27	0.27
1979	9.1	12.9	3.8	10.21	1.11
1980	10.2	14.25	4.05	12.48	2.28
1981	12.4	19.29	6.89	15.22	2.82
1982	10.9	15.81	4.91	14.26	3.36
1983	5.7	11.17	5.47	11.79	6.09
1984	4.4	12.06	7.66	12.95	8.55
1985	3.9	10.58	6.68	11.04	7.14
1986	4.2	10.52	6.32	9.52	5.32
1987	4.4	9.52	5.12	9.95	5.55
1988	4.0	10.83	6.83	10.22	6.22
1989	5.0	13.33	8.33	9.92	4.92
1990	4.8	14.06	9.26	10.85	6.05
1991	5.6	9.94	4.34	9.76	4.16
1992	1.5	7.48	5.98	8.77	7.27
1993	1.8	5.94	4.14	7.85	6.05
1994	0.2	6.88	6.68	8.6	8.43

Sources: Consumer Price Index StatsCan 62–001 1994; Economic Observer StatsCan 11–210, 1994/95, Table 12; Economic Observer—Historical Statement Supplement 1994/95 11–210.

High real interest rates perform a classic accumulation service in that they protect and even expand the value of money—a result that particularly benefits creditors and the affluent. This phenomenon is apparent in the increasing proportion of public resources devoted to servicing the public debt. Such payments represent transfers from the taxpayers in general to the minority of affluent taxpayers who hold the public debt (in the form of Treasury Bills, Canada Savings Bonds (CSBs), and other marketable bonds).[1] To the extent that debt-interest payments are levied through a regressive tax system, the transfer from average taxpayers to the affluent is accentuated; and, as we will see, the tax system has become more regressive in the neo-liberal era. In 1996–97, 33.2 percent of government revenues were devoted to servicing the public debt (Martin 1997:9). Once more the effect of such transactions is to fuel the belief among citizens that they are getting less and less value (or services) for their tax dollars. And this belief is absolutely correct. In 1973–74, for example, when real interest rates were far lower, and the tax system more progressive, only 11.4 percent of tax dollars went to service the debt.

To date, neo-liberals have managed to focus the public debate about debt servicing on its costs and on the need to reduce the role of government. Unsurprisingly, the role of neo-liberal policies in producing the costs and the advantages to some sectors of society that flow from these policies have not been highlighted. So far, critics of neo-liberal policies have been unable to win the battle of ideas on these points. Ideological success further serves the neo-liberal agenda in that it creates a receptive public mood for proposals to accelerate the dismantling of the public policy package, which, until the fairly recent past, served both as social cement and as a key component of the Canadian identity. The most spectacular effect of this is to abandon a central feature of the post-war social contract: full employment (McBride 1992).

The influence of inappropriately high interest rates is compounded by their association with economic slowdown and recession both in 1981–82 and in 1990–93. McQuaig (1995:ch. 3) focuses particularly on the Bank of Canada's anti-inflation war that intensified in 1988 under Bank Governor John Crow. She regards the high real interest rates imposed in the name of fighting inflation as the "driving force behind the deficit" (see also Krehm 1993). Similarly a Statistics Canada study—the Mimoto study[2] —found that 50 percent of the increased deficit incurred between 1975/76 and 1988/89 was attributable to revenue shortfalls relative to GDP, 44 percent to an increase in debt charges relative to GDP, and only 6 percent to higher program spending relative to GDP (McIlveen and Mimoto 1990).

Thus many of the problems associated with fiscal policy, such as the deficit, which provide the pretext for implementing neo-liberal policies, in fact have their origins in neo-liberal political choices made in the monetary policy area.

Even though revenues as a share of GDP have declined, the perceived incidence of taxation on average Canadians has not. This is because of the increased regressivity of Canada's tax system—another outcome brought about by neo-liberals. Canada's tax system has always contained regressive elements, and these have become more pronounced in recent years. Table 3.3 captures one aspect of these developments and shows the declining contribution of corporate tax, together with increased reliance on regressive taxes such as UI contributions—a reliance enhanced with the introduction of the GST. Reliance on personal income tax, normally considered the most progressive element of Canada's tax system, also increased. This development, however, coincided with changes to the personal income tax system that made it much less progressive. Brooks (1990:6) considers that tax changes under the Conservative governments reflect a major reorientation of the objectives of the tax system; away from its traditional goals of financing government expenditures and economic stabilization and redistribution, and towards facilitating economic growth and ensuring that Canadian business remains internationally competitive.

Table 3.3
Changes in Federal Budget Revenues as a Percentage of Total Revenue

	1975-76	1993-94	1997-98*	97-98 as %of 75-76
Personal income tax	40.3	44.0	47.7	118.3
Corporate income tax	18.2	8.5	11.3	62.1
Sales, excise tax, GST	21.1	23.0	18.7	85.3
UI contributions‡	6.5	15.7	13.8	212.3
Other revenues	14.0	8.9	8.4	60

Source: Public Accounts; 1996 Budget Speech Projections*
   ‡ Employment Insurance Contributions after 1996 percentages rounded.

These developments have been justified by a series of arguments derived from U.S. neo-liberal thinkers (Chorney and Molloy 1988:208–14). Essentially these arguments centre on the higher levels of private savings, economic activity, and personal incentives that lower taxes, especially on the rich and upon corporations, are presumed to stimulate. In the Canadian case this body of theory gave rise to several types of tax changes: reductions in the number of income tax brackets, thus producing a "flatter" tax system; reducing loopholes; and shifting the tax burden to consumption taxes (Chorney and Molloy 1988:207).

Tracing the impact of changes to the tax system is a complex business and here we can touch on only a few major points. The long-run trend to reducing corporate taxes has continued (and largely offsets the impact of the loopholes that have been closed). While the trend did not originate with the Tories, it did accelerate once they were elected. This development increased the tax pressures on average personal income taxpayers—thus contributing to the perception that the tax system is inequitable but, to the extent that these matters are poorly understood by the general public, fueling the demand for tax reductions rather than genuine tax reform. Introduction of a flatter income tax system had much the same effect; those earning more than $100,000 per year realized substantial tax savings, while for the rest the benefits have been minor or non-existent.

The Liberal Record
Elected in 1993 on a platform that stressed job creation as the route to deficit reduction, the Liberal government remained publicly optimistic for most of its first year in office about its prospects of reconciling deficit reduction and a jobs agenda. In retrospect the period can be viewed as a drift to a neo-liberal budgetary posture of "deficit *über alles*." The key developments were the budgets of 1994 and February 1995, and the "Purple Book"—*A New Framework for Economic Policy*—released by the minister of finance in October 1994.

Paul Martin delivered his first budget speech on 22 February 1994 (Martin 1994a). The sequence of topics in the speech, as revealed in its subtitles, provides an indication that the position crafted in the Red Book (Liberal Party of Canada 1993) was still serving as a guide to public policy. The speech spoke in succession of: Keeping Our Commitment to Canadians—Creating Opportunity; Economic Renewal and Revitalization; Towards Renewed and Responsible Social Programs; and Restoring Fiscal Responsibility. The aim, as in the Red Book, was to strike a balance between addressing unemployment and dealing with the deficit. The speech itself, and accompanying documents that responded to pre-budget consultations (Martin 1994b), outlined proposals to stimulate employment through assistance to small business (Manley and Martin 1994) and changes to the unemployment insurance system (Axworthy 1994b); all emphasized the government's two-track approach.

By October 1994 the balancing act that kept jobs and deficit reduction as co-equal goals in the mind of Finance Minister Paul Martin, with more jobs being seen as a route to a lower deficit, had been resolved in favour of giving deficit reduction greater priority. The concluding section of Martin's Purple Book (1994c) pledged that: "The commitment of the government to meet its fiscal targets—and to meet them on time—is ironclad. Those targets are not ends in themselves. Rather, they are a necessary *means* toward the overarching objective of providing more and better jobs for Canadians" (Martin 1994c). In the new ordering of priorities jobs would have to follow deficit reduction.

In the Purple Book the minister repeatedly returned to the theme that doing something about the debt/deficit combination of problems was a precondition for solving Canada's other problems. No one reading the document could be under any illusions that the "deficit *über alles*" mentality flourished in the Finance Department. In October 1994 there might still have been some uncertainty about whether the Finance Department line must necessarily triumph over the social policy reform position being advocated by Human Resources Development. The February 1995 budget provided the clarification.

Martin's 1995 budget speech completed the reversal of priorities from that presented in the Red Book: "This government came into office because it believes that the nation's priority must be jobs and growth. And it is *because* of that, not *in spite of* that, that we must act now to restore the nation's finances to health" (Martin 1995:2). The message was reinforced in the 1996 and 1997 budget speeches. Evoking the rhetoric of the Cold War battle against communism Martin's 1996 speech depicted the deficit as "a clear and present danger to this country—to our way of life, to our future" and pledged that "the attack on the deficit is irrevocable and irreversible" (Martin 1996).

The government sought legitimacy for its policy position in international comparisons. The outcome of the Detroit jobs conference in March 1994 and the Naples G-7 summit, it held, pointed to a near universal consensus among industrial country governments regarding both the nature of the jobs problem and the policy directions needed to address it. The Detroit summit was described by a senior British official as an event where emphasis on supply-side measures craftily disguised the fact Bill Clinton had effectively abandoned any hopes of boosting employment through expansionary macro-economic policies (Elliott 1995). Similarly the 1994 OECD *Jobs Study* could have served as a blueprint for the emerging Liberal position on employment and labour market policy.

Some policy analysts contend that with globalization national governments have reduced capacity to engage in macroeconomic management and thereby influence the larger environment. As a result, the real site of national policy action and debate has shifted toward a concern with labour-market regulation, human capital and the organization of the workplace —a trend confirmed by the July 1994 meeting of the G-7 in Naples. Indeed Canadian Finance Minister Paul Martin warned against attempts at economic management.

Thus international "conventional wisdom" reinforced the policy preferences of the Canadian government. In this context the June 1995 agreement among the G-7 countries at Halifax to hold a second jobs summit in 1996 largely served to affirm the "wisdom" of existing policies. In advance of the meeting a prescient journalist warned that "anybody who imagines for one moment that a jobs summit . . . will provide an alternative to the prevailing supply-side orthodoxy of deregulating labour markets and using the notion of job flexibility to justify chronic insecurity should think again" (Elliott 1995).

Privatization and Deregulation

Neo-liberal economic doctrine is concerned about minimizing state interference with markets. In seeking to roll back the boundaries of the state in Canada, Crown corporations and state regulatory activity have provided logical targets for neo-liberal governments. Clearly these developments have not been unique to Canada; many governments have divested themselves of state-owned corporations (Laux 1991:289–91). In this, as in associated endeavours, Canadian neo-liberals have been very much in tune with the rhetoric, fashionable worldwide, of achieving international competitiveness through enhancing the freedom of market forces. To some extent Canadian neo-liberals were impeded by the fact that their doctrines ran counter to a well-established national tradition: in this case, of public enterprise.[3]

Observers of various political stripes concur in regarding reliance on public enterprise as an historically important Canadian cultural characteristic (Hardin 1989:104; Stanbury 1988:120). As D. Wayne Taylor notes (1991:97–100), the public enterprise tradition has roots that pre-date Confederation, has been the product of necessity in that the state has undertaken works considered to be beyond the capacity of the private sector, and has encountered little ideological resistance.

Nor has public tolerance for public enterprise become entirely an historical phenomenon. One reason advanced by Allan Tupper and G. Bruce Doern (1988:32) for the Mulroney government's "slow and deliberate movement" on privatization is the fact that "Canadian public opinion is not overly critical of the current level and form of public enterprise."[4] Although government ministers have sometimes advanced ideological justifications for privatization measures—the "discipline and vitality of the marketplace will replace the often suffocating effect of government ownership" (quoted in Laux 1991:291)— ideological factors have usually been masked by a tone of pragmatic realism. As one government official interviewed by N.J. Baxter-Moore (1991:27) put it, "We always say that privatization in Canada is not ideological, since this helps us to distance ourselves from Margaret Thatcher or Ronald Reagan whose views would not be popular in Canada. But the fact still remains that privatization is a conceptual thing—one has to believe that the free market system works."

At first the government was so reticent in providing public rationalizations for its privatization program that there was considerable uncertainty, even among participants and those intimately affected by privatization, about its purposes: "There's no economic rationale, ideological or pragmatic . . . the thing that is still missing is the policy. Why are we selling these things and what do we want to achieve by selling them?" (quoted in Stanbury 1988:130–31).

In May 1987 the minister of state for privatization finally issued a comprehensive rationale for the program. There were five key points (for a summary see Stanbury 1988:131):

(i)   the public policy goals that led to establishing Crown corporations in the past either might have changed, or might be better achieved through other policy instruments;

(ii)   Crown corporations, being sheltered from market forces, may be less efficient than private sector organizations;

(iii)   Crown corporations constitute a drain on the public purse;

(iv)   the need for public accountability led to an inflexible and uncompetitive managerial style;

(v)   competition between Crown corporations and the private sector was unfair to the latter, because the competition was being partly financed by the private sector's own tax dollars.

As if to emphasize its pragmatic intentions, the Mulroney government attempted to distance itself from privatization's Thatcherite connotations (Laux 1991:296–97)—once more tacitly recognizing the strength of the public enterprise culture in Canada. Further, to protect themselves from British-style allegations that privatization was tantamount to "selling off the family silver to pay the rent," government officials initially and legitimately pointed to different accounting conventions in the two countries (Baxter-Moore 1991:22–23).[5] The 1991 budget, however, announced that future proceeds from privatization were to be credited to a special Debt Servicing and Reduction Fund. Canadian practice would henceforth approximate the British model.

Despite the pragmatic spin that the government placed on its privatization program, there are grounds for highlighting the ideological motivation. For example, a study of the privatization of Teleglobe, the most lucrative sale, noted that the corporation did not meet any of the government's criteria for privatization. The study concluded that the most important reason for privatizing Teleglobe lay "in the Government's ideological position that business activities should, whenever they are viable, be left to the private sector. . . . As one Minister put it, the sale of Teleglobe meant . . . giving back to the private sector its rightful place" (Charles Dalfen, quoted in Baxter-Moore 1991:32). This case seems to indicate that where the stated criteria cannot be found to apply, some other, unstated, criteria can be found. Indeed, as Baxter-Moore (1991:36) points out, even the apparently pragmatic government criteria are ideological: in particular, the judgement as to whether a Crown corporation continues to serve a public policy purpose is hardly based on objective criteria but, rather, lies "in the eye of the beholder." It is doubtful whether the free-market rationale for privatization, as opposed to a *private*-market rationale, has much bearing on the program. Jeanne Kirk Laux (1991:299–302) demonstrates that the effects of privatization include increasing concentration in the Canadian economy and conferring significant benefits upon a "select group of well-established companies." It is significant, too, that the state sought to retain a certain amount of control over privatized corporations. These included stipulations over levels of foreign ownership, location of headquarters, and employment levels. Such efforts testify to the public policy purposes served by Crown corporations and the political desirability of perpetuating these purposes through new organizational forms. Given the constraints faced by the Mulroney government, however, its privatization program was cautious and incremental.

Nevertheless, the push to privatization continued. Air Canada and Petro-Canada in particular represented "big ticket" items. In addition to the size of the assets represented by these corporations, they also serve as national symbols. Transferring the national airline or oil company to private hands is a symbolic action of major proportions; in conjunction with cutbacks in Via Rail services and CBC funding, it seemed that the traditional emblems of national unity were under concerted attack.[6]

Canadian statist tradition in the economic sphere extends to the extensive use of regulatory mechanisms, a tool "central to successive governments' attempts at nation-building and the promotion of economic development" (Schultz 1988:187–88). A certain dissatisfaction with some of the side effects of regulation became apparent in the 1960s but found little policy expression in the Trudeau years. The Mulroney governments showed considerably greater activity (Schultz 1988:192, 195–96), although, as in the privatization area, moving cautiously and preferring to avoid the term "deregulation" as far as possible in favour of the less ideologically loaded "regulatory reform."

In 1986 the Mulroney government announced its "Regulatory Reform Strategy," reassuring those who feared wholesale deregulation. The strategy promised that regulation would remain an important policy instrument, and it placed priority on its reform rather than its elimination. The tone of the document made it clear that the onus of proof would be on those who wished to regulate and that the government was sensitive to the economic and social costs of regulation. Moreover, it established new mechanisms to ensure careful scrutiny, review, and evaluation of new and already existing regulations. (For a summary of the strategy, see Kernaghan and Siegel 1991:244–45.)

Despite the effort to emphasize a pragmatic approach to regulatory policy, some of the government's early moves were highly charged in symbolic terms. The replacement of the Foreign Investment Review Agency by Investment Canada and the dismantling of the National Energy Program represented a frontal assault on the activist "new national policy" initiated by the Trudeau government. In other areas, such as air transportation, some initial deregulatory steps had been taken by the previous Liberal government, but the Conservatives moved much more comprehensively (see Strick 1990:134–35). In air transport (Strick 1990:140) there seems to have been a link between deregulation and the subsequent privatization of Air Canada. Much the same point can be made about the elimination of the National Energy Program and the partial privatization of Petro-Can that occurred some time later.

Richard Schultz (1988:200-01) argued that the government's moves were not based on ideology, but the consistency of its approach with the other themes of strengthening the market and downsizing the state suggests otherwise. This interpretation is reinforced by the effects of some of the moves to deregulation. Contrary to the claims advanced for reform of airline regulation, the major result has been increased concentration in the industry (a process that has not yet reached its logical conclusion). According to Statistics Canada, price increases for airfares increased 66 percent between 1987 and 1994 (compared to a general inflation increase of 25 percent). The cost of flying between smaller Canadian cities increased by an average 13 percent a year while travel between the three largest cities increased by an annual 2.6 percent (*Vancouver Sun*, 21 December 1995). This mirrors the pattern experienced with deregulation in the United States. Since the U.S. venture into deregulation preceded the Canadian policy by several years its effects were already known. The fact that the lessons were not drawn suggests an approach in which ideological considerations were a significant factor. Despite the incremental nature of the activity and a certain degree of governmental caution, this area fits the general pattern: the dismantling of structures of state interventionism that Canada has relied on to a marked degree.

Industrial Relations

In Canada the influence of Keynesianism on industrial relations has often been depicted as the result of a tacit rather than explicit class compromise between capital and labour. During the war years a much stronger labour movement emerged, generating intense pressure for reform of social and industrial relations (Panitch and Swartz 1988:18–22). In comparative terms, however, Canadian labour remained less powerful than many of its Western European counterparts, and the degree of recognition and the extent of the concessions it could extract were correspondingly more limited.

Nevertheless the adoption of a version of Keynesianism in Canada represented a major advance for labour. In particular, the full-employment commitment, truncated as it was, signaled a dramatically different policy environment than there had been in 1930s. And the Keynesian concern to sustain levels of aggregate demand carried connotations of a more benign attitude on the part of Canada's establishment to collective bargaining and spending on social programs. These considerations were, perhaps, reinforced by the legitimacy-creating effects of such concessions in an era of labour militancy—a point retrospectively recognized by the 1968 Task Force on Labour Relations, which noted the role of the collective bargaining process in "legitimizing and making more acceptable the superior-subordinate nexus inherent in the employer-employee relationship" (Woods 1968:9).

In the industrial relations sphere the key piece of legislation was a 1944 federal order-in-council (P.C. 1003), which was widely emulated by provincial governments. The approach accepted trade unionism and collective bargaining as rights, provided that evidence of worker support existed (Woods 1973:64–70, 86–92). Bob Russell (1991a:18) provides useful insights into the strategy behind the legislative concessions:

> The general intent of state labour policy was to enhance collective bargaining with duly certified trade unions. The object here was to avoid the scale of industrial militancy and disruption that had characterized industrial relations during the previous wartime demobilization (1918–20) and, more recently, in the latter years of the depression and throughout much of the Second World War. The calculation was that trade unions and employers, as responsible representatives of their respective interests, could be brought together through organized collective bargaining.

Together with the state's recognition of trade unions and collective bargaining went a highly restrictive legislative framework featuring elaborate certification procedures, legally enforceable contracts, no strikes during contracts, and unions' liability if illegal strikes occurred. The package meant that Canada's industrial relations system involved greater state intervention in collective bargaining than was the case in most comparable countries (McBride 1985). Further, the reconstruction of the legislative environment for trade union activities was accompanied by a purge of radicals from most labour organizations (Russell 1990:247), thus ensuring that labour's new rights would be exercised under relatively quiescent leadership.

These caveats notwithstanding, the industrial relations system introduced in the post-war period did enhance the status and rights of Canada's historically weak and fragmented labour movement. The fact that labour's new rights were to be enjoyed in a context of high employment for over two decades serves to emphasize the gains compared to any earlier period. The combination of relatively full employment with free collective bargaining strengthened labour's bargaining position vis-à-vis business. This factor is often cited in explaining the outbreak of labour militancy in the mid-1960s and continuous pressure both for higher wages and for greater trade union rights on the part of groups such as public servants. Certainly, the strike wave of the 1960s stimulated the state to a re-evaluation of the implications of collective bargaining. The Task Force on Labour Relations (Woods 1968)[7] identified some of the growing pressures on the post-war Keynesian system but remained well within the boundaries of Keynesianism. It saw collective bargaining as a crucial legitimation device in a modern industrial society (Woods 1968:9), and its recommendations seemed designed to perfect this role rather than to restructure it radically. But with the inflationary pressures and growing instability in the world economy, other schools of thought were devising more radical measures. By the 1970s, governments were implementing these measures, albeit in an ad hoc rather than theoretically-inspired manner.

Post-Keynesian thinkers began to consider the inflationary effects of sustaining demand at levels consistent with full or high employment. Their solution—one they believed would make possible continued high employment—was an incomes policy to restrain demand to levels justified by economic growth and productivity. Such a policy meant that the outcomes of the collective bargaining process would be controlled by the state. For labour and, as it turned out, capital, state intrusion into the centrepiece of the labour–capital relationship served to delegitimate the role of the Keynesian state. Although labour has yet to construct a theoretical alternative to Keynesianism, Canadian business found one ready-made: the updated version of pre-Keynesian orthodox economics known as monetarism, which would constitute a central ingredient of the neo-liberal agenda.

The implications of this approach for full employment, collective bargaining, and trade unionism were threatening. Implementation of monetarist policies would involve returning to a regime of high unemployment (McBride 1992), which in itself would cast a pall over trade union activities. Labour's social agenda could expect to gain little response from a state obsessed with retrenchment and restraint. The vigorous reassertion of the primacy of market forces called for by monetarist thinkers would also involve attacks on trade union rights. Unions were depicted in the theory as one of the chief impediments to the free operation of market forces. Despite neo-liberals' preference for a small state, they had no compunctions about a strong state when dealing with market-blocking institutions.

Thus Canadian business shifted to a theoretical posture inimical to the tacit post-war settlement between capital and labour. After considerable hesitation, reflected in conflicts between various arms of the state, state policy eventually came to reflect the same theoretical postulates.

While the shift in theoretical approaches is clearly discernible and is responsible, at least in the first instance, for the inhospitable environment faced by trade unions after the mid-1970s, it is important to connect ideological changes to the development of crisis within the economy and in the Keynesian mode of organizing it. As Russell (1991a:14) notes,

> if we take Fordism to stand for the dominant model of capital accumulation since 1945—and understand by this term a political-economic system of mass production premised upon increasing annual rates of labour productivity, low unit labour costs and historically high wages— then the evidence seems incontrovertible that this historic arrangement has become increasingly unstuck.

The theoretical conflicts between advocates of continued Keynesianism, post-Keynesianism, and monetarism should be understood as responses to developments in the real economy.

Leo Panitch and Don Swartz (1988:16) depict the neo-liberal era in industrial relations as one of "permanent exceptionalism" in which "rights established in the general legislation of the 1940s and 1960s were increasingly removed on an ad hoc basis, from particular groups of workers who sought to exercise them and eventually from large segments of the working class altogether for a 'temporary' period."[8] The assault on the status quo has involved periodic implementation of wage and price controls to regulate the outcomes of the collective bargaining process; use of ad hoc back-to-work legislation to end strike action; and amendment and erosion of the legislative regime governing collective bargaining. These trends have been apparent at both federal and provincial levels. In addition, judicial decisions have posed major problems for organized labour (see Mandel 1989:ch. 5).

The most sweeping example of wage controls was the Anti-Inflation

Program, in effect between 1975 and 1978, which covered federal and Crown corporation employees, public sector workers in participating provinces, workers in large private sector firms, and professionals. The wages of federal government employees were controlled under the "six and five" program in 1982–83 and, as with the earlier program, all provinces also introduced some form of wage restraint. The 1991 federal budget (Wilson 1991) announced another pay-restraint initiative for federal public employees. In addition to these examples, individual provinces resorted to this policy instrument at various points in the 1980s and 1990s. The effect of the wage-restraint policies was to severely circumscribe the recently obtained collective bargaining rights of public employees. For these workers in particular, the Keynesian era of unconstrained collective bargaining was indeed a short-lived phenomenon.

Nowhere was this truer than in Ontario under the NDP government of 1990–95. In 1993 the Rae government moved to reform the Crown Employees Collective Bargaining Act by extending the right to strike to public sector employees. On the same day, it introduced legislation imposing a Social Contract, essentially opening up thousands of collective agreements and suspending meaningful collective bargaining for a three-year period (Panitch and Swartz 1993). Extending the right to strike and simultaneously postponing the date of its implementation for three years in many ways typified the Orwellian symbolism of much of the Social Contract process—one that alienated many labour activists from their natural ally, the NDP.

The Social Contract was part of a package of measures designed to reduce Ontario's budget deficit. While the government was prepared to unilaterally cut $4 billion through an Expenditure Control Plan, it sought to negotiate an additional round of reductions, amounting to $2 billion, with public sector workers. The principles underlying this effort at legitimation were presented, on 23 April 1993, in the following terms:

> Real and enduring restraint is crucial to solving our fiscal problems. However, workers need assurances that the costs of restraint and restructuring are being distributed equitably across society. . . . Like the private sector, our public sector must adapt to the modern imperatives for continuous updating and productivity enhancement. . . . In exchange for voluntarily restraining compensation, public sector workers will expect to enter into long-term partnership arrangements for planning and implementing the future development of Ontario's public services. (Ontario 1993b:1–2)

In asserting the need for such measures while attempting to negotiate a partnership with labour, the Rae government was searching for a social democratic method of implementing neo-liberal policies.

The government argued that the $2 billion cut represented by the Social

Contract proposals could come entirely out of jobs, entirely out of wages or, as in the Social Contract proposal, occur through negotiation and "creative partici-pation" of the "stakeholders" (Ontario 1993b). In the negotiations that followed, the process envisaged by the government itself became a major issue, joining the size and significance of the deficit as a rock on which the government's expectations were to founder. (See McBride 1996b for a full account.)

During the negotiations the government used a standard brew of threat, inducement and exhortation. The attempt, however, proved counterproductive as participants came to perceive the process as one of cynical manipulation on the government's part. The unions found the threats—agree or suffer between twenty and forty thousand public sector layoffs—particularly difficult to accept because they were from a nominally social democratic government, which they had worked very hard to elect. The inducements—reforms to collective bargain-ing and partnership in neo-corporatist arrangements—were simply insufficient to compensate for draconian measures proposed under the Social Contract and the Expenditure Control Plan.

The public sector unions maintained their reservations against the proposed Social Contract proposals despite their generally favourable attitude towards the government's reform of the Ontario Labour Relations Act (OLRA), which represented a significant though modest reform to provisions related to union recognition and collective bargaining rights in the province. Promises to move public sector collective bargaining toward the OLRA model did, therefore, have some attraction. This was offset by the reality that any reforms would have no impact during the three years the Social Contract was in effect and that the post-Social Contract starting point would be inferior to the status quo. The episode was a botched attempt by a nominally social democratic government to manufacture consent for ad hoc suspension of collective agreements.

Public sector employees had been the most likely target of back-to-work legislation since the 1960s. The incidence of this type of legislation by both federal and provincial governments increased markedly in the 1970s and 1980s (see Canada 1985a, vol. 2:680). Again, this represented a retreat from the earlier extension of collective bargaining rights. Private sector workers were also affected by this type of legislation, but to a lesser extent; however, their bargaining power was undermined by the unemployment that resulted from the introduction of monetarist macroeconomic policies.

The legislative erosion of the post-war package continued in a variety of reforms and amendments to labour legislation at both federal and provincial levels (see Panitch and Swartz 1988: Appendix II). The federal government took full advantage of a 1982 Supreme Court decision giving it a virtually free hand in designating jobs as "essential"—thereby depriving the incumbents of the right to strike (Swimmer 1987). The Mulroney government pursued confrontational tactics with Crown corporation employees and, in 1991, with its own workers who sought to defy the wage restraints imposed in the 1991 budget. Similar trends can be observed at the provincial level, especially those governed by parties espousing neo-liberal doctrines (Shields 1991).

In Ontario one of the first actions of the neo-liberal Harris government was to repeal the Labour Relations Act passed by its NDP predecessor. Labour claims that the scope of the changes enacted goes well beyond a return to the previously existing situation. For example, the Ontario Federation of Labour considers that, in introducing an American-style electoral union certification process in place of a card majority system, the Harris government has broken with a non-partisan consensus dating back to the 1950s and, in the process, opened the way to employer intimidation and harassment during union organizing drives (see Ontario Federation of Labour 1995; Sack, Goldblatt, Mitchell 1995).

Still, Russell's earlier assessment of neo-liberal industrial relations policies probably continues to hold good:

> What we are presented with is not so much a total restructuring of the industrial relations system as a *de facto* renegotiation, *at the state's behest*, of some of the existing parameters. Once again, union security is exchanged for responsible union conduct *as defined by* existing political priorities. If anything has undergone fundamental revision, it is the nature of the contemporary political agenda and the relative benefits derivable from the trade-off." (Russell 1990:273)

While the impact of the state's actions has created a much more difficult environment, Canadian labour has certainly not been decimated in the way that the American labour movement has. In 1993 union membership stood at 3,768,000 or 32.6 percent of the workforce (compared to 30.8 percent in 1966) (Canadian Centre for Policy Alternatives 1996:3). However, the ability of Canadian unions to maintain or increase real wages has suffered, largely because of macroeconomic policies that create high levels of unemployment, which weakens labour's bargaining power generally, and because of public sector cuts, which have eliminated the job security that public sector unions formerly relied on.

Some governments in Canada have engaged in efforts to restore their legitimacy in labour's eyes.[9] In part the state has sought to achieve this goal through legislative reforms (and concessions on issues long demanded by labour) in such areas as workplace conditions and employment equity. Other initiatives have sought to generate legitimacy by involving labour, together with business, in various consultative mechanisms. One example is the Canadian Labour Force Development Board (CLFDB), dominated by labour and business representatives, set up to advise the government on how to use monies appropriated from the unemployment insurance fund for training purposes (see Mahon 1990). Under the Chrétien Liberals, however, the budget of the CLFDB was slashed and its advice ignored. Its Ontario equivalent, the Ontario Training and Adjustment Board was abolished by the incoming Conservative government in that province.

The general picture, therefore, is somewhat mixed; but it seems clear that governments have been gradually reshaping the industrial relations system that formed one cornerstone of the system of social rights introduced into Canada in the post-war period. For the most part, the changes have worked to disadvantage labour.

Regional Development

Janine Brodie (1990:164–65) has divided policies that explicitly address regional disparities into two types: compensatory, which compensate regions for their "underdevelopment"; and developmental, which attempt to remove the causes of "undevelopment." In addition she notes the existence of non-spatially targeted programs, such as unemployment insurance and other income security and welfare programs, which may have major redistributive effects between regions. Of this type of program, Banting (1987:97) commented, "National income security programs redistribute income between regions whenever greater proportions of elderly, unemployed or needy people, or children are found in some regions than in others, or whenever revenues to finance those programs are raised disproportionately from different regions." Each of these types of policy, as well as the impact of a government's general macroeconomic policy, affects the fate of regions.

In the 1960s and 1970s the general policy stance aimed at moving disadvantaged regions towards a national standard, itself defined in relatively egalitarian and Keynesian terms. While not always successful in achieving this goal, policy could be construed as contributing to national integration. Has this situation changed since the 1970s?

Between 1970 and 1984 income was redistributed regionally as much by national social programs as by explicitly regional equalization measures (Bickerton 1994). Taken together both forms of compensatory policies dwarfed spending on the developmental variety. For example, Harvey Lithwick (1982:139–40) reported that in the late 1970s the regional component of unemployment insurance alone delivered 80 percent more benefits to Québec and the Atlantic provinces than the entire annual budget of the Department of Regional Economic Expansion (DREE).

More generally, Donald Savoie (1992:200–02), in considering the 1961–87 period, notes a disproportionate increase in transfers to persons, as a percentage of total personal income, in the Atlantic provinces as compared to Ontario. Together with federal transfers to provincial governments, these expenditures enabled "have-not" provinces to narrow the gap, including the capacity to engage in public spending in areas as crucial to well-being as health and education. Similarly, federal transfer payments "have contributed to the virtual elimination of regional disparities in basic household necessities. They have helped greatly to narrow the regional gap in family income and in individual spending power" (Savoie 1992:202). Notwithstanding regular expressions of regional discontent and resentment at remaining disparities, policies that facilitated greater standardization of social services and opportunities did contribute to political integration and a sense of common nationhood. These policies have been the targets of fiscal restraint measures. Their impact can be projected to decline in the future.

Despite some improvements, significant regional disparities remained, especially as measured by indicators such as the interrelated variables of unemployment and per capita income. Developmental regional policies—designed to address the root causes of the problem—were devised to foster economic growth and employment in the regions and thus eliminate this type of disparity.

James Bickerton (1994) argues that the history of the developmental type of federal regional policy consists of three overlapping phases, each based on a different economic development model:

> Phase I, identified most closely with regional development in the 1960s, was primarily concerned with the problem of rural poverty in Atlantic Canada and with managing industrial crisis in Nova Scotia. Phase II began with the 1969 consolidation of regional development programs under the Department of Regional Economic Expansion and was characterized by the embrace of the urban growth centre approach and government support for the rationalization and modernization of resource industries. Phase III, which still can be classified as emergent, shifts regional development strategy away from its former focus on natural resources and economic infrastructure to nurturing local entrepreneurship and providing greater support for human resource development.

Phase III addresses the innovations of the Mulroney government that, for the most part, have been continued under Chrétien. The first two phases are characteristic of the federal government's regional development strategy in the Keynesian era.

Unlike other elements of the Keynesian policy package, regional development policies appear to have been poorly theorized (see Savoie 1992:ch. 1). The policy area tended to be characterized by successive "fashions and fads" (Savoie 1992:227). In the case of the first two phases of developmental regional policies at least, a nation-building ethic provided the motivation. For example:

> DREE was perceived as capable of reinforcing national unity, and of providing a new visibility of the central government. On the one hand, DREE would help to counteract Québec separatism and silence the disquiet of the Atlantic provinces by reducing regional disparities; on the other hand, it could bring regional policy into harmony with national objectives by asserting federal control over the spending of federal

monies in this area. Clearly, an expanded, centralized and politically sensitive regional development department was intended to counter these centrifugal economic and cultural tendencies and promote Canadian unity. (Gagnon 1991:8)

In the circumstances of the 1960s and 1970s, the federal government's nation-building concept of regional development came into increasing conflict with resource-based "province-building" strategies. Thus regional development became "a pawn in the continuing struggle between 'nation building' and 'province-building'" and a source of national conflict rather than national integration.

To some extent early federal efforts in regional development were predicated on strengthening the provinces. Bickerton (1994) argues that in the 1960s Ottawa sought to use the Fund for Rural Economic Development (FRED) to "transform the governments of the poorer provinces to enable them to do the kinds of things in the development field that were done in other provinces that already possessed the 'in-house' capability to do so." Other federal policies also contributed to province-building; cost-sharing welfare state programs augmented the capacity of provincial governments, and Ottawa's continentalist trade policies after the war tended to exert a decentralizing force (Brodie 1990:192). But clearly the demands for greater autonomy emanating from Québec, and later from resource-rich Western provinces, also had indigenous causes.

Initially province-builders tended to emphasize the province as the primary unit in which wealth could be maximized by a strategy of (decentralized) state interventionism. Later, especially among the Western premiers, denunciations of state interventionism *per se* (but especially interventions of the federal state) and calls for unfettered free enterprise and free trade became more common (cf. Brodie 1990:199–200). Such concepts were challenged by the federal government until the mid-1980s. For example, the 1982 Constitution Act contained a commitment to reducing regional disparities. Even an intermittent province-builder like Newfoundland Premier Brian Peckford periodically expressed the redistributive ethic: "Canada as a nation cannot survive if there are permanently rich and permanently poor provinces" (quoted in Savoie 1992:233).

The 1984 election of a Conservative government committed to a new era of federal–provincial cooperation permitted a new approach to the tensions that had emerged between the nation-building and province-building strategies. The Mulroney government initiated a series of decentralizing measures that repudiated the 1980–84 Trudeau government's concept of nation-building. As we will see in Chapter 6, the Chrétien government, as part of its quasi-constitutional strategy of accommodation towards Québec, has been an avid decentralizer as well.

In 1985 the Mulroney government signed agreements with Newfoundland

and three Western provinces, conceding greater control over resource revenues to the provinces. Two years later the federal government radically decentralized regional development policy; indeed, no national department of regional development now exists. Some of the new agencies (for example, the Atlantic Canada Opportunities Agency and Western Diversification Department) are located outside Ottawa. Savoie (1992:224) comments:

> Few can accuse them of being insensitive to regional circumstances. The departments are highly decentralized and regional offices have considerable scope to make decisions and to launch new activities. In addition the 'regional' departments have met head on criticism from Atlantic and western premiers that national departments tend to concentrate their efforts in central Canada.

Along with decentralization has gone a greater emphasis on market forces as a solution to regional development. This has been variously described as "nurturing local entrepreneurship through various types of support for small and medium-sized enterprises" (Bickerton 1994) and as downplaying and de-emphasizing "the social elements of regional development policies in favour of a more exclusively economic focus that aims to devote more of the available resources to fostering of opportunities for expanded capital accumulation" (Gagnon 1991:19).

Whether such an approach can produce more balanced regional development or outcomes is doubtful. Alain Gagnon, for instance, has predicted that the neo-liberal approach to regional development "is bound to ensure even greater regional disparities than those past policies were supposed to eliminate" (1991:21). Proponents of the new direction in the developmental type of regional development policy argue that the previous, more interventionist approach to the problem had failed to produce the expected results and that a new departure was therefore warranted. Such claims are hard either to prove or to refute: "There is probably no other field of government expenditure in which so much public money is committed but so little is known about the success of the policy. There exist very few objective research studies on regional development efforts in Canada" (Savoie 1992:3).

With respect to the impact of neo-liberal policy changes in other areas, there are stronger grounds for predicting the outcome. We saw earlier that compensatory policies (Keynesian welfare state programs and equalization grants) were more significant in ameliorating the symptoms of regional underdevelopment than developmental policies as such. Earlier we argued that such programs were being eroded and dismantled under neo-liberal stewardship. The effect can only be to undermine the equalizing impact of these programs on regional differences.

Other elements of the neo-liberal package will also exacerbate regional disparities. Fiscal restraint and tight control on public spending limit the funds available for regional development along with other areas. Reducing financial transfers to the provinces restrains their ability to respond to regional unemployment within their own boundaries. Reliance on monetary policy to curb inflation has two negative effects on provinces. Because the policy area is under the exclusive jurisdiction of the federal authorities, it is less susceptible than fiscal policy to provincial influence and, in any case, is less capable of being used to alleviate problems such as regional variations in unemployment rates. In addition there is evidence that reducing inflation primarily by monetary restraint tends to result in greater regional variations in unemployment than doing so by other means (Reeves and Kerr 1986). Most importantly, perhaps, the strategy of "continental rationalization" represented by the push to a Free Trade Agreement with the United States and Mexico (see Chapter 8) both "contradicts the logic of a regional development program" and "severely limits the ability of future Canadian governments to alleviate regional disparities and to contain regional conflict" (Brodie 1990:221, 223).

The Neo-Liberal Challenge
Everywhere the neo-liberal agenda has been implemented it has involved the reduction or removal of impediments to the operation of market forces. Accommodating markets is sometimes justified as the best—or possibly the only— response to irresistible competitive pressures emanating from an increasingly global economy. Sometimes neo-liberals emphasize long-held philosophical assumptions about markets being "inherently superior to any other way of organizing human societies" (Gamble 1988:38). At other times, moral factors, such as the claim that the welfare state creates dependency and a loss of freedom for its clients, receive greater prominence. Regardless of the justifications, the result of the neo-liberal policy package, to the extent that it is implemented, is the creation of a society in which market rationality is dominant. As some critics have noted, and some neo-liberals have conceded, this implies the dissolution of collective social relations in favour of an unbridled individualism based on the maximization principle (Macpherson 1962).[10]

Neo-liberalism is an attempt to readjust the tacit class compromise created in most Western countries during and immediately after the Second World War. The readjustment involves significant loss of concrete benefits for labour and for other subordinate social groups and strata. Important elements of the state's legitimation activities that had expanded in the Keynesian era have been attacked, cut back, or withdrawn. Part of the logic of neo-liberalism therefore involves increased social polarization along the lines of class and other cleavages in industrial societies. Yet for the most part class polarization has found little or no reflection in the political party system. This is as true in Canada as it is elsewhere.

In some respects, however, the Canadian case is distinctive. This is because an active role for the state, in partial contradiction to market forces, has been an instrument of nation-building and national identity, as well as of compromise between social classes. Indeed, some argue that the state's more activist role was entirely organized around national appeals: "The social compromises and institutionalized relationships of the welfare state were rationalized in terms of the needs of the whole nation and of the federal system" (Jenson 1989:84). In Canada the attack on the state's role and the promotion of unrestricted market relations involve a challenge to the definition of the country rather than merely to established social relations within it. While this country has fashioned tight connections between sovereignty and the state's economic and social roles, neo-liberalism purportedly consists of a set of universally applicable doctrines based on the primacy of the individual and of market relations. As such it has little to say about Canadian or any other national identity. Its target is what it sees as the unwarranted intrusion of the state into market relations between free individuals, and its proponents consider both the economic and social activities of the state to be intolerable. But if, to adapt Alexander Brady's observation, the role of the state in the economic and social life of Canada is really the modern history of Canada, the assault on the state's role carries broader implications than may be the case elsewhere.[11] Everywhere, the logic of neo-liberalism is to dismantle the state. In Canada this may involve dismantling the country as well. This means that both the social impact and the national impact of the neo-liberal agenda are of prime importance.

Notes

1. The most widely distributed component of public debt is Canada Savings Bonds. Yet in 1984 families with wealth over $100,000 owned almost three-quarters of the value of CSBs (Statistics Canada 1984:67–68).

2. For an account of the Mimoto study, its findings, and suppression under pressure from the Department of Finance see Klein (1996).

3. Whether this tradition has been rooted in values or in the recognition of necessity is less important than the fact of its existence.

4. See Baxter-Moore (1991:4) and Stanford (1990:2, 5–6) on public support for Petro-Can when threatened with privatization by the Clark government; and Graham (1986:371) for an account of the "political storm" occasioned by the sale of Crown corporations (notably deHavilland Aircraft) to foreign buyers.

5. For the peculiar accounting conventions in British public finance that enable proceeds from sales of capital assets to be viewed as negative public expenditure, thus reducing the deficit, see Vickers and Yarrow (1988:158).

6. An extensive list of assets that have been or are about to be privatized can be found in various budget statements and in Treasury Board's annual report to Parliament on Crown corporations.

7. For an extended discussion, see Russell (1990:246–55).

8. The extent to which "permanent exceptionalism" implies a thorough reconstruction of the post-war order in industrial relations has occasioned some debate (see McBride 1987; Russell 1990:ch. 7).

9. For a fuller discussion, see McBride (1992:206–11).

10. We have in mind here Margaret Thatcher's famous aphorism to the effect that "There is no such thing as society."

11. Brady's own observation was confined to the "economic" life of Canada (see Brooks and Stritch 1991:28).

Chapter 4

Dismantling the Post-War
Social Order

The establishment of a Keynesian welfare state was reviewed in Chapter 2. The system was largely complete by 1971. Some programs, such as unemployment insurance, were reduced in generosity during the 1970s but, for the most part, the main features of the Keynesian welfare state were little altered when the neo-liberal Mulroney Conservatives took office in 1984.

The precise impact of that government's neo-liberalism on existing programs was a matter of some debate in the 1980s and early 1990s. The prevailing view was that change was incremental and consisted of erosion rather than outright dismantling. In the late 1980s Keith Banting (1987:213) pointed to two contradictory trends: one was the ongoing extension of income support systems in response to societal needs; the other was the pressure for retrenchment emanating from neo-liberal ideas and a fiscal crisis. In his view, the federal system may have acted as a brake on the development of the Canadian welfare state, but it also acted as a brake on those who wished to shrink it. Others implied that ideological divisions within the Conservative ("blue Tories" or "hawks" versus "red Tories" or "doves") and Liberal (business versus welfare Liberals) parties, together with public apprehension about the government's intentions, may have slowed the implementation of a neo-liberal agenda (Lachapelle 1988).

In the 1984 election the Conservatives sought to calm the public's fears about their intentions by promising to maintain social programs and expenditures; in some areas (such as daycare) expansion was promised. Once the party was in office it became apparent that its chief priority was to be deficit reduction and that this would involve cost-cutting measures in the social policy area. But the government was forced to retreat on the issue of de-indexing old age pensions, and "by the end of 1986, it appeared to some observers that the government had abandoned its half-hearted attempt to break with the centrist consensus in Canada over social protection" (Mishra 1990:75). Proponents of this view were careful to point out that the absence of a major restructuring of the welfare state did not imply the failure of efforts to curb spending or alter the system; the universality principle had been eroded and the rate of increase of federal social expenditures considerably reduced (see, for example, Houle 1990:438).

The view that neo-liberalism's impact in social policy had been confined to erosion encountered criticism as the 1990s unfolded (for example, Mullaly 1994). But most contributors to this debate in the early 1990s could probably agree that the Mulroney government was restricted somewhat in its efforts to change social policy and that the changes would probably have been greater but for the constraints. Whether these constraints have now been removed is a question posed by the greater pace that Chrétien's Liberal government has achieved in paring back social provision—despite election promises that Canada's social programs would be in safer hands under the Liberals. The 1997 re-election of a government that effectively gutted social programs suggests that the public opinion constraint no longer operates as it once did.

One constraint was recognition, until recently, by federal politicians and officials that Ottawa's social policy role had served as a crucial instrument of political and cultural integration and a central means of legitimation (Banting 1987:119–20; Houle 1990:440–41). Although neo-liberal parties at the federal level sought to cut back on social services after elections, until the 1997 election they had been unwilling to risk campaigning on these issues at election time because "the heartland of the welfare state—universal social programs which serve the broad majority of the population—remains popular. . . . No party can hope to win elections on a platform which proposes their retrenchment" (Mishra 1990:77).[1] The difficulty that neo-liberals faced in trying to dislodge a Keynesian-style welfare state system from the public's affections led to the suspicion that important economic initiatives, such as the free-trade agreement, are Trojan horses that permit neo-liberal social policy to be introduced "through the back door" (Mishra 1990:99; Hurtig 1991:ch. 22).

The evidence of continued public support for social programs and the related perception that they are an important ingredient of national identity continued to be robust through the mid-1990s. In summarizing the findings of a 1995 *Maclean's* poll of Canadian attitudes, Alan Gregg concluded that:

> Canadians believe that virtually everything about Canada not only has got worse than it was in times past . . . but that we can expect continued deterioration. . . . Moreover, those areas where this deterioration is anticipated most are the same ones that best define Canadians' unique sense of identity and self: our social programs and social fabric, the opportunities for advancement afforded to our young people and our economic prosperity. In short, Canadians report that, not only is their outlook for the future negative, but also the aspects of Canadian life that have given us a common sense of purpose and character will exist—if at all—only as pale imitations of what they were. (1996:14)

Similarly an Ekos poll compared elite and popular attitudes towards government. It was apparent that the general public preferred strong active government, the hallmark of Canadians' traditional attachment to "statism," while the elite was attached to the concept of minimal government. Indeed opinions were distributed in a way that led Ekos to conclude that: "The country is riven by social-class differences. These are replacing regional and linguistic differences as the main cleavage in Canadian politics." Elites favoured goals such as "an unremitting focus on fiscal issues" over social and cultural priorities and felt governments should be concentrating on the goals of prosperity, competitiveness and minimal government. These goals were rejected by the general public (*The Globe and Mail*, 25 February 1995).

In a subsequent commentary on the Ekos poll Michael Valpy, in a column entitled "The war between the classes" (*The Globe and Mail*, 30 June 1995), drew attention to "the enormous chasm" that separated elite opinion from that of the general public. The latter continues to see

> government as a legitimate intervener in Canadian life and still accepts the goals of government intervention, but realizes that government has failed to deliver real progress toward those goals. Unlike the nation's elites, the public still sees government as a means for expressing core societal values. It still sees the country as a crucial source of identity and belonging, second only to the family. It still seems to be seeking a higher-order, moral community and not merely a rational articulation of economic interests.

Other polls, for example, a December 1995 Angus Reid survey for Southam News and CTV, reveal the same attachment to job creation and social programs in preference to deficit cutting—once again the distribution of opinion divided on class lines (*Vancouver Sun*, 28 December 1995).

The Liberal Party's election campaign in 1993 recognized the deep-rooted attachment of Canadians to social programs and their fears that these were threatened. The Red Book criticized the Conservatives for a "tendency to focus obsessively on one problem, such as the deficit or inflation, without understand-ing or caring about the consequences of their policies in other areas such as lost jobs, increased poverty, and dependence on social assistance" (Liberal Party 1993:10). With a more integrated approach to economic, social, environmental and foreign policy the Liberals believed that economic problems could be overcome without recourse to the Conservative scenario of "cutbacks, job losses and diminished expectations." In particular a continued priority to social pro-grams was envisaged:

> if Canada is to work as a country, Canadians have to see themselves as belonging not to a society composed of isolated individuals or of competing interest groups, but to a society of reciprocal obligation, in which each of us is responsible for the well-being of the other. (Liberal Party 1993:11)

Such assurances—continued commitment to social programs and a "jobs" orientation—played an important role in the campaign. A leaked draft White Paper on social policy and Prime Minister Kim Campbell's assertion that an election campaign was no occasion on which to debate such serious matters, coupled with her suggestion that Canada faced double-digit unemployment for the remainder of the century, were defining events. The leaked social policy document revealed plans to cut social program spending by 10 percent. This was to be accomplished through a massive overhaul of the income maintenance system including cuts to unemployment insurance and social assistance. Changes in the qualification criteria could exclude over half of those then qualifying for unemployment insurance benefits. Receipt of social assistance benefits was projected to be linked more tightly to labour market criteria—benefit payments, for example, might become contingent on participation in training programs (*The Globe and Mail*, 7 October 1993).

The goal of re-orienting social assistance and, particularly, labour-market programs from passive income support measures to more active measures formed part of the Liberal's own proposals. The Liberal's posture of putting their proposals into a supportive context as far as social programs generally were concerned, and the undoubted neo-liberalism and Mulroney-derived image of duplicity of the Tories, together with Campbell's refusal to debate the issue (see Erickson 1995:138–39), were damaging to the Conservatives.

Certainly the proposals leaked under the Campbell government were not dissimilar to those pursued by the Liberals, once elected. This is an indication that political and bureaucratic elites have jettisoned their earlier commitment to maintaining social programs as an element of national unity. The constraint of general public opinion, which, as we have seen, remains more attached to these programs, has weakened as it has become apparent that those holding these opinions are unable to coalesce around any political force committed to sustaining the Keynesian welfare state.

The second constraint is the federal system. Banting (1987:205–14) has reviewed two versions of the comparatively well-grounded argument that federalism exerts a conservative influence in social welfare politics. The first, and most familiar of these, is that federalism slowed the development of the Canadian welfare state, thus inhibiting the expansion of the state and preserving a broad arena occupied by the private sector and market forces. The second version of the argument is that federal systems are resistant to change *per se*:

> the fragmentation of power implicit in federal structures creates a set of checks and balances and veto points that increase the probability that any proposal for change—whether involving an expansion or a contraction of the public sector—will be delayed, diluted, or defeated. In effect, the additional opportunities for blocking change raise the level of

consensus required before new initiatives can be introduced on a nation-wide basis. (Banting 1987:206)

Banting provides evidence to support both versions of the impact of federalism: federalism clearly operated to impede *expansion* of the income security system and, in an asymmetrical way, to impede its *contraction*. The asymmetry arises from the fact that federal cost-cutting attempts encountered vigorous opposition from interest groups allied with provincial governments. At the provincial level, however, neo-liberal governments have been much less constrained in reducing the social services that are under their jurisdiction (see McNiven 1987; Mishra 1987). Such proclivities on the part of provincial governments were reinforced by the erosion of federal transfer payments (Johnson 1988:270–71). Nevertheless, the federal system continued to operate as a constraint in certain ways, as with the Canada Health Act's deterrence of practices like extra billing that some provinces wished to introduce.

The Liberal Record: Overview
It has been argued that the 1995 federal budget marked a fundamental shift in the role of the federal state in Canada. It marks the point where erosion of social programs ended and demolition seriously began. Even before the budget the trend was apparent to informed observers:

> All manner of rhetoric will be used to mask Ottawa's decline: 'reinventing government,' 'flexible federalism,' 'modernizing Canada.' . . . The essence of the matter, however, is this: the shrinking of the federal government, attempted by the Conservatives under the guise of fiscal restraint and constitutional reform, will now be accelerated by the Liberals through non-constitutional means. (Simpson 1995).

Others have defined the budget as the end of an era:"It is now clear that the Minister of Reconstruction's White Paper on Employment and Income of 1945 can be regarded as one bookend on a particular period in Canadian history, and Paul Martin's February [1995] budget as the other" (Kroeger 1996:21).

The case for 1995 as the termination point of the Keynesian welfare state rests on the primacy of deficit reduction over maintenance of the social safety net. Determination to reduce the deficit through spending reductions in the social policy area[2] has resulted in declining federal transfers to provinces. This has dissolved the glue that had bound some of them to national standards. Early projections that the cash portion of federal transfers would decline to zero by the fiscal year 2009/10 (*CCPA Monitor*, May 1995) and abolish federal constraint on provincial budget slashers completely were modified by the 1996 budget speech. The finance minister announced that the federal government was guaranteeing the cash portion of transfers would not fall below $11 billion in the period up to

Figure 4.1
The EPF System (1977–96)

Provincial program	Mechanism used by the federal government to help fund the program	Requirement that the provincial government must meet to obtain federal finding	The federal government's enforcement tool
Health care	EPF	Provinces must ensure that five principles of the Canada Health Act, specified in legislation, are maintained: public administration, comprehensiveness, universality, portability, and accessibility. This leaves them a lot of flexibility in determining which services are insured. Provincial variations can be significant.	There can be a dollar-for-dollar reduction of federal funding to the provinces for health care if a principle is violated.
Post-secondary education	EPF	None	None
Social services	CAP	A series of conditions are specified in the CAP Act, regulations, and individual agreements, and in the notes and guidelines that elaborate on specific policies. Aside from some overall conditions, there are separate conditions in relation to each of social assistance and welfare services.	A province does not obtain money unless it spends money on eligible services, within the requirements.

Source: National Union of Public and General Employees 1995.

2002/03. This would, he claimed, give the federal government the financial capacity to uphold the principles of medicare and other programs, including portability and accessibility. Nevertheless, even if the promise of a continuing cash component of transfer payments is fulfilled, the erosion of federal financial support for social programs has reduced the effectiveness of federalism as a constraint on dismantling the welfare state.

As money for social support has diminished there has been increased emphasis on "active" measures that would enable individuals to enter or re-enter the labour market rather than remain dependent on social assistance. As a result, as social policy's star waned, that of labour-market policy waxed—at least rhetorically. However, this area is in the process of being transferred from the federal to the provincial level. There it is likely to function, together with workfare, chiefly as a social control adjunct to residual social programs.

Transfer Payments
The main instrument of reduced federal commitment to social programs is reduced transfer payments and diminished federal conditions attached to the funds transferred. The major change occurred with the introduction of the Canada Health and Social Transfer (CHST) in 1996. Some of the main differences between the pre-1996 system of federal–provincial transfers and that which will occur under the CHST are summarized in Figures 4.1 and 4.2.

Federal funding in two social policy areas—post-secondary education and health care—was provided from 1977 to 1996 under a financial arrangement known as Established Programs Financing (EPF). EPF was introduced in 1977 and replaced earlier cost-sharing arrangements that had split health and post-secondary education costs on a 50:50 basis. The new formula was a "block funding" arrangement in which the federal contribution was partly cash and partly tax points transferred to the provinces. Its effect was to decentralize funds and therefore political power over these policy areas. It represented "the most massive transfer of revenues (and therefore the substance of power) from the federal to the provincial governments in Canadian history" (Taylor 1987:435).

Under EPF, increases in the federal contribution were tied to growth of GNP and population rather than, as previously, to increased real costs. Under the "six and five" anti-inflation program, EPF payments for post-secondary education were limited. Although the initial effect was minor, this measure eroded the base for future payments and led to a permanent loss in federal contributions—estimated at $2.4 billion over the 1984–91 period (National Council of Welfare 1991b:16). Further, in the name of deficit reduction the federal government imposed ceilings on EPF in 1986 (when increases were limited to the growth in GNP minus 2 percent, reduced to growth rate minus 3 percent in 1989); later, under Bill C-69, EPF was frozen for 1990–91 and 1991–92; and in the 1991 budget the freeze was extended until 1994–95, after which it was to revert to the constraint of GNP growth minus 3 percent (Canadian Council on Social Devel-

Figure 4.2
The CHST System (from April 1996)

Provincial program	Mechanism used by the federal government to help fund the program	Requirement that the provincial government must meet to obtain federal funding	The federal government's enforcement tool
Health care	CHST	Provinces must ensure that five principles of the Canada Health Act, specified in legislation, are maintained: public administration, comprehensiveness, universality, portability, and accessibility.	It has the authority to cut CHST funding, in part or in total, for infractions. Although it will attempt to consult with the relevant provincial government to work things out, it can act unilaterally. Because this is a block fund, if the power is used, provinces might apply the funding reduction to post-secondary education and / or social services, which have fewer standards than health care.
Post-secondary education	CHST	None. Unless the federal government and all the provinces reach unanimous agreement on the need for requirements and on what they should be, or the federal government unilaterally imposes its own standards in legislation.	None. This could change if requirements are agreed to or imposed. If that happens, the federal government will have the authority to cut CHST funding, in part or in total, for infractions. Although it will attempt to consult with the relevant provincial government to work things out, it can act unilaterally.
Social services	CHST	There is only one requirement—residency can't be used as a restriction. Other requirements are possible, if the federal government and all the provinces reach unanimous agreement on what they should be, or the federal government unilaterally imposes its own standards on the provinces. Remember that a stated goal of reform is provincial "flexibility" in providing social programs.	It has the authority to cut CHST funding, in part or in total, for infractions, in relation to the proposed standard or others that may be developed or imposed. Although it will attempt to consult with the relevant provincial government to work things out, it can act unilaterally.

Source: National Union of Public and General Employees 1995.

opment 1990; Wilson 1991:70–71). The Canadian Council on Social Development (1990:2) analyzed the effect of these measures:

> Since the money raised by the tax points continues to grow—it is not limited—all reductions in the growth of the block fund come out of the federal cash transfers. This means that the cash portion of federal block funding shrinks over time. . . . Federal cash to the provinces for medicare and higher education will shrink . . . to zero by about 2004 under Bill C-69. . . . Less and less federal money for medicare and colleges and universities puts the financial burden of these programs squarely on the shoulders of the provinces, and he who pays the piper calls the tune. The federal government's ability to influence national standards or guidelines will diminish.

To allay such concerns the federal government announced that it would be taking powers under the Fiscal Arrangements Act so that deductions from other cash transfers to provinces could be used to enforce national medicare standards in keeping with the way that, under the Canada Health Act, EPF transfers could be withheld for this purpose. Critics remained unconvinced: "It is only the federal spending power that allowed federal involvement in this area, and it is difficult to imagine how Ottawa could continue to maintain its presence once the money for medicare dries up" (National Council of Welfare 1991b:22–23).

In 1996 the EPF, which had provided federal funds for post-secondary education and health care, and the Canada Assistance Plan (CAP), which provided federal contributions to social assistance and welfare, were rolled into a single block funding scheme—the Canada Health and Social Transfer (CHST—see Figure 4.2).

A noteworthy feature of the CHST is a loosening of federal conditions attached to the transfer. Under CAP, for example, provinces had to spend their own money to receive federal funds. Under CHST this requirement does not exist. The other conditions attached to CAP, with the exception of that which prohibits residency requirements, were eliminated. The CHST contains no conditions as far as post-secondary education is concerned. And, as a comparison of Figures 4.1 and 4.2 reveals, federal enforcement mechanisms are either diminished or are less direct than formerly. Under these conditions the erosion of national standards can safely be predicted. There will be considerable variation, outside of health care, in the quality of benefits and in access to them. The effectiveness of the safeguards for health care are matters of dispute, as we see in the next section of this chapter.

As shown in Table 4.1, it is indisputable that the new funding mechanism will produce substantial reductions in fiscal transfers. Such reductions are additional to those that had occurred under the earlier funding mechanisms. The federal agenda in this area is certainly driven by the finance department and fiscal

Table 4.1
Federal Transfer Payments to Provinces, 1994–1999 (billions)

Budget Year	CST (pre 1996 -EFT & CAP)	Equal- ization	Terri- torial	Other	Alter- native	Total	Total Prog- ram Spending	Total Trans- fers as % of Total Pro- gram Spend- ing
98/99	11.8	8.4	1.1	0	-2.2	19.1	103.5	18.45
97/98	12.5	8.3	1.1	0	-2.1	19.8	105.8	18.71
96/97	14.9	8.5	1.1	0.1	-2.0	22.6	109.0	20.73
95/96	18.6	8.8	1.2	-0.2	-1.9	26.5	112.0	23.66
94/95	19.3	8.5	1.2	-0.4	-1.8	26.7	118.7	22.49

Source: Ministry of Finance 1997:43.

motives enjoy priority. However, as Battle and Torjman point out (1996:64), it also fits into a constitutional agenda of decentralization:

> Ottawa is seeking ways of 'renewing' itself and its relationship with the provinces—especially in light of the Québec referendum which threatens to break up the country. The Canada Health and Social Transfer has high symbolic value in that it represents a move by the federal government to retreat from provincial territory.[3]

Health
To date the best-protected social programs have been health and education. Even here, as public provision weakens, calls for partial privatization and increased use of market mechanisms have increased. Geoffrey Weller (1996:124–25) has depicted the supporters and opponents of medicare in the following terms:

> The groups and interests that support medicare in Canada are the New Democratic Party, a large section of the trade union movement (especially the health sector unions), many organizations representing pensioners, most academic commentators, and virtually all recent government inquiries into health care whether they be provincial or federal. Prior to the 1995 budget some included the Liberal Party in such a listing of medicare's supporters.... The domestic forces that oppose medicare, at least in anything like its present form, are the Conservative and Reform parties, a wide variety of business groups such as the Business

Council on National Issues, think tanks such as the Fraser Institute and the C.D.Howe Institute, most organized groups that represent physicians, and many members of what has been called the medical-industrial complex, that is, the pharmaceutical companies, insurance companies, medical equipment manufacturing companies, and the like.

Opponents of medicare criticize several of its key characteristics, including universality, public administration, and national standards enforced by a strong federal government. They also demand "user fees" to bring home to patients the cost of the services provided. A decentralized administration of the medicare system would make it easier for the other components of medicare to which opponents have objected to be dismantled. As we shall see in Chapters 5 and 6, this is consistent with a general neo-liberal preference for decentralization on the grounds that it will lead to less government and more scope for markets.

There have been serious concerns that NAFTA may undermine the principle of publicly-funded medicare. There is some evidence that the scope of privatization of hospital-related services, typically through contracting-out arrangements, has widened since the agreement took effect (CCPA *Monitor*, July/August 1995:5).

Notwithstanding claims that health care was protected, a union-based coalition, the Canadian Health Coalition, pressured provincial and federal governments to explicitly list policies, services and regulations as exempt from NAFTA. The coalition considered this necessary because in signing NAFTA, the federal government had failed to exempt health care in the financial services chapter of the agreement. In the face of this pressure, and the continued popularity of public health care, Ottawa finally acted and obtained an agreement with its NAFTA partners that considerably increased the ability of provincial governments to protect health and social services. This was a major victory for defenders of the public medicare system in Canada.

Yet as Fuller (1996:18) points out, Canadian legislation that echoes NAFTA provisions such as that on intellectual property rights is having a major impact on the medicare system. Under Bill C-22 patent protection for name brand drugs was extended from four to ten years. In 1993 the protection was extended to twenty years. The result has been rapidly escalating pharmaceutical costs, and some provincial health plans are beginning to reduce coverage in order to contain costs (CCPA *Monitor*, March 1995:9). It is likely that as other components of NAFTA come to be clarified they may serve to undermine the system (see also Chapter 8).

The 1977 change to block funding had the predictable effect of increasing provincial variations in medical coverage and billing practices. In 1984 the federal government responded by passing the Canada Health Act (CHA) which reaffirmed the conditions stipulated in the 1967 Medical Care Act—universal coverage, accessibility, portability, comprehensiveness, and public administration—and provided that federal funds would be withheld, on a dollar for dollar basis for every dollar of extra billing or hospital user fees that provinces permitted (see Silver 1996). Reflecting on the experience since 1984, Silver (1996:77) comments that the "'stick' of the CHA has been effective as long as the federal government has the political will and the financial means to enforce it."

In fact the Conservative government was constrained from making substantial changes to medicare by the Liberal decision to pass a new Canada Health Act just before the 1984 election and the immense popularity of the program (Weller 1996:130). The Conservatives were forced to vote for the measure or face the prospect of it becoming the main issue in the election. Having voted for it they were bound by its provisions as long as medicare itself retained its public support.

Although rhetorically committed to the principles of the CHA the incoming Chrétien government has undermined the ability of the federal government to sustain national standards in the health field. The diminishing cash portion of federal transfers for health care purposes diminishes federal capacity to oppose user fees, delisting of covered services, private health clinics and the variety of other means by which the market is being allowed to creep into a system previously based on quite different principles. The retention of a cash component to CHST transfers, announced in the 1996 budget, means that until 2002, or thereabouts, the federal government will continue to have the means to oppose these cuts—whether the political will is still there remains to be seen.

One leading observer of health policy has concluded that the political will of the Liberal Party is being exercised in an entirely different direction: "the Liberals have done an about face. . . . A government elected on the plank of preserving medicare is governing in a manner that will undermine and then destroy it. The end result for the Canadian health care system will be its eventual return to the private, profit-making market. That will inevitability lead to precisely what the Liberal Party itself said it would in the 1993 election campaign, namely a two-tiered, inequitable system—one that will be far more expensive and less efficient than the current one, and yet will suffer from most of the same problems" (Weller 1996:143).

Social Policy
Social policy in the 1980s had presented a mixed pattern; neo-liberal efforts to restrain and retrench programs were apparent in some areas, in others, modest expansion occurred despite the prevailing ideological environment. Banting (1987:186–92) contrasted the pensions area, which fared reasonably well, with developments in other areas of income security, such as family allowances, which experienced erosion and, ultimately elimination, with programs for the unemployed, which were targeted for more serious restraint. He noted the general similarity between this pattern and that experienced in other countries under neo-liberal governments in the 1980s. The differential treatment of programs was partly attributed to "the uneven political strength and popular support of different

beneficiary groups.... Programs that benefit the population as a whole have been treated more gently than those reserved for the unemployed and lower-income groups" (Banting 1987:192). The means of implementing changes in social programs are indicative of the cautious and incremental approach adopted by Canadian neo-liberals. Outright abolition of programs or draconian restructuring has not been characteristic of social policy reforms. Rather, other techniques have found favour: greater selectivity in programs that were previously universal, increased restrictiveness in determining eligibility for programs, and imposition of ceilings on program costs or, alternatively, attempting to make them self-financing (Houle 1990:432).

Developments in various branches of social policy show that however constrained the government has been, it has made significant progress in implementing its neo-liberal agenda. The change of government in 1993 has made little difference—if anything, the dismantling process has sped up. The increasing stringency of social programs can be seen clearly in the welfare system. Welfare or social assistance is provided by provincial and municipal authorities. Under the Canada Assistance Plan (CAP), Ottawa shared 50 percent of the costs, subject to certain conditions (see Moscovitch 1988). The number of social assistance recipients increased dramatically in the early 1980s, but although federal spending also increased (from 3.2 percent of total federal expenditures in fiscal 1982 to 3.5 percent in fiscal 1986), the expenditures did not keep pace with needs. The system was therefore subject to the erosion characteristic of other social programs. This process was exacerbated for the fiscally stronger provinces—Ontario, Alberta, and British Columbia—by the announcement, in 1990, that the growth in CAP transfers was to be limited for 1990–91 and 1991–92 to 5 percent a year. The 1991 budget extended this provision through 1994–95 (Wilson 1991). And the 1994 budget limited 1994–96 CAP transfers to their 1994/95 levels. The result is that the "have" provinces have seen a decreasing share of welfare costs covered by federal transfers.

Rates of assistance on CAP were low and recipients lived well below the poverty line (Johnson 1988:275). Since 1985 both federal and some provincial governments emphasized integrating the CAP with labour-market policy in order to get welfare recipients off the welfare rolls. To this end funds were diverted from the CAP to the Canada Jobs Strategy (CJS), and unemployed "employables" were encouraged to participate in job-experience and job-training programs (Russell 1991b:492). Such measures were limited in scope by the conditions under the Canada Assistance Plan. However, the replacement of CAP by block funding under the Canada Health and Social Transfer ended that constraint.

Under the new arrangement provinces are free to initiate social security reform without significant federal interference. It is already clear that the abolition of the CAP will lead to extensive use of workfare schemes in many provinces. Moreover, the inclusion of politically less popular welfare funds in the same mix as education and health will likely lead to welfare and social services having even lower priority than they did formerly. In addition, the ability of these programs to act as a countercyclical measure, already eroded by the "cap on CAP" imposed on the "have" provinces, will further diminish (see Battle and Torjman 1996:57–58).

Workfare[4] programs of various types—employability, job search, or job training—have been widely used in the United States and have been advocated by right-wing parties and organizations in Canada. Typically advocates of these programs claim they will produce cost savings and that participants will be re-integrated into the labour force. However, a careful survey of these programs concluded "there is no empirical evidence that education, job training, job search, or workfare programs are actually effective in putting people in jobs that will help them leave the welfare system. At best, these programs assist people who generally combine welfare with temporary, seasonal or part-time jobs to find work faster than if they had not enrolled in these programs" (Hardina 1997:144).

The best known examples of workfare in Canada, for which evaluations are available, are to be found in New Brunswick and Québec. Even in these cases definitive evaluation is difficult since, as with the New Brunswick Works program, caseworkers select participants on the basis of their potential to succeed in it, thus "creaming" from the available pool. There is no experimentally designed control group with which to compare the participants, and it is a far better resourced program than most of its type—costs per participant are about $100,000 (Milne 1996). One evaluation of NB Works, reflecting these concerns in part, concluded: "It is clearly cost-prohibitive to operate it on a national scale. Not only is it a very expensive program, it has an excessive dropout rate (approximately 70 percent of the first intake has exited from the program with a population that was selected on the basis of having the greatest potential for completing the program). This suggests, of course, that the retention rate would be even lower if the program was extended to include all employable persons in receipt of social assistance. In addition to the cost factor, there is no guarantee that persons completing NB Works will obtain a job. And even those who obtain jobs likely do so at the expense of another person, because the unemployment rates in New Brunswick remain very high. What really takes place is a kind of shuffling of the deck for the unemployed" (Mullally 1997:56). Very similar conclusions were reached about cheaper but equivalent programs in Québec (Shragge and Deniger 1997).

Emulation by other provinces such as Ontario and Alberta should therefore be seen as driven by ideological factors rather than by a track record of success for workfare.

In most workfare programs the training is of the most rudimentary kind, equipping "graduates" for the lowest-paid and most menial jobs—assuming these are available. Since the supply of such jobs is unlikely to increase as a result of employability training for welfare recipients, the most that such programs can achieve is rotation of more people through the cycle of low-wage jobs and the welfare system. This is only likely to fuel the hopelessness and desperation already experienced by these people.

If the empirical validity of workfare schemes is so problematic, what accounts for their current popularity? Historically, enthusiasm for workfare typically follows major structural changes in the economy that create high unemployment. As a result of such changes, welfare caseloads increase and economic "recovery" seems to do little to reduce them. Workfare is usually part of a broad set of coercive measures directed against the poor. Such measures might include cuts in benefits, allegations of widespread fraud, use of "snitch lines," and so on. Finally, workfare attempts to blame the victims of unemployment for their plight, rather than blaming the structural economic changes that led to it (Struthers 1996). Moreover, as Struthers asserts, workfare is always fraudulent in that

> through workfare, society insists upon the importance of testing the willingness of the jobless to work. But it is a cruel one-way exchange since such schemes, as the historical evidence suggests, have never been accompanied by guarantees that those who pass the test will in turn, be rewarded with legitimate employment. (Struthers 1996:7)

(Un)Employment Insurance
Unemployment insurance has been a principal target of the Liberal government's social cutbacks. From its inception in 1940 Canada's unemployment insurance system underwent regular amendment and modification in the direction of "almost unbroken expansion and liberalization" (Pal 1988:35) until the 1971 Unemployment Insurance Act, which had substantially more generous terms and conditions than its predecessors. After that, however, the trend of amendments and modifications was one of almost unbroken restriction and retrenchment. In unemployment insurance, as in a number of other areas, the neo-liberal era pre-dates the 1984 election (see McBride 1992:ch. 6).

Under the 1940 legislation, employees, employers, and government each contributed in the ratio 40:40:20 to an unemployment insurance fund out of which benefits were paid. When the fund was in deficit this was made up out of general government revenues, which were to be repaid from employer/employee contributions. During the 1970s, measures were taken to reduce the system's generosity and to finance it more regressively. The impact of these measures can be traced in the declining share of the costs borne by government. The major change implemented by the Conservatives was to cease government contributions to the fund. Figure 4.4 tracks the government's share (1972–86), from general revenues, of unemployment insurance costs and compares these with the scope of the unemployment problem. Compared with the situation in the mid-1970s, governments progressively insulated their general revenues from the direct impact of high unemployment. Since 1991 there have been no net

Figure 4.3

**Cost to Government of UI (as a % of GDP) Compared
to the Unemployment Rate, 1972–86**

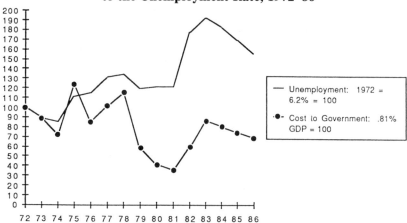

*Note: Costs are for fiscal years beginning with 1972–73. Source: Statistics
Canada, Canada Employment and Immigration Commission, Annual Reports.*

contributions from general revenues, so the insulation is complete.

Changes to the unemployment insurance system did encounter significant
opposition: "Any revision to unemployment insurance... engenders tremendous
counter-pressures from affected provinces, regions, unions, employers, and
social advocacy groups. Unemployment insurance is by now so deeply and
widely embedded in the Canadian political economy that fundamental change
would seem virtually impossible" (Pal 1988:11). Among the constraining factors
was the federal system. In retrospect, however, it is clear that Pal overstated the
impregnability of unemployment insurance and correspondingly underesti-
mated the power of Canadian business, whose pressure against the 1971 Act has
been unremitting and, incrementally, quite effective. On the other hand, he was
correct to point to the deep roots that the system established in Canadian society
and to the powerful coalition of class, governmental, and other interests that
periodically rallied to its defence. This serves to highlight the difficulty faced by
neo-liberals in dismantling Canada's welfare state and helps account for slow
progress. But it does not alter the fact that movement in this direction has been
taken.

During the 1993 election the Liberals made jobs a major priority: "Unless
Canadians get back to work, the cost of lost production, unemployment, and
welfare will inevitably increase the deficit, as it has in the course of the
Conservative mandate" (Liberal Party 1993:20).

Traditional infrastructure programs were to be launched to provide some immediate employment relief; however, the central initiatives would be longer-term—fostering trade and exports, promoting research and development, support for small and medium-sized business, and measures to enhance the productivity and competitiveness of the labour force through training and skill development.

Government's role in the new global economy, the Liberals claimed, would be different than in the past. Canada had relied on its natural resources and on a degree of integration in the North American market in which proximity to American markets, assisted by managed trade agreements such as the Autopact, made a Canadian version of Keynesianism feasible. In the new economy of the 1990s

> it is the information and knowledge-based industries with their new products, new services, new markets for both old and new products, and new processes for existing businesses that are providing the foundation for jobs and economic growth . . . comparative advantage now hinges . . . on our technological prowess—on the sophistication of our infrastructure, our ability to innovate, and, most important, the education and skill levels of our population. (Liberal Party 1993:29)

Thus the Liberal Party appeared to buy into the concept of an information economy and the related concept of human capital development as a necessary condition for success. Similarly, the Liberals argued that some sort of neo-corporatist "partnership" between business, labour and government offered the best means of promoting the training, education and investment necessary for success in the new economy—a version of the "progressive competitiveness" strategy often posed as an alternative to neo-liberalism (for an analysis and critique, see Albo 1994).

The Liberals promised federal support for provincial efforts in education though, given lack of federal jurisdiction, these were predictably minor. Funding to support apprenticeships in areas such as information technology, telecommunications and broadcasting technology, computer services, environmental services, and medical and biotechnology skills was promised. These areas were targeted because they were seen as high growth areas in the new economy. The approach was to be cooperative, with the federal government working closely with the provinces, business, and labour. Similarly, the program envisaged a Canadian Youth Service Corps to provide work skills and experience to those under twenty-five who were experiencing employment difficulties. The program was to start on a small scale, however, with about ten thousand places per year initially. Also promised were increased efforts to overcome illiteracy and increased provision of child care, to remove a barrier to labour force participation, especially for women provided that the provinces also agreed to participate.

In the area of workplace training the Liberal manifesto reflected the conventional wisdom that too little training was being performed. It undertook to encourage more private-sector training and to work together with labour, business and the provinces to increase the volume of training performed. To ensure that the expertise of labour-market partners was procured and that the right sort of training was performed, it proposed to transfer greater authority to community training boards, which, it was felt, could best advise on appropriate training ventures and promote a training culture. In this context funds from the unemployment insurance fund were to be designated for more active use (Liberal Party 1993:ch. 2). This initiative was entirely in line with Conservative policy, which had established the Canadian Labour Force Development Board and a system of local boards for precisely this purpose.

The standard and plausible objection to such labour market strategies is that while they are bound to work for capital—through providing increasingly skilled and flexible labour power—it is unclear how they can work to labour's advantage or to that of individual nation-states. This is because the strategy is becoming so widespread that it is unlikely to confer a comparative advantage on national labour forces unless matched by an expansionary demand-side strategy. Indeed, in the absence of a demand-side component, the more widely supply-side strategies are pursued, the more likely it is that existing comparative advantages will be broken down and the existing connection between high skill, high wage, and high value-added production severed. There are, in any case, grounds for doubting that Canadian policy produces the kind of advanced training essential to such a strategy (see McBride 1992:154–57). Other analysts (see Livingstone 1996) have cast doubt on the notion that a skills deficit, in relation to the type of jobs being created, exists at all.

At the rhetorical level, however, supply-side strategies retained some appeal—they certainly sounded more optimistic and active than the guarantee of low wages and permanent insecurity contained in the neo-liberal paradigm. It is apparent, moreover, that labour-market policy and social security are becoming intertwined. Active labour-market policy is often defended as a means of getting people off passive income support and into jobs. More critical analyses concede this may happen, though not necessarily, but view the emphasis on active policy as an instrument to destroy the Keynesian welfare state system, leaving people with no option but to enter the labour force and fill the low-wage, temporary and insecure jobs increasingly characteristic of our labour force (see Shields 1996).

In a speech soon after the 1993 election, Lloyd Axworthy (1994a), the new minister of human resources development, outlined an approach that linked social security, labour-market policy and education to the economy. Axworthy interpreted the election result as an overwhelming mandate to use the tools of government to put people back to work—"No more passivity, indifference or avoidance. The message was clear. Jobs was the issue, and they [the electorate] wanted action" (1994a). In devising his "Action Plan," however, the minister emphasized the structural nature of some of the high unemployment Canada was experiencing and the need for structural measures, including a re-focusing of the income security and labour-market policy systems, and greater coordination between orders of government in order to restore employment as the central goal of economic policy. In criticizing the failures of existing social programs— continued unemployment, poverty and illiteracy, duplication among government programs—Axworthy sought to distance his proposals from the "slash and trash" variety. Instead the purpose of social policy reform would be to remove perceived disincentives to individuals to seek or firms to create employment; promote the employability of those receiving various forms of social assistance and of those who were in transition from school to the labour market; and maintain an essential social safety net, while searching for more efficient means of delivering programs. These themes were developed further in the Green Book, *Agenda: Jobs and Growth* (Canada 1994), which sought to confer a comparative advantage on Canada through human capital development. According to this theory, countries will be successful in creating jobs to the extent that they are able to attract investment, international as well as domestic. To create jobs in sufficient quantities, the Green Book argued Canada must become an "investment magnet." Key to this is overcoming Canada's 'skills deficit'—offering the best-educated, best-trained workforce in the world" (Canada 1994:10). Reforms to the social security system must contribute to this goal as well as providing support for the "most vulnerable" in a fiscally responsible way. However, the document stressed repeatedly that the best form of social security came from having a job and that, in the context of structural unemployment caused by technological innovation and global pressures, existing social programs were ill suited to deliver this result.

The Green Book argued that the existing system of passive income support supplemented by specific programs was geared to an environment where rapid change was the exception rather than the rule. From this perspective, long-term unemployment and the phenomenon of "repeat claimants" of unemployment insurance benefits were indications that the system was failing to enhance the employability of those concerned. Over time the Green Book took second place to the finance department's "deficit *über alles*" agenda. However, most of the Green Book proposals in the unemployment insurance area were consistent with neo-liberalism and were represented in the eventual reform of unemployment insurance.

The direction of Liberal labour-market policy became clearer with the passage of the Employment Insurance Act in 1996. The Act was tabled in the House of Commons on 1 December, 1995, and was intended to replace both the Unemployment Insurance Act and the National Training Act. A press release (Human Resources Development Canada 1995) claimed the bill represented a "fundamental restructuring" of the unemployment insurance system since it redesigned income benefits and combined them with active measures to promote re-entry into the labour force while respecting "provincial responsibility for labour market training."

The restructured system would provide two kinds of benefits. Income benefits would serve as basic income replacement during unemployment. Employment benefits would be more active instruments to assist claimants find jobs.

In recognition of provincial responsibility for training, the government stated that it would no longer purchase training courses and that it would withdraw from apprenticeship training and cooperative education. The active portion of employment insurance, employment benefits, might include wage subsidies, earnings supplements, assistance to individuals starting their own businesses, job creation partnerships with provinces, the private sector or local communities, and skills loans and grants to help individuals finance their own training. However, these would "only be offered in a province with the agreement of the provincial government." The federal government envisaged different arrangements with different provinces—a kind of practical version of asymmetrical federalism that could cater to both the Québec agenda as well as to generalized demands for decentralization.

One implication of the changes is that federal financial contributions to provincial employment or training measures will henceforth come exclusively from employment insurance. Until recently money from the "developmental uses" of unemployment insurance had been accompanied by funds from general revenues, under such programs as the Canadian Jobs Strategy. Thus total federal funding will decline further. This is likely to stimulate further privatization of the training industry unless provincial governments use their regulatory power to protect public provision of training.

A major purpose of the restructuring of unemployment insurance is to reduce costs. The government itself claims a 10 percent reduction in expenditures but trade union critics allege the savings are likely to be in the order of 15 to 25 percent (National Union of Public and General Employees 1996). The instruments of expenditure reduction are reduced benefits to be achieved through increased eligibility requirements, lower benefit rates, more exclusions from collecting benefits, clawbacks of benefit payments, penalties for repeat claimants, and a reduced cap on insurable earnings. Currently less than 50 percent of the officially unemployed manage to collect benefits compared to 87 percent as recently as 1990 and 64 percent when the Liberals assumed office (Ecumenical Coalition For Economic Justice 1996:8). Benefits are of shorter duration and the benefit rate has fallen steadily from 66.6 percent to 55 percent and, for repeat claimants, as little as 52 percent.

Cultural Policy
Though hardly part of social policy, state involvement in culture, particularly in areas such as broadcasting, has long been part of the nation-building tradition in

Canada. Like social policy it has been one of the means by which a distinctive identity in the northern part of North America has been shaped. In the 1920s it became apparent that left to the private sector Canadian radio would either be an inferior copy of U.S. radio, which could rely upon a much larger and more concentrated market, or would be swept away by it altogether (Hardin 1974:254). Indeed this prospect led Graham Spry to coin his classic formulation, "The State or the United States?" (Hardin 1974:257). In 1929 the Aird Royal Commission on Radio Broadcasting advocated a publicly-owned and -operated broadcasting system to provide the nationwide coverage that the private sector would not. The Aird Commission recognized the new media as a potential shaper of national identity and consciousness and argued that in the absence of public intervention much of the shaping would be done by U.S. private stations (Siegel 1983:166).

These themes were echoed by Conservative Prime Minister R.B. Bennett in 1932 when he provided a rationale for the Canadian Radio Broadcasting Act: "This country must be assured of complete Canadian control of broadcasting ... by which national consciousness may be fostered and sustained and national unity still further strengthened.... No other scheme than that of public ownership can ensure to the people in this country ... equal enjoyment of the benefits and pleasures of radio broadcasting" (quoted in Hardin 1974:256-57). Arthur Siegel (1983:167) noted that in many subsequent inquiries and four broadcasting acts (1932, 1936, 1958, and 1968) there "is a consistent philosophy of national consciousness and purpose" as well as a recognition that the Canadian Broadcasting Corporation is the key instrument for the development of Canadian culture.

In 1985 the past president of the CBC, A.W. Johnson, argued that Canadian broadcasting had been "Americanized" by the importation of U.S. television through cable and by the privatization and fiscal deprivation of the Canadian public broadcasting system (Raboy 1990:304–05). To these must now be added the potential impact of the Free Trade Agreement with the United States. Although "cultural industries" were ostensibly exempt from the agreement, a "notwithstanding" clause provided that either side could retaliate with "measures of equivalent effect in response to actions that would have been inconsistent with this agreement but for (the exemption)." As Raboy comments (1990:333), "Under this provision, *every* Canadian cultural policy, program, or mechanism, existing or future, could be subject to retaliation."

The early goals of Canadian broadcasting and cultural policy—to use publicly-operated electronic media as a tool of nation-building—have been dramatically eroded. Obviously much of the erosion occurred prior to the neo-liberal election victories, but equally obviously those victories only served to accelerate the trend. A prime example came with the closure of a number of CBC outlets that had "united distant parts of this far-flung country" (Finkel, Conrad and Strong-Boag 1993:607).

Despite regular affirmation of the ethos of public broadcasting, its primacy soon came under pressure from the "for profit" sector of the industry, and the

Table 4.2
CBC **Parliamentary Funding 1994-1999 (millions)**

Budget Year	Parliamentary Appropriations	Total Program Spending	% of Total Program Spending
98/99	694.0	103.5	0.67
97/98	694.0	105.8	0.66
96/97	855.0	109.0	0.78
95/96	974.0	112.0	0.87
94/95	951.0	118.7	0.80

Source: Ministry of Finance. "Budget Chartbook" (http://www.fin.gc.ca), March 1997:43. CBC Mandate Review Committee. "Historical Financial Information and Current CBC Forecasts" (http://canada.gc.ca/whats/heritage/ anglais/chap2/ch2s6.htm).

desire to have exclusively Canadian broadcasting gave way to an effort to sustain minimum Canadian content in the face of the "Americanization" process. Both of these developments pre-date the election of neo-liberal governments in Canada, but they have intensified since 1984. As Marc Raboy puts it, "The evolution of Canadian policy clearly placed economic considerations in priority over cultural questions, and the election of a Conservative government in 1984 put people in power who appeared prepared to carry that policy forward, or backward, as the case may be" (1990:14). Raboy analyzed policy developments in the 1980s under the chapter heading "The Eclipse of Public Broadcasting" and documented the increasing favour shown to "market considerations" by the Canadian Radio-Television and Telecommunications Commission (CRTC)—the government's regulatory agency in the communications field; the greater governmental enthusiasm for the private sector's broadcasting role after 1980; and the enhancement of this after 1984.

Table 4.2 summarizes CBC funding in the 1990s. Comparing this situation to the 1980s on a per capita basis, the CBC's funding had been reduced in real terms by 37.5 percent between 1984 and 1996. Taking into account projected cuts CBC funding on a per capita basis will decline, in constant dollars, from $32.19 to $19.11 in 1997/98—47 percent lower than in 1984/85 (CCPA *Monitor*, December 1996/January 1997:3).

The Battle to Restrain the State
Neo-liberal ideas challenged the legitimacy of an active, interventionist state engaged in managing the economy, organizing the collective provision of social benefits, and recognizing and integrating the claims of subordinate social groups, such as labour and disadvantaged regions. The basic themes espoused by neo-

liberals have focused on reducing, restraining, and retrenching state activities in these areas. The corollary is that market forces are intended to prevail in an ever larger sector of social life.

The process of restraining the state and expanding the role of the market is hardly neutral in its effects on social classes. Neo-liberal restraint is closely associated with the reallocation of benefits in favour of the affluent and wealthy. The various justifications advanced by neo-liberals need not detain us at this point; we are concerned merely to point out that this result is inextricably linked to the various policy initiatives favoured by neo-liberal theory. We can detect this trend in the increased regressivity of the tax system, the erosion of social benefits and regional development initiatives, the conversion of formerly universal benefits into targeted means-tested benefits, the uncoupling of the unemployment insurance system from the marginally more progressive general tax revenues in favour of the regressive contributions system, and, not least, in the legislative assault on trade union rights.

These policy initiatives represent an attempt to dismantle the various elements of the Keynesian welfare state that were introduced gradually in the 1945–71 period—a process that has been at least as gradual as the construction of the Keynesian welfare state. Is the structure so unsound that its continued viability is unlikely? In the policy areas we have examined erosion has been succeeded by demolition.

The failure to advance the neo-liberal project more rapidly was attributed to two types of constraint: the Canadian value system, which continues to demonstrate affection for many of the concrete benefits characteristic of the Keynesian era, so that public opinion constitutes an obstacle; and federal institutions, which operated to impede the implementation of a neo-liberal agenda by the national government, although they presented much less of an obstacle for neo-liberal provincial governments. The restraining influence of both of these constraints has diminished in recent years.

The first constraint indicated that neo-liberal values were far from hegemonic in Canada. While this remains true in the sense that opinion polls regularly indicate a preference for the outcomes of the Keynesian era, it is unaccompanied by any recognition of how such a situation might be re-established. The results of the 1997 election indicated that NDP proposals aimed at restoring full employment and the integrity of the welfare state failed to convince more than a fraction of that portion of the public who might agree with the goals. As a result, many of those who are dissatisfied with the results of neo-liberalism voted for parties that espouse that ideology. Such is the condition of Canadian democracy at the close of the twentieth century. Under these conditions public opinion, traditional Canadian values and so on are not viewed by neo-liberal parties as offering much of an impediment to the implementation of a neo-liberal agenda.

The second constraint is federalism. We have seen, however, that the role of the federal government is being systematically reduced to a point where its ability to insist on national standards is minimal. The measures taken by the Chrétien government, since the October 1995 referendum (see Chapter 6), to deal with the threat of separation have hastened this process.

Notes
1.   Obviously a statement that is no longer true, particularly at the provincial level.
2.   The case for addressing the deficit through alternative measures has been made best by Stanford (1995).
3.   For more on the theme of decentralization see Chapter 6.
4.   The section on workfare is excerpted from Rehnby and McBride (1997:18–20).

Chapter 5

Neo-Liberalism, the Constitution and Canada's Federal Condition[1]

The necessity of responding to economic globalization and intensifying international competitive pressures provides a standard rationale for neo-liberal policies. An important component of the neo-liberal response is to downsize the state and liberate market forces from the state's regulatory constraints.

Restraint and retrenchment of state activity can, of course, be accomplished without constitutional change. The role of the state can simply be reduced by normal political processes. However, there is a corresponding danger that such processes will, in a later period, lead to an expansion of the state's role—thus reversing the neo-liberal revolution. To prevent this requires a continuing ideological battle to convince the electorate of the rectitude or inevitability of the neo-liberal response. Such an ideological endeavour will be reinforced by the operation of market forces. Once those market forces are freed from state control, whether by privatization or deregulation, or through participation in a free-trade agreement, the costs of reimposing control over them will be high and might even seem prohibitive. Nevertheless, there is another possibility; to render the neo-liberal assault on the state's role permanent through constitutional change.

A number of analysts have noted the challenge posed for all nation-states by the growing power of transnational corporations and the markets they operate in (for example, see Simeon 1991:47–49); and in light of Canada's free-trade "solution" to these pressures, it is worth noting the widespread perception that North American integration and Canadian disintegration are directly correlated (for example, see Simeon 1991:51; and Mel Watkins, quoted in Norman 1991:27). Thus the impact of globalization on Canada's political system has increased the constitutional strains generated by Canada's internal and idiosyncratic cleavages based on nations, language, and region. (For an insightful review of the interconnections between continentalism and the constitution, see Laxer 1992).

Because the institutional arrangements of the country are far from settled, there has been an opportunity for neo-liberals to initiate constitutional reforms designed to reflect their political and economic agenda—even though the process of constitutional change itself has been driven by a different agenda expressed in the discourse of Québec's demands, provincial powers, and the dissatisfaction of regions. Indeed, according to Jane Jenson (1989, 1990) the connection between the two agendas may be quite intimate:

> The paradigm which helped to stabilize the fordist mode of regulation in Canada after World War II was organized around national identities. . . . The social compromises and institutionalized relationships of the welfare state were rationalized in terms of the needs of the whole nation and of the federal system. Therefore, when the fordist paradigm began to dissolve, it would do so around the issues of national existence and proper state forms." (Jenson 1989:84)

Be this as it may, there is certainly a conjunction between the development of a crisis in Canada's institutions and the desirability, from a neo-liberal viewpoint, of using the constitution to bind the state to a role consistent with the goals of classical liberalism. In this context it may be worth recalling the argument advanced earlier in the book that existing institutional arrangements such as federalism served to impede cutbacks in social spending.

Reducing the role of government generally, and in particular reducing the role of the welfare state, is a central feature of the push towards "restraint" (Marchak 1991:ch. 5; Shields 1990; Whitaker 1987). Whatever other differences they may have, neo-liberal theorists are united in the "rejection of the state as the source of the good life" (Arthur Seldon, quoted in Marchak 1991:97).[2] Still, students of some neo-liberal governments, especially those of Margaret Thatcher and Ronald Reagan, have noted a predilection to use the state to overcome opponents. Reg Whitaker (1987:2) points to their prominent use of coercion, both at home and abroad. In certain spheres of state activity they have tended to rely on a "strong state."

To a degree, Thatcher's penchant for a strong government found expression in changes to the machinery of government. She was quick to dispense with the informal, neo-corporatist institutions that her predecessors had depended on to integrate organized labour into the decision-making process (see McBride 1986, 1991). She also left her imprint on the formal state machinery. Bob Jessop and his co-authors (1988:87) provide a useful summary:

> The state has been Thatcherized through civil service reorganization and politically motivated promotion to key official posts; through the enhancement of Treasury control over all areas of government; through a much reinforced policing apparatus and redefinition of "subversion"; through the radical centralization of government power and the assault on local government; through a programme of denationalization and competition which would be difficult to reverse; through privatization in the welfare state—thereby constructing new interests around private provision both among clients and within the professions and supply industries; through the radical restructuring of education . . . and so forth.

Not all of these are constitutional changes in the strict sense; many fall under policy headings. Others are quasi-constitutional changes and do seem to indicate a centralizing and authoritarian trend that runs counter to much of the new right's rhetoric.[3] One problem for British neo-liberals, who might have wished to use the constitution as a barrier against the unraveling of their counter revolution in public policy, is that the British constitution is an uncodified and flexible instrument. None of the changes put in place by neo-liberal governments are immune, or even protected by any form of entrenchment, from the counterthrusts of a determined successor.

In the United States, which has a codified and rigid constitutional structure, the same drive towards an authoritarian, strong state in some policy fields was exhibited, for instance, in the mass firing of striking air-traffic controllers, and there were efforts to escape the confines of the constitution in the illegal manoeuvres known as Irangate. But the centralization of power within existing institutions, characteristic of Thatcherism, was impossible in the U.S. context. The U.S. case is of particular interest because, since the passing of Canada's 1982 Constitution Act, our own constitution has become rather more codified and rigid. In addition, both countries are federal systems, complete with the limits these systems pose to the implementation of policies of restraint or, indeed, to any other political agenda carried by the central government.

Neo-liberal constitutional change in the United States is largely confined to the quasi-constitutional area of federal–state relations. In 1981 President Reagan told a conference of state legislators:

> Today the Federal government takes too much taxes from the people, too much authority from the States, too much liberty with the Constitution. . . . The steady flow of tax dollars to Washington has something to do with the fact that things don't seem to work out anymore. The Federal government is overloaded, musclebound, if you will, having assumed more responsibilities than it can properly manage. (quoted in Robertson and Judd 1989:354)

The solution was to *decentralize* the U.S. system: since the neo-liberals saw the states as being more responsive to their citizens and as more efficient providers of services, they put forth proposals for a "new" federalism. The various versions of new federalism advanced by the Reagan administration involved transferring programs to the states. But because there appeared to be inadequate financial provision for these programs, enthusiasm at the state level was muted and, considered as a coherent strategy, new federalism was eventually abandoned, although Reagan did succeed in drastically pruning federal transfers to the states (see McKay 1989:72–74).

In a detailed review of U.S. public policy, David B. Robertson and Dennis R. Judd (1989) cast doubt on the neo-liberal rationale for decentralization. They concluded:

In nearly all cases, state policy is superior to national policy only if one defines 'good' policy as *conservative* policy—that is, less activist, less redistributive, and less regulatory. Despite its rhetoric, the Reagan administration did not enhance policy performance or responsiveness. Instead, it reduced government capacity and coherence in policy areas outside the conservative agenda. In effect, the Reagan administration sought a "new" federalism that would strengthen the structure of policy restraint. (355)

Similarly, they depict the decentralizing thrust of the Reagan administration as being quite instrumental: "Usually, decentralization efficiently served the administration's conservative ideology. But when this turned out not to be the case, the goal of decentralization was abandoned (Robertson and Judd 1989:377).

On the surface, the contrasting stance of Thatcher and Reagan to subnational governments suggests a certain promiscuity in the neo-liberal approach to constitutional arrangements. However, the underlying unity would seem to be that neo-liberals favour whatever constitutional arrangements they deem necessary to protect the primacy of the market. If a strong state is necessary to remove the obstacles necessary for the market to operate freely, so be it; if a weak and decentralized state better serves these objectives, this can be easily accommodated by neo-liberal theory and rhetoric. Beyond the ultimate goal of fostering market forces, however, is it possible to identify a body of neo-liberal constitutional theory that might serve as a benchmark in evaluating the extent to which the Mulroney and Chrétien governments' constitutional initiatives have been shaped by this ideology?

Three themes can be emphasized. The first one is the genuine desire to confine the state to a much more restricted sphere of activity than was characteristic of the Keynesian era. In particular, state intervention in the economy and social policy is to be reduced significantly. While this might be accomplished by normal political activity, it is also conceivable to restrict the state's role in these areas by constitutional or quasi-constitutional provisions. One benefit of the constitutional route is that by prohibiting the state from certain activities it can be insulated from democratic pressures (Shields 1990:162).

Second the state must be strong enough to confront and defeat the "special interests" that will work to defend the welfare state. In addition it will require sufficient power to police and protect the market order.[4] Strong government is necessary to uphold authority in society—this clearly implies a role for the state in defence of the institution of private property and, perhaps, of institutions such as the family (see Gamble 1988:35–36).

Third, in federal political systems we can presume that neo-liberals will have a greater concern to limit the power of government *per se* rather than a principled or rhetorical position in favour of assigning powers permanently to a particular level of government. In practice, neo-liberals will see decentralization as more likely in most cases to mean "less government in general and less redistributive activity in particular" (Boadway 1992:3).

Obviously these are general guidelines and we should take care in attributing a particular constitutional proposal to any of them. However, they do provide a profile of the general constitutional preferences of the neo-liberals. How are these preferences connected to the basic economic strategy favoured by Canadian neo-liberals? What kinds of specific constitutional proposals are likely to emerge from the conjunction of the neo-liberal economic and constitutional preferences? In this chapter we discuss the Mulroney years. The Chrétien government's approach to these issues—post-Meech, post-Charlottetown and post-1995 Québec referendum—is dealt with in the following chapter.

The Neo-Liberal Constitutional Agenda
In his book, *Federal State, National Economy* (1987:especially ch. 9), Peter Leslie comprehensively analyzed the interplay of economic strategies and constitutional preferences. He outlines the constitutional and political implications of three potential economic strategies: interventionist–nationalist, interventionist–provincialist, and liberal–continentalist. The first option implies an expanded role for the federal government, which would produce a greater intervention in the economy—clearly a strategy incompatible with neo-liberalism. The second option is also highly unattractive in neo-liberal eyes; yet its decentralization of contemporary federalism makes it more appealing than the nation-building and strong federal role contained in the first. The third, liberal–continentalist option means minimal government intervention and would include the possibility of continental free trade. It is the economic strategy recommended by the Macdonald Commission and, in broad terms, adopted by the Mulroney government, and it is the strategy that most recommends itself to Canadian neo-liberals. What are its constitutional correlates?

Neo-liberals generally favour a reduced role for the state in the economy and in social policy. However, given the constitutional principle of the supremacy of Parliament, according to which legislative authority over these areas must reside with one or the other level of government, the initial question for neo-liberals is to decide on the level that is most preferable.[5] For neo-liberals the answer is some combination of limits on federal powers and transfer of jurisdictions to the provinces. Through decentralization and deference to the market, the neo-liberal ideal of a limited and constrained state might be approximated.

However, Leslie (1987:167–70) argues that even the liberal-continentalist option requires a strong state for certain purposes: "The market-enhancing policies advocated by the [Macdonald] commission are anything but anodyne in their constitutional effects. Indeed, they demand more extensive limitations on provincial powers than anything proposed by the federal government during the [constitutional] negotiations of July to September 1980" (24). For example, the divided jurisdictions over fiscal policy (both the power to tax and to spend) that is involved in any federal system of government open the possibility for one level of government to use its fiscal powers to offset initiatives taken by the other. Fiscal restraint at the federal level may lead to compensatory activity by unsympathetic provincial governments. Reductions of federal taxes may encourage provincial governments to move into the tax room created. (It was precisely this sort of activity by British local authorities that led to Thatcher's onslaught against local autonomy). Some form of coordination would seem necessary to ensure that a low-tax and low-spending policy would prevail. Under the existing constitution no such mechanism is available. One might therefore expect some initiative in this area from a neo-liberal government.

Similarly, for a truly free market to prevail in Canada it would be necessary to form a more complete economic union than the one guaranteed by Section 121 of the British North America Act. Section 121 provides that "All Articles of the Growth, Produce, or Manufacture of any one of the Provinces shall . . . be admitted free into each of the other Provinces." Although this creates a free-trade area, it has not prevented the creation of barriers to interprovincial trade. Usually these have been the handiwork of provincial governments using devices such as marketing boards or preferential procurement schemes. To strike down such obstacles would seem to require strengthened national institutions. Finally, the Macdonald Commission anticipated that the federal government's lack of a treaty implementation power in cases in which treaties touched areas of provincial jurisdiction might hinder the implementation of continental free trade with the United States (see Leslie 1987:108–09). In fact this seems to have been less of an obstacle than anticipated. The failure of any province to challenge the Free Trade Agreement in the courts is, perhaps, a reflection of provincial suspicions that the Supreme Court might take the opportunity to reverse earlier jurisprudence.

Given the Canadian neo-liberals' preferred economic strategy, two sorts of constitutional initiatives might be anticipated. The first is a general predilection to weaken the powers of the central government, especially in any possible economic and social intervention. The second is a selective strengthening of the federal government's ability to overcome interventionist proclivities on the part of the provinces. Finally, neo-liberals could be expected to rely upon the external U.S. connection, as manifested in the Free Trade Agreement, to provide the support for a free-market economy that is denied by domestic politics in Canada. This kind of agreement could serve to "lock in" market reforms. We examine the Free Trade Agreement in Chapter 8.

The Meech Lake Strategy
One round of constitutional reform was completed in 1982 when the Constitution Act 1982 became law. As a result of the changes, Canada's constitution was "patriated" and the remnants of British supervision were discarded. Canadians acquired a new Charter of Rights and Freedoms, which, in English Canada at

least, rapidly became a "sacred symbol" of nationhood (Cairns 1991:244), and a new amendment procedure was adopted, along with other changes. The separatist government of Québec remained bitterly opposed to the provisions of the 1982 Act and engaged in a variety of actions aimed at demonstrating that Québec remained "outside" the constitutional order (see Milne 1991:ch. 6). Although this stand had no legal significance it did help to establish a public mood to the effect that Québec should eventually be induced to "rejoin" the federation by formally accepting the new document.

As long as the chief protagonists of the 1982 constitutional fracas were in office, however, there seemed little incentive to initiate this process. Trudeau's retirement in 1984 and the subsequent election of a federal Conservative government, which espoused "national reconciliation" and wished to consolidate its electorate support in Québec, changed parts of the equation. The retirement of René Lévesque, the subsequent defeat of the Parti Québécois, and the election of Robert Bourassa's Liberals changed the remainder. By 1985 the preconditions for another round of constitutional negotiations—the Québec Round—were in place.

Some of the actors most closely associated with the 1982 constitutional changes could not accept the idea that Québec had in some way been excluded and that efforts from the rest of Canada to bring about its inclusion were necessary. Pierre Trudeau cited the Supreme Court's validation of the 1982 Constitution Act as legal and constitutional. He pointed to the Act's endorsement by Québec's elected federal representatives, cited the unwillingness of a separatist government to sign any new constitution for Canada, and concluded that there was no need for a "Québec round" to draw the province in: it was already in.[6]

After the Meech Lake Accord was signed in 1987, Trudeau's views served as a basis for criticism of its contents. Critics saw the accord as decentralizing; in light of Trudeau's account, the decentralizing provisions had been quite unnecessary. Moreover, the fact that offers of more power had mistakenly been made to Québec enabled the other provinces, in the name of the principle of equality of provinces, to acquire many of those powers for themselves as well (see Behiels 1989:5–6; Bowker 1990:18–19).

The contrary view has been well expressed by Patrick J. Monahan (1991:22):

> The constitutional package of 1982 was achieved with a price attached, namely the need to negotiate a subsequent accommodation with the government of Québec. It may have been appropriate to dispense with the consent of Québec in 1982, but this omission would have to be remedied sooner or later through negotiations designed to bring Québec 'back in' to the constitution.

The central point in Monahan's argument is that the 1982 constitution failed to address Québec's traditional constitutional aspirations, that it broke faith with the promises made for a "renewed federalism" during the 1980 Québec referendum, and that, whatever the legal aspects of the matter, the refusal of the provincial government of Québec to sign the constitution denied it political legitimacy. From this point of view, then, it would be necessary at some time to undertake the task of "bringing Québec back in."[7] The propitious circumstances of the mid-1980s explain why the attempt was made when it was.

Our concern here is not with the Québec issue or Meech Lake *per se*, but with the opportunity that Canada's unfinished constitutional agenda afforded for implementation of the neo-liberal view of the "good" constitution. Meech Lake may represent the Québec Round, and it may have been driven by the territorial and linguistic cleavages characteristic of Canadian federalism, but is there also evidence of an effort to incorporate a neo-liberal agenda? In view of the failure of Meech Lake and the subsequent, and broader, round of constitutional negotiations, this is also a question we will ask of later developments.

Beginning in 1985, and with greater precision in the spring of 1986, the Québec government identified its conditions for agreeing to the 1982 constitution. These consisted of recognition of Québec as a "distinct society," more powers over immigration, participation in the appointment of judges to the Supreme Court, limits on the federal spending power in shared-cost programs, and a veto over constitutional amendments affecting Québec (Bowker 1990:17). The federal government sensed that success on the constitutional front, a considerable political prize in its own right, would be enhanced to the extent that the agenda was limited (see Monahan 1991:50–54). This means that the agenda was restricted, as far as possible, to the specific points raised by the Québec government, and that the Conservative government worked to avoid an explicit commitment to neo-liberal constitutional principles. The most that one can expect to find in the negotiations is a correspondence or consistency between the federal government's position in the Meech Lake discussions and its general ideology. In this particular round of constitutional reform the general ideology was at best a conditioning factor, and not a determining factor. In the subsequent set of constitutional negotiations of 1991–92, with their broader range of issues, the federal government felt itself able to promote its ideology overtly.

To begin with the element of spending power, much of the fabric of Canada's post-war welfare state was developed at federal initiative but operated in areas of provincial jurisdiction, and the federal government's "spending power" was used as an instrument to create shared-cost social programs. While the precise arrangements varied by program, a common feature was provincial delivery of the service, but with significant financial contribution from the federal government, which also imposed conditions designed to produce national coherence (although not uniformity or absolute standardization) to the programs. The constitutional basis for the exercise of federal spending power was inferred from a number of sections in the British North America Act, notably the powers of taxation (s.91.3), of legislating with respect to public property (s.5.9 1[A]), and of appropriating federal funds (s.106)(Banting 1988:S82). Banting (1988:S82) comments that although the

> legal status of this doctrine has never been settled authoritatively, especially in the case of conditional grants to provincial governments . . . a vast edifice of public spending has been constructed on the basis of the spending power . . (which) was especially critical in the development of the welfare state.[8]

Under the Meech Lake Accord a new section (106A) would have been added, reading:

> (1) The Government of Canada shall provide reasonable compensation to the government of a province that chooses not to participate in a national shared-cost program that is established by the Government of Canada after the coming into force of this section in an area of exclusive provincial jurisdiction, if the province carries on a program or initiative that is compatible with national objectives. (2) Nothing in this section extends the legislative powers of the Parliament of Canada or of the legislatures of the provinces.

The opposition to federal spending power originated with Québec. In the 1950s Premier Maurice Duplessis resisted federal support for universities. During the 1960s Québec pressed, for the most part successfully, for the right to opt out of some shared-cost programs with compensation. Québec nationalists recognized the nation-building potentiality of social programs and strove to make sure that these contributed to Québec's sense of identity rather than to Canada's. It came as no surprise, therefore, when the demand to limit federal spending power emerged as one of Québec's five conditions for accepting the 1982 constitution. Significant support for this proposal existed among the other provinces. Some of them had argued for years that Ottawa's social policy initiatives distorted provincial priorities and that in an era of fiscal restraint the federal government had become an unreliable financial partner. Once established, social programs were politically difficult to terminate. As the federal government pared back its financial support the provinces were left to sustain some very expensive programs. Provincial sensibilities in this area were inflamed by the 1984 Canada Health Act, which imposed penalties for provincial violations of federal conditions. Québec, therefore, could rely on considerable support from other provinces on this issue.

The actual text of the new section was sufficiently ambiguous to sustain major variations in interpretation. (Much the same comment can be made about the Meech Lake Accord generally.) Critics argued that it would inhibit the creation of further national social programs and hence serve to decentralize the federation. Some supporters disputed this; others conceded the point but argued that it was a justiciable and, indeed, overdue measure.

Deborah Coyne (1989:246–48) argued that the ability to opt out of future national programs, without financial disincentive, would erode Ottawa's ability to build a national identity based on relatively standardized access to social provision. Further, the ambiguity in such terms as "national objectives" and "compatible with" would further judicialize our political system (see Coyne 1989:260–61). Finally, Coyne stated that the effect, when combined with other provisions in the accord, "involves a substantial devolution of power to the provinces and significant shift of political dynamism on matters of national importance away from the federal Parliament, as well as the undermining of the Charter of Rights and Freedoms" (1989:247). For Stefan Dupré (1989:279), "Section 106A will have minimal consequences for the conduct of federal–provincial fiscal relations." Similarly, Thomas Courchene (1988b:572) emphasized the criteria that must be met for a province to receive financial compensation, and the Business Council on National Issues (BCNI) (1990a:2) highlighted the fact that Meech explicitly recognized, "for the first time in Canada's constitution, the power of the federal government to exercise its spending power in areas of provincial jurisdiction." The remainder of s.106A, according to the BCNI, simply provided for flexibility and the ability of provinces to respond to local needs. Central to the debate, then, was the question of how decentralizing an effect the accord would have.

Probably the most controversial item in the Meech Lake Accord was the inclusion in the constitutional draft of an interpretive clause recognizing Québec as a distinct society and specifying that the role of the Québec legislature and government was to "preserve and promote" Québec's distinct identity. Balancing this injunction, and in the same section of the constitutional draft, was "the recognition that the existence of French-speaking Canadians, centred in Québec but also present elsewhere in Canada, and English-speaking Canadians, concentrated outside Québec, constitutes a fundamental characteristic of Canada." The Canadian Parliament and the provincial legislatures were charged with the preservation of this "fundamental characteristic of Canada."

Much of the debate around the accord was concerned with the impact of these clauses. Because their final meanings would have been settled by the Supreme Court, the debate was largely speculative. But, whatever "distinct society" might mean, initially at least its consequences in terms of the centralization/decentralization dynamic would be limited to Québec. If, as most anticipated, it would decentralize Confederation, it would do so by accentuating aspects of asymmetry already present in the Canadian constitutional structure (see Bowker 1990:ch. 12). If the concept was as elastic as some feared, and others hoped, it might have led to significant differentiation in the economic and social powers of the provinces.

To a degree such a development would be consistent with neo-liberalism:

if such powers were transferred to a province, they would no longer be available to the federal level as far as that province was concerned. Given the strong attachment in the other provinces to the concept that "all provinces are equal," this could fuel demands for the further decentralization of Confederation. Such a process would be indirect and long-term. The neo-liberals' conditional preference for a decentralized federation may have played a minor role in making asymmetrical arrangements palatable to them, in a way that those arrangements could never be for the nationally-focused Trudeau Liberals. But this consideration was not the prime motivation. That motivation is probably to be found in the political and partisan imperatives of the Mulroney strategy of building a coalition between Western provincialists and Québec nationalists.

Other elements of the Meech package appear to demonstrate the strength and impact of the "all provinces are equal" doctrine. In making these concessions to provincial pressure, neo-liberal tolerance for a decentralized federation is probably of greater significance; quite simply, there were few purposes for which neo-liberals required a strong national government (although there were some) and many uses to which a strong national government could be put that were inimical to the neo-liberal project.

The Charter of Rights and Freedoms has also had an impact on the course of constitutional events. The charter has placed the value of individual rights far ahead of notions of collective rights—an ideological direction that neo-liberals are comfortable with. It has also promoted the principle of provincial equality in opposition to constitutional asymmetry for Québec. This reflects an increasing tendency in Canada to stress the first two values, liberty and equality (or at least one reading of equality), that emerged out of the French Revolution to the neglect of the third value, fraternity (Watts 1991:17). Fraternity has been downgraded both in the sense that collective social provision (social services) has experienced governmental assaults, and in the sense that the role for government in society, and especially the federal government, is being undermined. The process of provincializing state power will result not only in a weakening of universal Canadian standards for public services, but also in a general reduction in the capacity of governments at all levels to act for fraternal purposes.

As part of its five conditions for accepting the constitution Québec had demanded more powers over immigration, more control over nominations to the Supreme Court, and "restoration" of its traditional veto over at least some constitutional changes. Meech addressed all these issues, extended them to all provinces, and went beyond them by extending the provincial role in nominations to the Senate and by entrenching annual first ministers conferences—one on the economy, another on the constitution. Again the details of these provisions are of less concern to us here than the general perception that they represented a diminution of the powers of the national government (immigration), an increased provincial role in choosing the personnel of national institutions (Supreme Court and Senate), and institutionalized annual opportunities to exert pressure on the national government (first ministers conferences). Taken together with the restrictions on federal spending power and the distinct society clause, these provisions point to a significantly reduced role for the national government and, indeed, for a national identity.

For the Mulroney Conservatives, Meech Lake represented a policy response to national reconciliation. It promised all things to all regions. In addressing Québec's demands for more powers the federal government was willing to transfer such authority to all the other provincial actors. But while the Mulroney administration was willing to devolve powers to the regions, it was unwilling to financially support the infrastructure of Canadian unity. As Frances Abele aptly observed, "Federal initiatives and federal spending are the traditional glue in the Canadian federation" (1991:23). Under Meech Lake the federal government seemed willing to transfer such initiatives to the provincial level, yet it failed to outline an adequate structure for financially supporting the power shift. Deficit reduction and governmental restraint remained the higher priority (Abele 1991:24). Ironically, some commentators perceived the growing ineffectiveness of the federal government as a reason for its loss of legitimacy in Québec (for example, see Simeon 1991). If the federal state is increasingly relegated to a secondary actor providing ever less services, francophone Québecers may be more inclined to question the relevance of the federal union—a perception that seems to have had some impact in the 1995 referendum (see Chapter 6).

This interpretation of Meech is reinforced when it is considered in tandem with the Free Trade Agreement. Richard Simeon has forcibly expressed the connection between the two:

> The Free Trade Agreement is far more significant a restraint on governments in general than Meech Lake is, and more of a restraint on the federal government than it is on the provinces. . . . Each does have this one element underlying it: a sense of the need to limit and constrain the state in the modern era. . . . One can at least make the argument that both in the long-run are likely to increase domestic fragmentation and certainly to inhibit a strong nation-building policy led by the federal government. . . . For the many who argue for both, the two are tied together by hostility towards an activist, interventionist, national state, both in its nation building role and in its economic development role . . . decentralization and a degree of non-interventionism go together. (1989:4–6)

To what extent, then, can the Meech Lake Accord be viewed as an expression of a neo-liberal constitutional agenda? Let us first reiterate a disclaimer; Meech was for the most part the product of the Mulroney government's constitutional inheritance, its own political agenda for consolidating support in various parts of the country, and the traditional demands of most provincial governments for greater power. Within that context, though, there is an obvious consistency, if not an absolute one, between the accord and elements of the neo-liberal agenda.

Alan Cairns (1991:158) views the accord as the outcome of an intergovernmental process and, consequently, as reflecting the interests of governments. To those who argue that the accord would have led to greater interdependence and cooperation between governments, he responds:"The new stress on interdependence is purchased almost entirely at the cost of reducing the autonomy and discretion of the federal government, and of strengthening the role of provincial governments in virtually every area touched by the Accord." In this sense at least the accord was decentralizing and could be viewed with favour by neo-liberals, even if the strengthening of provincial governments was somewhat problematic.

At one level, the process may have been unavoidable if Québec was to be brought "back in." This is because of the governmental self-interest of other provincial elites "who enhanced the status of their governments on the coattails of Québec" (Cairns 1991:155).[9] Federal compliance may be explained either by principle—attachment to a different view of federal balance based on a vision of Canada as a "community of communities"; alternatively, it might be explained as driven by political opportunism—decentralization was the price of constructing a new political coalition that would establish the Conservatives as Canada's party of government. A third explanation is that provincial governments were less likely to impede realization of a neo-liberal economic and social agenda—a perception based on the historical roles played by the two levels of government.

Banting (1988:588–89) views the debate over Meech Lake as one between those committed to a nation-building, centralist view of federalism in which a strong central government is the key instrument of national integration and those who view Canadian politics as being about the reconciliation of regional, territorial, and linguistic differences. The latter view favours a decentralized federation, because the cleavages it is sensitive to require locally-differentiated policies and programs. Meech Lake, therefore, involved asserting the primacy of linguistic and territorial cleavages over those class-based cleavages that had led to an agenda of social reform and national integration. Neo-liberals would clearly prefer placing linguistic and territorial cleavages over the class-based. Both sides of the debate could probably concur with Michael D. Behiels's historical observation:

> The creation of a political culture conducive to the creation of a social service state was slow to emerge. Governments, particularly those at the provincial level, preferred to spend their tax revenues on private and

public projects that contributed directly to capital accumulation. Provincial governments saw little or no political advantage to involving
revenues in projects of legitimization, such as health and social welfare
programs. (1989:236)

When this situation began to change, it was primarily as a result of federal
government initiatives.[10] Transferring powers to the provinces might reasonably be expected to lead to policy outcomes consistent with neo-liberal and
business preferences.[11]

Certainly, these calculations could help to account for a striking feature of
the federal government's negotiating posture: an apparent indifference to the
maintenance of federal authority.[12] One provincial premier reportedly said that
Mulroney "kept asking if we had a deal. . . . It was as if he didn't have any idea
what the deal was or he didn't care that much as long as he got one" (quoted in
Cairns 1991:252). Yet a journalist's account, also cited by Cairns (1991:153),
points to the underlying substance of an otherwise incomprehensible attitude.
According to this account, the prime minister gave Senator Lowell Murray,
Minister of Federal–Provincial Relations, "carte blanche to negotiate away
whatever federal powers were necessary to get Québec into the constitution."
Obviously there was no shortage of willing takers. Moreover, as Trudeau
pointed out (1989:90), Mulroney had already made major concessions of
powers to the provinces before the constitutional talks began (for instance,
abolition of the National Energy Program, granting of offshore resources to
Newfoundland). A willingness to bargain away federal authority was also a
feature of the subsequent round of constitutional negotiations.

There are some interesting parallels between the government's negotiating
strategy at Meech Lake and the one adopted in the free-trade negotiations with
the United States. In Stephen Clarkson's view (1991:116), Mulroney

> put Canada in the weakest possible bargaining situation. As *demandeur*
> in the negotiations, Canada laid its cards on the table. . . . The United
> States made no concessions but sat back and waited. When the
> bargaining crunch came, the Canadian negotiators were under instruc-
> tions to do anything to get a deal. The ultimate document represented
> an astonishing gain for American trade diplomacy while surrendering
> virtually no American sovereignty. . . . Canada had made enormous
> concessions that limited the federal and provincial governments'
> capacity to make industrial policies to promote their exports, to
> husband their energy reserves, or to foster their cultural industries.

How can we explain the negotiating stance of the federal government? Was
it monumental incompetence? Or, as the substance of the agreements suggests,
was it the practical extension of the logic of neo-liberal theory? In our view the

latter is the more realistic position. Both Meech and the Free Trade Agreement constrained governments—the federal (and most interventionist) government most severely. And although the Meech Lake Accord strengthened provincial governments, the exercise of some of the new powers would be constrained by the Free Trade Agreement. Taken together the two agreements may not represent the perfect situation from the viewpoint of neo-liberal constitutional theory, but they do represent a situation preferable to the one inherited by the Mulroney government.

Awkwardly, from the point of view of this happy scenario, the Meech Lake Accord was not ratified, and in 1991–92 the constitutional question had to be reopened.

Business and the Constitution: Macdonald, Meech, and Post-Meech
The Business Council on National Issues's brief to the Macdonald Commission (BCNI 1983:67) emphasized the linkages between the need for economic competitiveness, a more "realistic" set of social policies in which programs would be available to "assist those truly in need of public support," and institutional reforms to improve "the effectiveness, accountability and representativeness of our major political institutions."[13] One proposal to increase representativeness was a reformed Senate—elected, and with an equal number of senators from each province, although with fewer powers than the House of Commons (BCNI 1983:62–65). Such a reformed Senate, the BCNI felt, would significantly improve regional representation in central institutions.

The Macdonald Commission itself devoted most of the third volume of its report to political institutions and reforms to the political system. Many of its recommendations found their way, in one form or another, into either the Meech Lake Accord or the federal government's 1991 constitutional proposals, *Shaping Canada's Future Together* (Canada 1991a). Some of them continue to influence the Chrétien government's strategy today. The Macdonald Report (Canada 1985a, vol. 3:385–408) recommended senate reform to enhance regional representation, recognition of the distinctive character of Québec, a form of constitutional veto for Québec, and opt-out rights with compensation to all provinces. The existence of barriers within the Canadian economic union occupied the attention of the commissioners, and the report called for an amendment to extend the provisions of section 121 to include services and for a code of economic conduct to help eliminate non-tariff barriers to trade in goods and services. The commission proposed an intergovernmental agency to police the economic union and foresaw that if a code of economic conduct were eventually made legally enforceable it would become "a regulatory agency . . . that regulates governments" (Canada 19485a, vol. 3:393). Thus there would be greater coordination, and ultimately governmental self-restraint from interfering with the economic union would become a legal or constitutional restraint. The commission also recommended a constitutional amendment to make enforceable international treaties to which Canada was a signatory, even when their substance lay in areas of provincial jurisdiction. This recommendation was subject to the proviso that the relevant sections of the treaties be approved by the legislatures of seven provinces containing 50 percent of the population (that is, the general amending formula). As far as federal spending power was concerned, the commission stopped short of recommending formal limitations, but its future use ought, in the commission's view, to be subject to conditions and guidelines.

Some of the commission's thinking clearly found its way into the Meech Lake Accord. The accord, in turn, was supported by the Business Council (BCNI 1990a). The accord's demise, though regrettable to the business community among others, did provide an opportunity to initiate a new constitutional round. It was widely conceded that the agenda in this—the Canada Round—would need to be broader than the Meech agenda. As a result, one would expect to find a more consistent expression of neo-liberal goals.

Certainly documents issued by the BCNI became more specific about the linkages between the economy and political system, and the ways in which the political system might be restructured to more adequately serve the economy:

> Competitiveness is the foundation upon which an improved social, economic, and environmental order will be built. In the quest for competitiveness, the Canadian political system must be an ally and not an impediment. First and foremost, the reforms to our federal system must ensure that the Canadian common market is established in fact and that the Canadian economic union is strengthened. The free movement of labour, capital, goods and services must be guaranteed under any new constitutional arrangement, and in this area, we see the federal government having a strengthened role. (BCNI 1991:8)

But the tolerance for centralization had limits. Elsewhere the BCNI cited with approval the argument that

> Increasing global interdependence in economic and security matters has perforated the reality of political sovereignty and made the concept of the nation state as the ultimate political reality increasingly obsolescent. . . . There have been potent concurrent pressures, for larger political units capable of fostering economic unity and enhancing security and, at the same time, for smaller political units more sensitive to their electorates and capable of expressing regional distinctiveness and ethnic linguistic or historically derived diversity. (BCNI 1990b:1–2)

Clearly, the BCNI's perception was that global pressures required both centralization (as in the case of the Canadian Economic Union) and decentralization (primarily in the non-economic areas). In some cases the council felt that the decentralization that had already occurred had led to unproductive duplication for which greater coordination and cooperation between levels of government might provide a solution. In fact by the early 1990s the BCNI was deeply worried about the consequences of excessive decentralization for economic stability. So while the council was prepared to countenance "meaningful decentralization or a reduced federal government role in fields assigned to the provinces under the current Constitution or a revised Constitution," this was subject to the proviso that "any decentralization must be accompanied by concrete arrangements to assure greater coordination or cooperation—otherwise, the existing Canadian economic union, and the benefits it confers, will be threatened" (BCNI 1992:24).

The "Canada Round," 1991–92
The demise of the Meech Lake Accord and the sense of crisis it occasioned eventually led to another round of federal constitutional proposals.[14] This initiative was undertaken in the face of impressive polling evidence that suggested such a constitutional project was "unpopular, unnecessary, and likely to fail." Polls also suggested that any perception that Ottawa was seeking enhanced economic powers would be opposed (*The Globe and Mail*, November 19, 1992). Despite this, the federal government devoted much of its constitutional document, *Securing the Future*, to "prosperity-enhancing" proposals. Ostensibly, however, federal strategy was a response to an agenda emanating from Québec.

Having made a set of modest proposals in 1986, Québec responded to its "rejection" by English Canada by establishing some very far-reaching conditions for its future accession to the constitution.[15] These were reinforced by legislation to hold a referendum by the fall of 1992. The referendum might either be to approve or reject a new constitutional offer from the rest of Canada or, alternatively, be on the issue of political sovereignty. As it turned out the vote was held on the "offer" contained in the Charlottetown Accord.

The federal government's first initiative was to establish the Spicer Commission to take soundings of public attitudes throughout Canada.[16] The reports of the federal and Québec governments were only the tip of an iceberg. There was intense and widespread activity on the fate of the constitution, featuring initiatives both by governments and by private individuals and organizations.[17] In large part the demand for citizen input in any new round of constitutional renewal sprang from the widespread perception that the Meech Accord had been hatched in the "back rooms" or, more formally, that it was the result of executive federalism rather than popular participation. Reflecting on the process, a special edition of *The Network* (1991) identified five main issues: the distinct society, aboriginal self-government, the division of powers, official languages, and the reform of institutions. Each of these categories contained many sub-issues and possible divergences of opinion. The federal government unveiled its own constitutional proposals in September 1991.[18] These were intended to be followed by several months of public hearings before a joint committee of the Senate and House of Commons and subsequently to become the subject of intergovernmental negotiation.

The federal government made twenty-eight specific proposals organized into three parts: "Shared Citizenship and Diversity"; "Responsive Institutions for a Modern Canada"; and "Preparing for a More Prosperous Future." The first two parts consisted of thirteen of the twenty-eight proposals and addressed the Québec, aboriginal, and regional issues through such measures as "recognition of Québec's distinctiveness and Canada's linguistic duality," entrenchment of a "general justiciable right to aboriginal self-government," Senate reform, and provincial participation in appointments to the Supreme Court. For those who felt that all the jostling for sectional advantage had lost sight of Canada's identity, a so-called Canada clause, which sought to symbolize what Canada is and stands for, was also included.

Quantitatively, at least in terms of the proportion of proposals dealing with "prosperity," the government seems to have accorded greatest priority to the third part of the proposals, which focused on transforming the constitution into the helpmate of economic success. The federal proposals in this part of the package, together with property rights (included in the part of the document dealing with citizenship) and diversity, represent the core of the neo-liberal constitutional agenda. This aspect of the constitutional proposals can be divided into six discrete, though interlinked, sections: (i) competitiveness as a rationale for renewed federalism; (ii) strengthening the economic union; (iii) harmonizing federal and provincial economic policies; (iv) reforming the Bank of Canada; (v) redistributing powers between federal and provincial governments; and (vi) property rights. Only the fifth of these agenda items survived intact. And it is the only one that continues unambiguously into the Chrétien era.

(i) Competitiveness as a Rationale for Renewed Federalism

In a series of booklets containing and accompanying its constitutional proposals, the federal government sought to explain the proposals and also to win public support for its approach to constitutional renewal. One major justification for the government's economic proposals was the impact of globalization on national sovereignty and the desirability of harmonious and effective political relationships. In the past, the government argued, the mutually supportive combination of a federal political system and an economic union had enabled Canada to become one of the world's most prosperous countries. For these benefits to be maintained the basic combination must continue—"economic and political integration go hand-in-hand" (Canada 1991b:9). Although this statement can be interpreted as an argument against Québec separatism, it also found service in the dispute over strengthening the economic union. A

variety of challenges, internal and external, meant that continuity was insufficient—"to prosper we must change" (Canada 1991a:29).

More specifically, the external challenge of globalization and technological change required "greater adaptability and more effective approaches to how
federal and provincial governments interact with each other and with the private
sector" (Canada 1991b:1). Internally, the existence of barriers to the free flow
of goods and services, combined with the phenomena of federal and provincial
policies working at cross-purposes to each other, pointed in the same direction.
In the government's view one of the key ingredients of future competitiveness
lay in strengthening the free-market basis of the economic union:

> At the heart of effective economic integration must be the absence of
> restrictions to the free flow of people, goods, services and capital and
> the existence of a common currency, which encourages this free flow
> by removing exchange rate uncertainty and transaction costs that can
> impede trade. Also important are uniform business framework laws,
> uniform work and product standards, coordinated and harmonized
> economic policies, and a coordinated and harmonized tax system.
> (Canada 1991b:9)

(ii) Strengthening the Economic Union

The government's view of how to strengthen the economic union was not an
absolutely non-interventionist one. It recognized the impact of various government policies as ongoing and the need as one of harmonization and predictabil-
ity. However, the core of its proposal was the *laissez-faire* notion that, as far as
possible, governments should be constrained from interference with the operation of markets. This viewpoint, dear to the hearts of neo-liberal economic
theorists, found expression in the text of the proposal to amend section 121, the
common-market clause of the existing constitution:

> (1) Canada is an economic union within which persons, goods, services
> and capital may move freely without barriers or restrictions based on
> provincial or territorial boundaries. (2) Neither the Parliament or
> Government of Canada nor the legislatures or governments of the
> provinces shall by law or practice contravene the principle expressed in
> subsection (1).

Although some exceptions follow, the core of the proposed article is clear:
the principle that *no* government can legitimately interfere with market relations
would be constitutionally entrenched. It is a clear case of the Canadian
government seeking to constitutionalize a particular economic theory or ideology.

The exceptions are interesting in terms of the federal–provincial relationship. Some deal with regional development and equalization and need not detain us here. But general exceptions could be made by the federal government, with the consent of seven provinces totaling at least 50 percent of the population: (a) to exempt any barrier from judicial review, by declaring it in the national interest; (b) to legislate on anything related to the efficiency of the economic union.

Thus the substance of the proposed amendment was decentralizing in that it generally prohibited any level of government from interfering with the free flow of economic activity; it was centralizing, though, in its impact on federal–provincial relations. If a province, or several of them, wished exemptions they must obtain federal permission (plus that of sufficient other provinces—a mechanism bound to encourage "log-rolling, or horse-trading of exemptions between governments"). On the other hand, the federal government "has almost unlimited capacity to *interfere* with democratic outcomes within a particular province, as long as enough other provinces agree" (Howse 1991:15). Traditionally, centralization in the Canadian political economy has been a formula for an active government and for nation-building projects. Under the Mulroney government, centralization seems to have been envisaged as an instrument to enforce a minimalist conception of government. If we bear in mind the "free economy, strong state" depiction of neo-liberal political economy, any paradox is only apparent.

In taking up the cause of a free-market economic union, the neo-liberals are, of course, simply seeking to apply the postulates of neo-classical liberal economics. In this sense there is nothing new about neo-liberalism. Neo-classical economic theory posits that large, barrier-free markets permit economies of scale, more efficient use of resources, and thus maximize the general welfare. There is no shortage of documentation indicating that existing provincial and federal practices deviate from the neo-classical ideal. Provinces use non-tariff barriers such as preferential purchasing programs, subsidies, beer and liquor regulations, and so on. Federal policies include energy policies, tariffs, various regulatory policies, freight rates, the tax system, and more (Dunsmuir 1990:15). Many of these policies have been the stock-in-trade of the nation-building (and province-building) efforts of activist Canadian governments. Their prohibition, and its entrenchment in the constitution, would represent a strong defence for the market order against democratically-elected governments seeking to satisfy their electorates by moderating market outcomes.

Proposals to strengthen the economic union gathered strength in the 1970s and 1980s (Safarian 1974; Canada 1979; Courchene 1986). Indeed, this had featured as part of a much earlier round of constitutional negotiations when it had achieved symbolic status as an element of national unity (see Chrétien 1980). We have noted the growing enthusiasm of business groups such as the Business Council on National Issues.

Critics of neo-liberal proposals to strengthen the economic union by constitutional entrenchment have made a number of points. For one thing, they say that such a development entrenches one value—efficiency—as the prime goal of social activity in the country. Entrenchment constrains potential democratic majorities that may favour a different value—for instance, equity—from achieving their ends. The effect is to insulate from democratic control something that ought to be subject to it. Further, in the context of a federal system a watertight economic union may be incompatible with the theory of federalism:

> The very purpose of fiscal federalism . . . inevitably leads to differences in the levels of taxation and public services. The resulting differentiation in tax levels may interfere with the most efficient allocation of resources and location of industry for the region (nation) as a whole; such is the cost of political subdivision. (Richard Musgrave, quoted in Courchene 1986:204)

Further, the assumption that free trade, whether internally or internationally, will produce a net increment in welfare depends upon assumptions, such as full employment, that are demonstrably not present in Canada (Jackson 1992:73-75; Furlong and Moggach 1990).

(iii) Harmonization Measures

A related measure was designed to achieve better coordination of federal and provincial fiscal policies and to improve the harmonization of these with Canada's monetary policy. In part the proposal was simply one of process, albeit one that would have the result of applying moral suasion to a province pursuing disharmonious policies. The government proposed to develop, in consultation with the provinces, an annual timetable to allow for greater visibility in the budget-making process. Such procedures would include a relatively fixed annual budget cycle; a fixed annual schedule of finance ministers meetings; the publication by all governments of pre-budget economic-fiscal outlooks; and common accounting conventions (Canada 1991a:32). Beyond that, the government foresaw the use of "guidelines" to coordinate policies. If approved by the federal government and seven provinces with at least 50 percent of the population, meeting in a new Council of Federation, the guidelines would be set in federal legislation under the new economic-union power. Although up to three provinces could opt out, with a 60-percent vote in their legislative assemblies, the opt-out was only for three years and it was unclear, in the federal proposals, whether such measures were renewable.

The federal government also favoured establishing an independent agency

> to monitor and evaluate the macroeconomic policies of the federal and provincial governments. Such an agency could perform a role for Canadian governments not dissimilar to that performed by the OECD and

the IMF for their members. The monitoring function would furnish an indispensable information base that would be publicly available to assist the task of policy coordination and harmonization. (Canada 1991a:32)

The effect was clearly centralizing (albeit requiring substantial provincial consent). Certainly a common reaction in Québec was that the proposals represented a federal "power grab." More generally, it is reasonable to infer that the ability of any province, or small number of provinces, to deviate from a national majority viewpoint would be circumscribed under these proposals. In the context of Canadian electoral history this might be expected to be more of a problem for provinces with left-leaning governments than for those with more conservative administrations.

(iv) Reforming the Bank of Canada's Mandate
In its constitutional proposals the government included a number of ideas for changing the Bank of Canada's mandate and for changing the appointments system to the board and governorship of the bank. Since the bank is under the exclusive jurisdiction of the federal authorities, this could be accomplished without provincial involvement and without amending the constitution in any way. Its inclusion in the proposal helps to indicate the pattern of changes in economic institutions and objectives that the government had in mind.

The changes in appointment procedures involved regional representation on the board of directors of the Bank of Canada, consultation with the provinces over appointments, establishing regional consultative panels, and making the appointment of governor of the bank subject to ratification by a (reformed) senate. The impact of these structural changes must be seen as largely symbolic. This is because the bank's mandate, under the rest of the federal proposal, would be focused on a single goal—the preservation of price stability.

The bank's mandate has been much broader:

> to regulate credit and currency in the best interest of the economic life of the nation, to control and protect the external value of the national monetary unit and to mitigate by its influence fluctuations in the general level of production, trade prices, and employment, so far as may be possible within the scope of monetary action, and generally to promote the economic and financial welfare of Canada. (Canada 1991b:38)

Nothing in the package demonstrates more clearly the influence of neo-liberal economic theory and ideology upon the government's constitutional agenda than the argumentation surrounding this proposal:

> The only contribution the Bank of Canada can make to the well-being

of all Canadians in the long run is to pursue policies which maintain the purchasing power of the nation's money. . . . The references to mitigating fluctuations in production, trade and employment and other objectives should be eliminated as they represent objectives either that history has taught us a central bank cannot achieve or that can only be achieved through price stability. (Canada 1991b:38–39)

This is, of course, a somewhat selective and theoretically blinkered reading of what "history" has to offer. Pierre Fortin (1991:3) commented that the new mandate, zero inflation, would

force our central bank to support a priori a scientific position that is highly controversial at best and, at worst, completely in error. . . . Although the achievement and maintenance of the lowest possible inflation rate is desirable, it is nevertheless illogical to relieve the central bank of its responsibilities to concern itself with the stability of employment and other 'real' variables.

(v) Redistribution of Powers

The decentralization of federal powers contained in the Meech Lake Accord was replicated and expanded in the 1991 proposals. A number of areas were to be recognized as being within exclusive provincial jurisdiction: training, tourism, forestry, mining, recreation, housing, and municipal and urban affairs. A number of other areas were identified for review to see which level of government could best provide them. With respect to immigration and culture the federal government was prepared to negotiate and constitutionalize agreements with individual provinces. In addition, the government proposed a constitutional amendment to permit the delegation of legislative authority between the two levels of government. It was also willing to remove the federal declaratory power from the constitution and to recognize provincial possession of the residual power on "nonnational matters not specifically assigned to the federal government under the Constitution or by virtue of court decisions." Finally, the Meech objective of limiting the federal spending power found a place in the 1991 proposals. The government committed itself to obtaining the approval of seven provinces containing 50 percent of the population before launching new shared-cost programs or conditional transfer payments in areas of exclusive provincial jurisdiction. The federal government would also provide reasonable compensation for those provinces that wished to opt out but established their own programs meeting the objectives of the federal initiative.

When taken together with the other measures, there is little doubt that the result would be major decentralization of Canadian federalism (Johnson 1992). Most of the decentralizing measures were consistent with neo-liberal principles, and for the most part this particular federal government's desire to rid itself of these responsibilities was not surprising. However, the decision to provincialize labour-market and labour-training policy struck some observers as curious, in light of other government policies that have and will create the need for major labour-adjustment programs (Simpson 1992). It may best be explained as a concession to Québec that became generalized in view of the "equality of provinces" doctrine.

(vi) Property Rights

The government failed to advance any rationale for its proposal to include a guarantee for property rights in the Charter of Rights and Freedoms, and its motivation remains unclear. Joel Bakan (1992:118) offers three possible reasons: a desire to undercut Reform Party support, to give itself a bargaining chip in the constitutional negotiations, or a desire "to elevate their market ideology to constitutional status." Earlier attempts to introduce guaranteed property rights into the constitution foundered on the concern that such provisions in the United States had resulted in striking down laws regulating hours of work and child labour, and prohibiting discrimination against unions. Speaking about the 1991 Canadian proposals, a spokesperson for the Canadian Environmental Law Association expressed the fear that its provisions would protect business from regulations imposed by democratically-elected governments. Similarly, David Milne argued that property-rights provisions are a "favourite vehicle for conservative interests resisting social legislation and the welfare state" (quoted in Mittelstaedt 1991). Such comments demonstrate the consistency of the property-rights proposal with the general neo-liberal constitutional agenda.

The Process

Following publication of the federal government's constitutional proposals in September 1991, the process of debate and discussion intensified. Much of the opportunity for public input focused initially on the Special Joint Committee (of the House and Senate) on a Renewed Canada. Ultimately, the committee held seventy-eight meetings across Canada, heard testimony from some seven hundred individuals, and received three thousand written submissions before presenting its report in March 1992 (Beaudoin and Dobbie 1992:3). Because of major organizational difficulties being experienced by the Special Joint Committee in the fall of 1991, the federal government asked a number of major research institutions to organize constitutional conferences to debate the federal proposals. Five of these were held, in January and February 1992, and they focused national attention on the constitutional debate. The conferences each consisted of around two hundred delegates, some of them experts or selected because of their membership in various groups. Others were randomly selected from interested "ordinary" Canadians who applied to participate (Canada 1992a, b, c, d). Although hardly representative in any scientific sense, the participants in the conferences did establish a sense that they spoke in some way for the average Canadians who had been left out of previous constitutional negotiations.

In general the neo-liberal items in the federal constitutional proposals were not well received by the constitutional conferences. The principle of a strong economic union seems to have been largely accepted—possibly because of its symbolic appeal. However, the federally-proposed mechanisms for achieving it were more controversial. One example was the proposed section 91A, granting Parliament (subject to provincial approval on the 7/50 formula) the right to make laws it declared to be for the efficient functioning of the economic union. The conferences rejected this section virtually unanimously on the grounds that it was unnecessary, illegitimate, and inappropriate (Canada 1992a:10–13, 19–22). The proposals for greater harmonization of fiscal policies, and of fiscal policy with monetary policy, received the same response. Delegates to the conference were suspicious of rigid and constitutionally-entrenched mechanisms for dealing with problems that they believed should be addressed flexibly (Canada 1992a:14–16). They unequivocally felt that the Bank of Canada reforms ought not to be part of the constitutional process and that the bank's mandate should not be narrowed to focus only on price stability (Canada 1992a:17–18; Canada 1992b:11). The Conference on Identity, Rights and Values overwhelmingly rejected the inclusion of property rights (Canada 1992c:15–16). But, the proposal to include a social charter in the constitution, clearly neither part of the federal government's proposals nor a neo-liberal preference, surfaced in a number of the conferences, and it was apparent that the idea enjoyed substantial support. Finally, although the results of the Conference on the Division of Powers could not be construed as a repudiation of the federal proposals, there was clearly substantial support for a strong central government, national standards, and a willingness to deal with Québec's aspirations through asymmetry rather than through generalized devolution (Canada 1992d:21).

Given its composition, one could expect the Beaudoin-Dobbie Committee to be generally supportive of the federal proposals. While this expectation was met, even the Conservatives who belonged to it were influenced by the process of public discussion. In a number of areas the report suggested alterations to the federal package. The committee felt further consultations with the artistic and cultural communities should take place before the government proceeded with the proposal to transfer jurisdiction over culture to the provinces (Beaudoin and Dobbie 1992:77). It favoured a non-judicial dispute-settlement mechanism for policing the economic union (Beaudoin and Dobbie 1992:87); the inclusion in the economic union of undertakings to pursue the goals of full employment and of ensuring that all Canadians have a reasonable standard of living (Beaudoin and Dobbie 1992:88–89); and the inclusion of a "social covenant" (Beaudoin and Dobbie 1992:87). In addition, the report recommended that the issue of the Bank of Canada's mandate not be part of the constitutional discussions.

Enter the Provinces: The Charlottetown Agreement
However widespread the public consultations, the amendment of the constitution remains an intergovernmental process. A number of provinces had well-defined constitutional demands to pursue once the negotiations began in the spring of 1992. These included Alberta's advocacy of a triple-E senate, Manitoba's concern to see a "Canada clause" expressing the underlying values of Canadians and thus helping unify the country, and Ontario's demand for a social charter to guarantee social programs and national standards. A number of provinces had differing concerns about aboriginal issues and the proposed recognition of an inherent right to self-government. The most detailed, longest, and most public list of constitutional requirements came from Québec, which declined to participate in the negotiations until the rest of Canada produced an acceptable "offer"—a position Premier Bourassa had adopted after the unraveling of Meech.

Despite the complexities and the clash of agendas, nine provinces and the federal government arrived at an agreement covering a wide range of topics on July 7, 1992. On this basis Québec rejoined the constitutional negotiations and on August 28, in Charlottetown, the federal government, all provinces, and the Native and territorial leaders reached an agreement.

A number of the federal government's original proposals, including measures to harmonize fiscal policy, change the Bank of Canada's mandate, and entrench property rights, were absent. A number of the items that were included were either undesirable from the viewpoint of classical liberal political economy or, at best, a mixed blessing. A non-justiciable provision described the commitment of the governments and legislatures to preserve and develop Canada's social and economic union and called for a monitoring mechanism to be established by a future first ministers conference. Presumably such a mechanism could apply moral suasion against any government deviating from the policy objectives of the social and economic union. The policy objectives themselves, however, provided little joy to the neo-liberal political economist. In addition to a commitment to strengthen the economic union and the free movement of persons, goods, services, and capital, which were obviously acceptable, the clause included items that were not greeted with enthusiasm.

Under the social union, governments and legislatures would be committed to maintaining a health care system that met the criteria established by the Canada Health Act, provision of adequate social services and high quality and accessible education, together with protection of workers' rights to organize and bargain collectively. Under the economic union the goals of full employment and a reasonable standard of living for all Canadians were prominent. Another provision, which was to be justiciable, strengthened the federal government's commitment to regional equalization under section 36 of the Constitution Act. Henceforth the federal government would be charged with ensuring that "provincial governments have sufficient revenues to provide reasonably comparable levels of public services at reasonably comparable levels of taxation" and to provide "reasonably comparable economic infrastructures of a national nature in each province and territory." Although the precise impact of this language was difficult to predict, its fiscal consequences were potentially contrary to the goals espoused by the neo-liberals. Certainly the "wish list" of policy objectives in the non-justiciable clause could have served to legitimate Keynesian policies as easily, or more easily, than neo-liberal ones.

In the July 7th accord, section 121, the common-market clause was to be strengthened by preventing any interprovincial trade barrier "by law or practice that arbitrarily discriminates on the basis of province or territory of residence, origin or destination and unduly impedes the efficient functioning of the Canadian economic union." The provision was to have been policed by an independent tribunal that, to strike down a barrier, would have to find that it (a) was arbitrary and (b) unduly impeded the economic union. Neo-liberal political economists were quick to denounce this language as weak and limited (for example, Corcoran 1992). In addition there was a lengthy list of areas in which interprovincial trade barriers could continue to function. This included subsidies or tax incentives aimed at encouraging investment, "reasonable" public sector investment programs, agricultural marketing and supply management programs, consumer and environmental protection, and the establishment and maintenance of government-owned monopolies. Clearly these were much weaker measures than originally proposed by the federal government.

During the summer's negotiations a number of changes were made to the provisions regarding the common market. Under the August 28 agreement section 121 would remain unchanged and a future first ministers conference would discuss how best to implement a number of "principles and commitments related to the Canadian Common Market" that were included in the accord. These principles included a prohibition against governments erecting interprovincial trade barriers, and the criteria to be used by a possible future enforcement agency were strengthened slightly. Instead of having to find that an arbitrarily discriminatory measure *unduly* impeded the efficient functioning of the Canadian economic union, it would be sufficient merely to find that such a measure did impede its efficient functioning. However, a lengthy list of exemptions continued be appended to this section.

Only in the area of transferring powers to the provinces did the Charlottetown package reflect the federal agenda. Although decentralization is consistent with the preferences of neo-liberal political economy, it is a second-best solution unless combined with measures to prohibit market intervention by all levels of government. This clearly was the purpose of the strong economic union proposals. Without those proposals decentralization represents only a partial victory for neo-liberal political economy, because the interventionism it abhors at the federal level could continue at the provincial level. Also, the non-justiciable but highly symbolic language on the social and economic union could be used to legitimate provincial or popular pressures for federal interventionism.

The Obstacles to a Constitutional Agenda

The defeat of the Charlottetown proposals brought the process of constitutional reform to a conclusion, however temporary. In explaining the defeat of the accord many factors were at work and their interaction was complex (see McRoberts and Monahan 1993). What can be stated with some certainty is that the 1991–92 constitutional process highlighted some of the obstacles to implementing a constitutional agenda based on neo-liberal political economy.

Since the introduction of the Charter it was apparent that a great many Canadians, especially in English Canada, had become attached to the (primarily liberal) individual rights it contains—they had, as Alan Cairns has put it, become "Charter Canadians." But there was little evidence of attachment to the idea of extending liberal political rights to the neo-liberal economic values expressed in the federal government's constitutional agenda. If the views of the Renewal of Canada conferences can be taken as in any way representative of informed Canadian opinion, it would seem that Canadian political culture was still inclined towards collective social provision and tolerated reasonable levels of governmental intervention in the economy to moderate the effects of market forces. The Canadian government may have become "true believers" in neo-liberal political economy, but in this respect their position was incongruent with the broader political culture.

A second obstacle, of course, was the federal system itself. Although many provinces were prepared to accept some decentralization of the federal system, this process was often accompanied by a desire to maximize the powers of the particular provincial government rather than by repudiating the powers of government in general. Certainly many of them found the attachment to pure market economics represented in the economic-union proposal to be unacceptable in practice. Further, a number of provinces continued to support and demand a strong federal role in some areas. In taking this position they seemed to agree with the general preferences of Canadians, at least those outside Québec: opinion poll data regularly demonstrated a preference for a strong federal government.

Canada's continuing constitutional crisis provided an opportunity for Canada's neo-liberals to attempt to shape the outcome along the lines of their ideology. But by the end of Mulroney's time in office it appeared that Canada's traditionally statist political culture, combined with its federal institutions, had been strong enough to dilute that effort to a very significant degree. Yet the neo-liberal effort continued. Having failed to strengthen the Canadian economic union by constitutional means, the federal government, spurred on by business pressure (*The Globe and Mail*, December 5, 1992:B3), began trying to achieve it through a new approach to intergovernmental negotiations. In practice the

Agreement on Internal Trade turned out to be a non-binding political accord that provided little enforcement to back up the stated goals of removing internal trade barriers in Canada (see Howse 1996). For neo-liberals this is a disappointing outcome. The weakness of the enforcement mechanisms, the result of provincial resistance for any supervisory powers for Ottawa, stands at odds with the provisions of international trade agreements to which Canada is signatory: "The more and more we get into international trade agreements, the onus falls on the federal government to ensure that the provinces play by the rules" (trade consultant Peter Clark quoted in the *The Globe and Mail*, 13 November 1995).

More generally, many of the goals pursued in the constitutional talks may prove in the end to have been achieved by other routes: the provisions of the Free Trade Agreement—and its NAFTA successor; the Multilateral Agreement on Investment that is currently under negotiation; and the quasi-constitutional administrative changes and intergovernmental agreements initiated by the Chrétien government.

Notes
1. An earlier version of this chapter was published as McBride (1993).
2. For a useful survey of these aspects of neo-liberal theory see Green (1987:chapters 2, 3 and 4).
3. See also Gamble (1988:129–38).
4. More than ten years before the Free Trade Agreement was signed Garth Stevenson (1977:82) made the prescient suggestion that the Canadian economic elite considered "their" strong government to lie in Washington rather than in Ottawa.
5. This concern may be overridden by the provisions of trade agreements that reduce the powers of both national and sub-national governments.
6. Others have pointed to opinion-poll evidence to critique the notion that Québec, as opposed to the Québec government, was hostile to the 1982 Constitution. Frances Russell, in an article headlined "Meech Lake Shows The Tories Have Learned Nothing" *(Winnipeg Free Press,* July 4, 1992) cited two Gallup polls taken around the time of the patriation of the Constitution. The first, in December 1981, reported that 46 percent of Québecers disagreed with their government's refusal to sign the patriation package; only 30 percent agreed with the government's stance. By April 1982, 49 percent of Québecers told Gallup that the Constitution was "a good thing for Canada"; only 16 percent thought it was not.
7. For a balanced account of the "Québec was betrayed" thesis, see Cairns (1991:226–37).
8. The obverse of Banting's presentation of this issue is that the legal status of federal spending power had never been repudiated and that its use was legitimated by federal–provincial agreements.
9. According to some critics of Meech, this process entrenched the substantial provincial gains already made in the 1982 constitution (see Trudeau 1989:73).
10. Obviously there were some exceptions to this rule as with the introduction of health care by the CCF government of Saskatchewan.
11. This point was not lost on some critics of Meech Lake who depicted tight connections between the accord, the recommendations of the Macdonald Commis-

sion, and the corporate agenda. See United Electrical Workers (1988).

12. This is a factor that casts doubt on "state-centred" interpretations of the Meech affair.

13. According to its own press releases, the Business Council on National Issues "is the senior voice of Canadian business leaders on public policy issues in Canada and abroad." Composed of the chief executives of 150 leading Canadian companies, the BCNI carries out an active program of research, consultation, and advocacy in four principal areas: the national economy; foreign affairs and the global economy; the environment and sustainable development; and political governance. The member companies of the BCNI are active in every major sector of the Canadian economy, employ over 1.5 million Canadians, and manage approximately $1 trillion in assets. The view that the Macdonald Report reflected the prevailing consensus of the economics profession has been expressed by, among others, Carmichael, Dobson and Lipsey (1986) and Simeon (1987).

14. The sense of crisis was the result, in Cameron's view (1992:3–5), of the federal government manipulating the Meech process to put pressure on dissident premiers and other opponents of the deal.

15. These conditions can be found in the Québec Liberal Party's Allaire Report and in the report of the National Assembly's Belanger-Campeau commission. Both reported in March 1991 and called for transferring major powers to Québec. However, both reports also argued for continued economic cooperation and economic union between Québec (whether it remained part of Canada or opted for independence) and the rest of Canada.

16. For a useful summary of the report, see *The Globe and Mail*, 29 June 1991, A7–A10.

17. A sense of the scope of this activity can be gleaned from surveying issues of *The Network,* a non-partisan newsletter designed to stimulate informed debate on the constitutional options available to Canada.

18. Canada 1991a.

Chapter 6

Quasi-Constitutional Change Under Chrétien

Elected in 1993, the Chrétien Liberals understood clearly that the country was suffering from "constitutional fatigue" as a result of protracted involvement in the Meech and Charlottetown Accords. The Red Book made few concrete references to constitutional or federal–provincial issues (Brooks 1996). Indeed, even after the election of a Parti Québécois government in Québec and the prospect of a 1995 referendum on separatism moved from the realm of conjecture to reality, the Liberals' constitutional posture could be characterized as being one of an "advanced state of denial" (Johnson and Stritch 1996b:298).

Insofar as a constitutional strategy was apparent, it was one of devolution of powers that involved implementing aspects of the Meech and Charlottetown Accords by administrative means or intergovernmental agreements. After the narrow federalist referendum victory this policy was intensified and joined by symbolic recognition of Québec as a distinct society and rhetoric about a harder federal line in the event of a future referendum and/or separatist victory.

The Referendum Campaign
No definitive account of the campaign or its aftermath can be attempted here. However, a brief narrative can be provided and, consistent with the theme of this book, we will emphasize the implication of neo-liberalism in the results and consequences. We recognize that this is a minor aspect of a debate that has far deeper roots and ramifications. However, in this, as in other areas, neo-liberalism has made its own distinctive contribution to dismantling a nation.

Buoyed by opinion polls that initially seemed to point to a federalist victory, the Chrétien government displayed overconfidence until late in the campaign followed by panic when it appeared that the "Yes" forces were on the verge of winning.

On the Yes side two events laid the foundation for a good result. The first was the adoption, after a summit meeting of Premier Jacques Parizeau, Bloc Québécois Leader Lucien Bouchard and Mario Dumont of the Action Démocratique du Québec in June 1995, of a relatively soft question. The question asked, "Do you agree that Québec should become sovereign, after having made a formal offer to

Canada for a new Economic and Political Partnership, within the scope of the Bill respecting the future of Québec and of the agreement signed on June 12, 1995?" This question made it possible to argue simultaneously that the vote was on the issue of sovereignty and that independence was not necessarily the final outcome. Arguably the ambivalence of the question made possible the well-documented instances of Yes voters who believed that they would continue to be Canadian citizens, holding Canadian passports, using Canadian currency and so forth. Certainly polling evidence indicated that a soft question, with its promise of an offer of partnership, was a necessary condition for a majority vote (*The Globe and Mail*, 25 October, 1995).

However, until Lucien Bouchard became the *de facto* leader of the Yes forces, the soft question alone seemed insufficient to propel the sovereignist vote much above its traditional levels. The charismatic Bouchard, playing upon the historical and recent grievances of Québec within Confederation, was able to transform the tone of the campaign, to rally activists and soft nationalist voters alike, and to come within an ace of victory. The result was 50.6 percent for the No (federalist) side to 49.4 percent for the Yes (sovereignist) side—a difference of only 53,000 votes out of 4.756 million cast.

Until very late in the campaign the federalists had stuck to economic arguments, long after Bouchard had dismissed the proposition that the issue could be settled on cost-benefit lines, or that, to the extent it could, the balance sheet favoured the federal forces. Federal predictions of dire economic consequences were not widely believed and the threat that no new partnership would be forthcoming[1] was also regarded as implausible by many. In the last week of the campaign Prime Minister Chrétien bowed to pressure and began to promise constitutional changes, including some form of recognition of Québec as a distinct society and a possible constitutional veto for Québec. Commenting on the changed federal strategy, Michel Auger, writing in *Le Journal de Montréal* observed: "The No side is suddenly presenting itself as the real champion of change. And to convince itself, it needed only listen to the speech of Mr. Chrétien, who repeated the word 'change' no fewer than twenty times, as if the incantation-like repetition would magically make people forget that he has steadfastly refused to broach the topic for the past two years" (cited in the *The Globe and Mail*, 26 October 1995). And, equally belatedly, the federal side followed Bouchard's lead and began to speak to the emotional issues of national pride—to the heart rather than to the head—a shift that culminated in the huge rally in Montreal on October 27.

The Role of Neo-Liberalism
What role did neo-liberalism play amidst this conflict of national visions, language-based nationalism, and conflicting historical interpretations of French–English relations in North America? The answer must be: a secondary, but not insignificant role.

Québec's declaration of sovereignty (*The Globe and Mail,* 7 September 1995) included a blend of nationalist appeals and commitment to social democratic principles. Thus the document appealed to national and social solidarity and pledged that the purposes of a sovereign Québec included compassion for the destitute, a commitment to full employment, guarantees of social and economic rights including the right to education, health care and other social services. These sentiments reflected popular demands for a *projet de société* that had emerged during public consultations on the referendum. This enabled sovereignist spokespeople to argue that anyone who wanted to preserve social services should vote "yes" in the referendum.

The federal government's priority to reduce the deficit meant that it was less able than in 1980 to play the role of defender of social programs. Given its fiscal priorities, any attempt to do so would be implausible. Under federal proposals for devolution Ottawa would play a decreasing role in social provision. The federal authorities were thus in a contradictory position. Remaining in Canada no longer meant attachment to the social democratic principles espoused in the sovereignty declaration; increasingly it would be up to the provinces whether these or neo-liberal principles would prevail in social policy. All that could be said with certainty was that Ottawa's fiscal policy would make it hard for provinces to maintain social programs at the existing level. As a result of federal neo-liberal policies the case *for* belonging to Canada was weaker than it might have been. And the risks of separating from a decentralized and, in social policy terms, "hollowed out" country were correspondingly less.

In reality the depiction of the Parti Québécois (PQ) as social democratic has always been problematic. There were real grounds for doubting that social democratic principles would inform its policy once the referendum was over— doubts which have since been confirmed. However, uncertainty about which way the PQ might lean did not offset certainty about the neo-liberal tenor of federal policy. This gave the sovereignist side an advantage they had not had in the 1980 referendum. Jean-Jacques Samson, an editorial writer for *Le Soleil* warned that the No side must counter the myth that a "No vote means a shift to the right for Québec society and that a Yes is the way to resist the dismantling of our social-security system. . . . Whether they vote Yes or No, Québecers, will not escape the Draconian cuts that are coming to government programs. . . . Too many Québecers are voting Yes because they think it will be like winning the lottery. But they're buying into a dream, a mirage" (quoted in the *The Globe and Mail,* 26 October 1995). Despite the validity of the warning there is no doubt that federal policies made it much harder to win the "socially concerned" vote in the referendum.

The social factor was seen as sufficiently central to the result that in the days immediately following the referendum there was media speculation that the Chrétien government would be forced to back off or postpone its drive to reduce government expenditures (see Maclean's, 6 and 13 November 1995 and the *The*

Globe and Mail, 31 October 1995). In the event, however, the federal strategy came to consist of continued focus on the deficit combined with further devolution, symbolic action on distinct society and the veto, and threats of a harder line towards Québec sovereignty by way of Plan B.

Pursuit of this option was made easier as the PQ government, by now under the premiership of Lucien Bouchard, demonstrated that it was as little committed to social programs, when forced to prioritize them against the imperatives of deficit reduction, as its federal and most provincial counterparts. By the spring of 1997 the Québec government had embarked on "the deepest cuts in social spending in the province's history" with major strains being caused in the sovereignist coalition as a result (*The Globe and Mail*, 19 March 1997). Thus part of the advantage that federal neo-liberalism conferred on Québec sovereignists was cancelled out by the actions of the PQ government in the post-referendum period.

A veto for Québec and recognition as a distinct society came in the form of federal legislation. Since it is not entrenched in the constitution the distinct society provision has only symbolic value. It takes the form of a resolution urging the executive and legislative branches of government to be guided by the reality that Québec is a distinct society. Perhaps significantly, no mention is made of the judicial branch of government. The legislation also binds the federal government, but not in any constitutionally entrenched sense, to support constitutional changes only if it has support from Québec, Ontario, British Columbia, two of the four Atlantic provinces, and two of the three Prairie provinces. Effectively, therefore, Québec is granted a veto, albeit one dependent on continued federal commitment to this formula. Moreover, expert opinion is divided on the constitutionality of this device. Some consider that it is an unconstitutional attempt to change the amending process (Andrew Heard in *The Globe and Mail*, 3 February 1996); others believe that because the legislation is focused on the ability of the executive to introduce constituyional changes rather than on the legislature's ability to dispose of them, it is constitutional (Patrick Monahan in *The Globe and Mail*, 3 February 1996). Predictably the changes were denounced by the Bloc and Parti Québécois as an "empty shell," devoid of content, and further proof that Ottawa could not deliver on its referendum campaign promises to offer real change (see *Toronto Star*, 29 November 1995).

The third element of the federal government's conciliatory approach, designed to woo "soft" nationalists to the federal cause was further decentralization of powers within the federation. Whether this demonstrated the need to stay in Canada, because Canada was a flexible federation that could meet Québec's needs for greater autonomy, or showed that there was little point in remaining, because the federal government was an empty vessel that did little for its citizens, remained an open question.

Decentralization and Devolution: Intergovernmental Agreements as a Surrogate for Constitutional Change

Federal proposals to further decentralize an already highly decentralized federal system have found willing takers in provincial capitals. It quickly became clear that some provinces were interested in more than the transfer of items such as training, tourism and forestry that had featured in the Charlottetown Accord.

For Alberta and Ontario provincial control over health care was now viewed as a desirable and possibly achievable objective (*The Globe and Mail*, 3 November 1995). A background study for the Ontario Ministry of Intergovernmental Affairs (Courchene 1996) outlined a model for a federal system in which there would be full provincial responsibility for the design of health, social services and education. National standards and equivalencies would be the product of an enforceable interprovincial accord. The paper seemed to enjoy the support of the Harris government whose intergovernmental affairs minister, Diane Cunningham, has argued that provinces will assume greater leadership in social policy and that national standards do not have to be federal standards (Fafard 1997:14). Discussions of the particulars of the Courchene model moved out of the public eye after pressure for continued federal guarantees for the medicare system from some provinces, and Alberta Premier Ralph Klein's clarification that, while guidelines might be acceptable, they should not be enforceable. Such developments were indicative of how far some of Canada's larger provinces were prepared to go in a decentralist direction.

Much of the real action has been concentrated in the areas identified in the Charlottetown Accord as ripe for transfer to the exclusive jurisdiction of the provinces. However, the redesign of transfers for social assistance, health, and education under the Canada Health and Social Transfer, the deep reduction in the size of the fiscal transfer, and the elimination of most conditions that formerly applied to Canada Assistance Plan money, has reduced federal leverage in seeking to maintain national standards in the one area—health—where conditions continue to apply. Provincial autonomy in the areas covered by the CHST is correspondingly enhanced.

Some of the *de facto* decentralization pre-dates Chrétien—a point that emphasizes the substantive continuity between the Mulroney and Chrétien governments. After the failure of the Meech Lake Accord the Mulroney government concluded an immigration agreement with Québec in 1991—an early attempt to demonstrate the flexibility of federalism outside the area of formal constitutional change. The agreement enhanced the role of the province in the selection of immigrants, and it was given exclusive responsibility over independent immigrants and provided generous funding to assist with resettling and acculturating immigrants in French. Faced with criticism from other provinces that the funding provided to Québec was excessive[2] the federal government offered, in 1997, to conclude similar agreements with those provinces where heavy concentrations of immigrants tend to settle—Alberta, British Columbia and Ontario. The new agreements would transfer greater power to the provinces in the selection of immigrants and control over resettlement programs, as well as making more money available to them for resettlement purposes (*The Globe and Mail*, 27 February 1997). Ottawa also announced that regulations governing the immigrant-investor program would be changed to give provinces responsibility for monitoring compliance and enforcement of the program and the ability to direct up to 40 percent of the money to provincial investment priorities. Under the terms of a 1986 agreement, Québec already had its own investor program so the effect, consistent with the agenda of decentralization, was to extend its provisions to the other provinces (*The Globe and Mail*, 22 March 1997).

Efforts to achieve major decentralization of the environment portfolio seemed on the verge of success in October 1995 when the Canadian Council of Ministers of the Environment released a draft Environmental Management Framework Agreement (EMFA). Kennett (1995:4) commented that if "decentralization, rationalization and elimination of overlap and duplication are indeed the new watchwords of Canadian federalism, the EMFA appears to be on the forefront of change." In the event, however, the draft was altered as a result of pressures from environmental groups who opposed federal withdrawal from the area (see *The Globe and Mail*, 20 January 1996); mixed reviews from business groups, some of which were concerned that too much regulation and duplication remained; and uncertainty about how the issue would play in Québec. The upshot, when a revised draft was eventually circulated and endorsed, was little change in the division of responsibilities (Fafard 1997:9).

In the natural resources area the federal authorities withdrew funding from forest resource development agreements and mining development agreements but retained some role in aspects of forestry that affected international trade and investment, federal Crown lands, science and technology, aboriginal issues, and national statistics and environmental linkages (McLellan 1996). In another demonstration of "flexible federalism" Ottawa concluded an agreement with British Columbia ceding the province an increased role in the management of the west coast fishery (*Vancouver Sun*, 17 April 1997).

Labour-market policy has been one of the Liberals' central priorities for devolution of powers. The policy fits into a general argument for avoidance of duplication but is driven primarily by Québec's demand for control over training and "manpower" policy. The commitment to withdraw from training and seek new partnerships with the provinces was promised by Prime Minister Chrétien on November 27, 1995, and made official in the 1996 throne speech. Details of what the federal government had in mind were outlined more fully in May 1996 (see Human Resources Development Canada (HRDC) 1996a).

The federal government proposed to transfer to the provinces the responsibility for active employment measures funded through the employment insurance account. Such measures would include wage subsidies, temporary income supplements, support for self-employment initiatives, partnerships for job creation and, where provinces request, skills loans and grants. Provinces that assumed responsibility for delivery of active measures could also opt to provide labour-market services—screening, counselling, and placement—currently delivered by the federal government. The proposal also involved federal withdrawal from labour-market training over a three year period, or sooner if provinces wished. The federal government would no longer be involved in purchase of training, funding apprenticeships, co-op education, workplace-based training, or project-based training (HRDC 1996a and 1996b).

Federal officials acknowledge that asymmetry will result (interview HRDC official, July 1996). In some cases provinces might prefer co-management rather than full devolution. In other cases, provinces remain undecided and are still deciding whether to take up the federal offer (interview HRDC official February 1997). In these cases the federal government will still be involved in active employment measures, though to different degrees. In cases where agreements have been signed the federal presence will be reduced significantly and transfers of personnel to the provinces are a feature of these agreements. In an effort to limit asymmetry federal negotiators point to the inclusion of an equal treatment clause. A federal official explained that, "if another province was seen to have a markedly better agreement, ones that we had already signed could be opened up—not something that the federal side would want. So federal negotiators have established certain benchmarks in the existing agreements" (interview HRDC official February 1997).

As well, the federal offer to the provinces contained a number "guidelines" for the intergovernmental agreements. According to these, active measures must be: "results-based (i.e., help individuals obtain or keep employment); reduce individuals' dependency on government assistance; promote cooperation and partnership with other labour-market partners, such as other governments, employers and community-based organizations; feature local decision-making; eliminate unnecessary overlap and duplication; encourage individuals to take personal responsibility for getting back to work; [and] ensure service to the public in either official language, where there is significant demand" (HRDC 1996b:2).

The existence of these guidelines or conditions has led some to argue that

> the federal "withdrawal" is neither total, unconditional nor absolute. . . . The federal government has no desire to let go of its responsibilities of conception, orientation, evaluation and control. The provinces are still called upon to collaborate with the federal government for the implementation of training programs and seeing its management/operational powers increase. (Rocher and Rouillard 1997:126; see also Bakvis 1997)

While some federal conditions certainly remain, the result of transferring employment insurance funds to the provinces for active labour-market purposes and the agreements already signed indicate that the conditions are not seen as particularly onerous by provinces that are bent on the maximum possible decentralization. At the time of writing, labour-force development agreements had been concluded with most provinces, including Alberta and Québec, both strong proponents of decentralization.

The new Employment Insurance legislation and the associated labour-force development agreements with the provinces will leave the federal authorities with a limited range of labour-market policy responsibilities. These include employment insurance benefits, provision of a national system of labour-market information and exchange, support for interprovincial sectoral development and developing responses to national economic crises, jurisdiction over a one-time Transitional Jobs Fund of $300 million from the consolidated revenue fund to be spent over the next three years, and some continued involvement in aboriginal and youth programs (HRDC 1996b:1; interview HRDC official February 1997).

Since, at the time of the Charlottetown Accord, the federal authorities contemplated transferring unemployment insurance to the provinces (interview, former HRDC official, July 1996), it is possible that further devolution on these lines will occur eventually. Certainly this eventuality seems more probable than reoccupation of the labour-market area by the federal authorities. Further federal withdrawal from labour-market policy has been made more likely by the major shift toward radical decentralization of federalism now favoured by Ontario, traditionally an upholder of a strong role for Ottawa. The province's most recent position paper on the constitution calls for unemployment insurance to be run jointly by the federal and provincial governments or by the provinces alone (*The Globe and Mail*, 16 August 1996). Should this materialize, the process of harmonizing Canada's unemployment insurance system with that of the United States, predicted by opponents of the Free Trade Agreement, will be largely complete.

The intention of symbolic recognition of distinct society, a veto for Québec, and decentralizing measures is to address some of Québec's historic demands for more control, while maintaining for the most part the equality-of-provinces approach that has become entrenched in much English Canadian public opinion. Periodically federal spokespersons indicated that a harder position—the so-called Plan B—existed in the event that the conciliatory measures, outlined above, were insufficient to avert another referendum in Québec.

Plan B
While no document labeled "Plan B" has been issued by the federal authorities its main feature appears to be one of challenging the notion that Québec can determine the circumstances under which it might leave Canada. Succinctly expressed by Intergovernmental Affairs Minister Stéphane Dion, Plan B is the "rules of secession" while Plan A is the "plan of reconciliation" (*Maclean's*, 12 February 1996).

The federal government has expressed a wish to see a "fair" question posed in a future referendum; has floated the idea that a higher threshold than 50 percent plus one vote should apply, given the momentous consequences; has held out the possibility of a national referendum to allow all Canadians to have their say on the issue of Québec's separation; and has raised the spectre that the partition of Québec could occur as part of the secession settlement. Partition would cater to the expressed preferences of the aboriginal population of northern Québec and those areas of the province that rejected the separatist option in the referendum. Prime Minister Jean Chrétien asserted that, "If Canada is divisible, Québec is divisible" (*Vancouver Sun*, 30 January 1997)—a view that declined to take into account differences that might exist between the right to self-determination of people and that of minorities. Since Québec sovereignists refused to compare their right to self-determination to those of aboriginal peoples living in northern Québec or to ethnic minorities living in the province, Plan B contains a potentially explosive mixture.

Independent of the federal government, a legal challenge to the proposal to unilaterally declare sovereignty was launched in 1995 by Québec City lawyer Guy Bertrand. While declining to grant an injunction against holding the referendum, a Québec Superior Court judge ruled that: "The constitutional changes proposed by the Québec government would lead to a break-up of the justice system which would clearly be contrary to the Constitution of Canada. . . . The evidently illegal process undertaken by the government leads the court to conclude that the claimant (Guy Bertrand) is entitled to relief" (*The Globe and Mail*, 9 September 1995).

In the fall of 1996 Federal Justice Minister Alan Rock referred the question of Québec's right to separate unilaterally to the Supreme Court. The government requested the Supreme Court "to clarify the issue of unilateral secession so that Québecers and other Canadians can understand clearly the legal framework that would govern any process that could possibly lead to secession." The government noted that Québec legislation provided that the National Assembly could unilaterally declare Québec to be sovereign but, from the federal viewpoint "such a change in the structure of our country could not be taken unilaterally" since, under the Canadian constitution there are no provisions, other than matters internal to a province and its institutions, that provide for unilateral provincial amendments to the country's constitution. The federal government also asked the court to reject the argument that under international law Québec had the right to self-determination. The federal government argues that such a right "has never included a right to secede from democratic independent states" (all details taken from Department of Justice 1997). Manitoba and Saskatchewan joined the federal reference. The provinces argued that any secession must involve talks with all provinces, not just the federal government, and, according the Saskatchewan Premier Roy Romanow, be agreed to, as a minimum, by seven provinces representing 50 percent of the population, and Parliament (*The Globe and Mail*,

15 April 1997). At the time of writing the Supreme Court had yet to arrive at a decision.

Conclusion

The inclusion of neo-liberal constitutional proposals in the Meech and Charlottetown Accords—packages driven by another agenda, that of recasting federal arrangements to facilitate Québec's continued membership in the Canadian state—was not at first glance a resounding success. The accords went down to defeat and with them such neo-liberal prescriptions as they incorporated.

Failures though they were, the contents of the accords continue to influence current strategies. Current strategies are, in Gibbins's words (1997:12), "path dependent on past failures." And, he argues, the strategy should be re-assessed "before it takes the country too far down the path to a destination that may neither keep Québec in Canada nor serve Canadians well should Québec leave" (Gibbins 1997:1).

From the perspective of this book the move to radically decentralize Confederation is partly driven by neo-liberal preferences for a highly restricted role for government. Neo-liberalism is implicated to a greater extent than commonly acknowledged in the constitutional dismantling of the nation.

Notes

1. See the speech of Paul Martin as reported in *The Globe and Mail*, 27 September 1995.
2. By 1997 Québec received about 12 percent of immigrants to Canada but received 37 percent of the money that Ottawa allocates for resettlement (*The Globe and Mail*, 27 February 1997).

Chapter 7

National Policies, Continentalism, and the New Global Order

The history of Canada has been one of a constant tug between ongoing efforts to maintain national autonomy against the pulls of continental integration. The emergence of the new global economic order has introduced an additional layer to the complex relationship of sustaining national cohesion in the face of external disunifying economic forces. As explored more fully in Chapter 8, one of the shapes that globalization has assumed in North America is greater continental assimilation in the form of regional free-trade associations.

Much of Canadian public policy has been debated and contested through the prism of nationalism versus continentalism. "Continentalism is a term used to describe the theory of closer ties (e.g., in the form of closer trade links, energy sharing or common water-use policies) with the United States. An impressive number of crucial turning points in Canadian political history," Clarkson reminds us, "have pitted the forces of nationalism against those of continentalism" (1996). This chapter examines the evolution of the Canadian economy and economic policy from the vantage point of the interplay between nationalism and continentalism, and considers the shifting role which the Canadian state has played in this process. Moreover, we explore the challenges to public policy that globalization poses for the Canadian political economy.

Structuring the Economy: From the National Policy to the NEP
The Canadian state played a formative role in constructing a "separate" economy north of the 49th parallel. The Macdonald National Policy of 1879 was a project in which Canadian business worked closely with the state to create a "national" economy and to solidify the new Canadian political unit. Significantly, nationalism in Canada has of necessity been primarily economic in its orientation because of difficulties in making appeals centred around a common language, a common culture, and a common history (Smiley 1975:39–41). Hence, the National Policy was much more than simply an economic strategy; it went to the heart of defining the purpose behind the new nation-state.

The precise linkage between the first National Policy and the nature and structure of Canadian capitalism has occasioned considerable debate. Some writers contend that the National Policy was directed in the interests of a mercantile elite against the aspirations of indigenous industrial capital (see, for example, Naylor 1975; Watkins 1980a); others maintain that the policy was aimed at fostering the development of a fully mature and rounded Canadian capitalist economy (see, for instance, Ryerson 1973; MacDonald 1975; Williams 1979; McNally 1981).

For Tom Naylor the National Policy was a political measure devised by the commercial bourgeoisie to advance their interests at the expense of a domestic industrial bourgeoisie. The domestic bourgeoisie, centred in natural resource extraction, transportation, banking, and merchandising, controlled state policy with the goal of solidifying the dominance of a staples-based trading economy in Canada. This commercial faction of capital, according to Naylor, bound the Canadian economic strategy to supplying the industrial-centre economies in Europe and the United States with staple products.[1] This created a policy environment that discouraged the emergence of a strong domestic industrial base. The industrial formation that did occur in Canada was largely fostered through heavy foreign investment. Manufacturing came to be controlled and shaped by foreign interests for their benefit. Consequently, the Canadian economy remained tied to more industrially-advanced nations, especially the United States. In short, for Naylor (1975), the Canadian economy was marked by its "dependent development" character, and Canadian economic policy was, consequently, not nationalist in origin but continentalist.

In contrast, others have concluded that while the National Policy did have significant "continentalist ramifications," this was "because of unforeseen circumstances" (Hutcheson 1978:11). Thus, although the National Policy was designed to unite Canada on an east–west axis, in fact it also served to integrate the country into the "international colonial system" (Phillips 1977:43). While the Canadian industrial sector was ultimately distinguished by U.S. domination, the explanation for this effect does not lie in a conscious policy emanating from merchants and politicians but rather in the changing nature of capital itself, specifically the emergence of the multinational corporation (Hutcheson 1978:95). Foreign economic domination in the 1870s and 1880s was not seen as a "real threat." During this early period there was an influx of U.S. investment, "but not in amounts that would raise fears."[2] If later Canadian leaders did not readjust the National Policy to react to the foreign economic threat, one cannot blame the negative consequences of their failure on John A. MacDonald (Clement 1975:66).

In fact there was nothing unusual about foreign long-term investment in manufacturing in the early stages of industrialization. In the U.S. case, for instance, industry was largely financed from Britain, and this condition was not reversed until the second half of the nineteenth century (Macdonald 1975:272–73). No doubt the Canadian strategy was to follow the U.S. example of utilizing foreign capital with the future aim of repatriating it. The weakness of the strategy was the failure to realize the qualitative change in the nature of capitalism. U.S.

industrial investment in Canada was of a branch-plant variety; it was direct investment rather than the portfolio investment that British capital predominantly used. The difference is significant because portfolio investment entailed simply a transfer of a bond that gave the "holder a claim to a sum of money and interest payments" and did not involve the ownership of physical assets as in direct investment (Naylor 1973:45).

Hence the high level of U.S. foreign ownership in Canada had little to do with a conspiracy on the part of merchant capital, but rather resulted from the Canadian misfortune of being situated next door to the major twentieth-century capitalist power at the very time it was attempting to industrialize and expand its international presence. International capitalism was fundamentally reshaped in the early twentieth century by the process of the monopolization of capital:

> The younger and smaller units of Canadian capital appear to have been the victims of an historic phase of capitalist competition, which culminated—as must all such phases—'in the ruin of many small capitalists, whose capitals pass into the hands of the conquerors, and partly vanish completely.' (McNally 1981:55)

Hence we concur with Wayne Roberts: "Any reading of the . . . National Policy debate reveals a group of Canadian manufacturers who wanted control of the Canadian market. They were simply incapable of doing so" (1977:32).

By creating a transcontinental economy out of British North America, in large measure centred around the building of a national railway, the fathers of Confederation hoped to foster the development of a national community as well. The transcontinental railway nurtured a "national dream," even if that dream was initially shared only by an economic and political elite.[3] The National Policy, "aimed at extensive growth and economic diversification, was a defensive reaction to the threat of U.S. expansionism balanced by the desire to emulate U.S. industrialization and westward expansion" (Eden and Molot 1993:235). Constructing a political community was essential for this economic strategy. Creating a nation, at least in English Canada, would thus be a top-down process promoted by the Canadian state, especially through its economic policies (see Laxer 1992:202–03; Resnick 1990:207–20).

As for French Canadian nationalism, in the first century of Confederation, it took on a predominantly traditional conservative and defensive posture, captured in the concept of *la survivance*. French Canada remained more weakly attached to the economic nation-building project, especially as the effective boundaries of French Canada came to be ever more associated and "restricted" to the province of Québec. The presence, however, of an ever larger continental anglophone threat to the south did much to reinforce the logic of the Canadian "unequal union" from the francophone perspective. This was especially the case given that the economic activity and the jobs generated by the National Policy helped to stem the tide of francophone emigration to the US. Still, Lord Durham's dictum, "two nations warring within the bosom of a single state," captures much the reality of the uneasy co-existence between French and Anglo relations in Canada. The French Québec component of Canada's national "equation" has been and remains highly problematic (see, for example, McRoberts 1995, 1993; Gagnon 1993; Moniere 1981).[4] Having set forth this qualification, however, it remains true that economic nationalism has been one of the central pillars to the Canadian unity project.

In part national integration was strengthened by the nature of the Canadian staples trade, which served a trans-Atlantic market in the first decades after Confederation:

> From a nation-building perspective, the sequence of staples exports—furs, then square timber, then grains—had the virtue of unifying Canada on an east–west axis: national transportation systems carried staple exports in a west-to-east direction on the way to their ultimate, European markets, and central-Canadian and European goods and immigrants in an east-to-west direction on the return trips. (McDougall 1991:397)

In the initial post-National Policy years, the trans-Atlantic nature of Canada's staples trade served as something of an integrating force, partially able to offset the influence of U.S. foreign investment that resulted from the policy of "industrialization by invitation." But as the leading staples trade of Canada shifted to new mineral resources destined for U.S. markets, economic activity was pulled in a north–south direction. Over time this pull contributed to decentralizing tendencies (Stevenson 1981:115). By the 1990s, as John McDougall noted:

> All that is left of the original trans-Atlantic relationship is a reduced European grain trade, while the exploitation of the "modern staples"—metals, hydrocarbons, and forest products—has been predicated heavily on exports to the *American* market. It has, hence, contributed a North–South, rather than an East–West flow of trade and, if anything, has accentuated regional fragmentation by integrating parts of Canada with adjacent regions of the United States while dissociating them (relatively speaking) from one another. (1991:397)

Some of the very transportation networks constructed to unite the economy on an east–west basis, over time, came to be utilized for Canada's integration into the U.S. economic system. Easterbrook and Aitken's observations on the fate of the St. Lawrence Seaway is instructive in this regard.

The creation in Canada of a transcontinental national economy was essentially the end-product of a series of forced extensions of the east–west axis until it reached the Pacific Coast, the impelling motive in each case being the determination to counteract the decisive north–south pull of the United States. In a sense, the construction of the St. Lawrence Seaway is a continuation of this same national policy. But whereas formerly the St. Lawrence River carried Canada's foodstuffs and raw materials to Europe, now a large part of the traffic which passes along it consists of exports of raw material to the United States. . . . The St. Lawrence River, traditionally the symbol of Canada's economic orientation to Europe, now serves in part at least to strengthen Canada's ties with the United States. (1956:556–57)

Under these circumstances the Macdonald National Policy failed to foster an independent, nationally-controlled economy—a development that can be characterized as the failure of conservative nationalism. The approach was based on a Canadian nationalism that rejected free trade and economic union with the United States. The policy fostered a strong political connection with Britain along with a trade orientation with Europe to "correct the imbalance of power on the North American continent," but it failed to concern itself with the threats posed by foreign investment (Laxer 1989:6–9).

Canada's economy became closely integrated into the U.S. metropole during the twentieth century, but the framework of the National Policy of 1879 remained the core of the Canadian government's economic development strategy. The 1911 federal election fought over reciprocity with the United States was a clear victory for this conservative nationalist approach (see Granatstein and Hillmer 1991:46–56). Even though free trade was rejected as a policy, and anti-American rhetoric remained high, the lines of commerce and communication were nevertheless pulled southward as the British Empire continued to decline and the base of the staples trade shifted.[5] A new foundation for Canadian east–west unification would have to be discovered.

The Second National Policy,[6] grafted on the old National Policy, came to be fully articulated following the Second World War.[7] A Keynesian demand-management strategy complemented by the construction of a social welfare state became the centrepiece of this policy formula (Brodie and Jenson 1988:293; Smiley 1975:47–48). This new "railway" that would now unite the country had strong social and cultural components (Courchene 1992:A4).[8] There were new features: one part of the old conservative nationalism—anti-American rhetoric—was jettisoned with the arrival of the Cold War. In the new ideological climate, "anti-Americanism seem[ed] disloyal to the 'western' way of life" (Laxer 1992:217). Further, continental economic integration came to be accepted, promoted as it was by the links generated by U.S. branch-plant industry and the southern destination of the new Canadian staples. What remained as a constant force linking the Second National Policy to the first was an activist Canadian state fostering east–west ties. Canadian statism helped to counterbalance the disunifying effects of the economic continental shift in the twentieth century. Policy-makers in the period of the first two national policies "used the state as a catalyst to nudge the market towards public ends" (Axworthy and Trudeau 1992b:40–41).

The Keynesian set of policies developed in the post-war period began to unravel in the 1970s. Two different approaches to dealing with the crisis of the Second National Policy emerged, and a major difference between them concerned the role of the state. One, adopted at least in part by the Liberal Party, was a nationalist-inspired industrial strategy that would actively use the state to stimulate the economy and promote domestically-controlled capital accumulation. The Progressive Conservatives, by contrast, came to view the state as a major cause of the crisis and based their cure in free-market solutions (Brodie and Jenson 1988:294).

The set of policies adopted by the Liberal governments of Pierre Trudeau represented an embryonic, state-directed industrial strategy, with a highly interventionist role reserved for the federal government. The federal state, as in the first National Policy, would be utilized in an attempt to restructure the national economy (Leslie 1987:8). The core of the industrial strategy eventually came to be the National Energy Policy (NEP), adopted in 1980; it attempted to base economic strategy upon "a resource driven restructuring of the industrial sector." This was part of the Liberal government's on-going nationalist policy, as evidenced by its earlier creation of the state oil company Petro-Canada and the Foreign Investment Review Agency (FIRA) (Brodie and Jenson 1988:314).[9]

The Trudeau energy policy "was interventionist, centralist, and nationalistic" (Pratt 1982:27). The NEP aimed to achieve energy self-sufficiency and hence insulate Canada from international oil crises (Lalonde 1992:107). Energy security would also provide strategic advantage to Canadian-based capital. One effect would be to enhance the federal government's control over energy and to increase its revenue intake from this commodity, thus strengthening the central government's fiscal capacity. Another aim was "to lower the costs of entry for Canadian capital pools into the oil and gas industries, the fastest-growing area of accumulation, and to encourage the formation of large Canadian-owned petroleum companies" (Pratt 1982:28). The goal was to achieve 50 percent Canadian ownership in the energy sector by 1990 (Lalonde 1992:107). A further anticipated result of the NEP would be "to shift the pattern of oil industry capital spending from the Western Canadian provinces to the federally-owned Canada lands in the north and offshore, thereby accelerating the exploitation of frontier oil and gas resources" (Pratt 1982:28). Moreover, the federal government would be reserved an automatic 25 percent share in all frontier land development for energy purposes (Lalonde 1992:110). Thus energy would become "a strategic commodity for nation building" purposes (Lalonde 1992:107). As Ian Stewart notes:

The National Energy Program was not only an energy policy narrowly defined. In the proposed allocation of its revenues, it addressed significant industrial policy and conservation issues, allocated funding to economic development generally and eased pressure on the government's fiscal posture outside energy. (1992:165)

The NEP was the first attempt by a Canadian government since the Second World War to reclaim for Canadian ownership a key foreign-controlled sector of the economy. The NEP was also aimed at strengthening the fiscal hand of the central state, a process designed "to prevent the further balkanization of the Canadian economy." Further, the policy was geared towards giving "the national state far greater control over one of the real commanding heights of the Canadian economy." But while the core of the Liberal government's energy policy was Canadianization, it was far from socialistic.[10] While the NEP utilized the federal state to promote indigenous capital over foreign business interests, the state was employed primarily to advance the interests of private capital accumulation (Pratt 1982:28, 40–41).

This new, third national policy failed largely because it was dependent upon the fortunes of the international commodities market. To sustain the strategy and support the energy megaprojects, oil prices had to keep rising, a scenario that failed to materialize. Additionally, post-war Canadian economic strategy had been premised upon increased Canada–U.S. trade, which made the economy vulnerable to U.S. policy (Brodie and Jenson 1988:318). U.S.-based capital successfully encouraged the U.S. state to pressure Canada to abandon its new national policy. Indeed, Canadian business generally, both indigenous and foreign-owned, had become quite nervous about the degree of state interventionism inherent in the Liberal strategy and evident in such initiatives as the Anti-Inflation Program and the NEP. Such concerns had prompted business to increase its representative capacity—hence the formation of the Business Council on National Issues in 1975 (Langille 1987). The susceptibility of the Canadian state and economy to this pressure became more evident as oil prices fell.

The collapse of the Trudeau Liberals' new national policy opened the door to the Conservative Party's neo-liberal economic agenda based on free-market principles. In the energy field this meant abandoning a national energy policy in favour of the continentalist approach eventually embodied in the North American Free Trade Agreement. Underlying this policy shift was ideological disapproval of the Canadian quest for a national policy. For neo-liberals the country was born in original sin and needs to be cleansed of its statist preoccupations. Neo-liberals see state-directed policy as the cause of economic distortions and problems rather than as a means of economic development. For them, *laissez-faire* economics and free trade formed the only true "national" policy to guide the country towards prosperity. Consequently, the advocates of *laissez-faire* have attempted to divorce Canadian nationalism from its association with economic policies. Nationalism is, for the classical economic liberal and modern neo-liberal, a state of mind and thus independent of economics (Smiley 1975:49–50). Neo-liberal economic doctrine leads in the direction of embracing continental economic assimilation; its policies represent an "anti-national policy."

Ironically, a second plank in Trudeau's nationalism involved constitutional reform, which has helped to move the Canadian political system in a direction that is closer to the U.S. system of governance. The 1982 Charter of Rights and Freedoms was packaged as a "people's charter" and one which would promote a strong independent sense of Canadian nationhood (see, for example, Laforest 1995:126–7); Alan Cairns (1995) refers to manifestations of this within English Canada in terms of the creation of "Charter Canadians." The politics of the Charter, however, is also one which has helped to transform the language of political discourse in the direction of individual rights and freedoms and has profoundly judicialized the Canadian political process. This has had the effect of making public policy more vulnerable to the influence of monied interests. In these ways Canadian politics have become more Americanized (see for example Mandel 1994). Hence, the Trudeau legacy is a multifaceted and contradictory one with respect to its continentalist and democratic ramifications.

Canada as a Staples Economy
We have mentioned the importance of natural resources—or staples—to Canadian economic development and to the national question. Canada's position in the international division of labour is intimately connected to the role that natural resources have played in "national" wealth creation (Clement and Williams 1997:59–61). Indeed, the "staples approach" has been the major theme running through Canadian economic historiography (Easterbrook and Watkins 1967:ix). Harold Innis, the leading proponent of this approach, contended that the motor of the Canadian economy did not rest in the development of a manufacturing base but rather in the exploitation of key domestic natural resources for export. The Canadian economy was set in motion by a series of staple products—first fish, then furs, timber, wheat, industrial minerals and finally energy resources. Staple exports were the key to growth and prosperity; they were "the leading sector of the economy and set the pace for economic development" (Watkins 1967:53).[11] The economic relationship that this reliance generated was unequal: Canada occupied a hinterland position in relation to metropolitan economies. The task of the staples society was to perform the function of "hewer of wood and drawer of water." As Innis put it: "The economic history of Canada has been dominated by the discrepancy between the centre and the margin of western civilization" (1975:385). Canada's economic role was to provide a succession of staple products to the manufacturing industries of the metropole. The staple trade served to prime the industrial pump of advanced industrial nations (Drache 1978:33).[12]

Industrial development in such societies is at best only "partial because of the long-term danger inherent in export-led growth" (Drache 1982:36). This danger includes boom–bust cycles and the high degree of foreign economic control; export-dependent peripheries are characterized by their greater vulnerability to economic disruption and crisis due to volatility in resource markets and prices and a dependent industrial structure. Economic diversification, such as extensive development of the tertiary sector, can occur in staple societies, but it will be dependent on a healthy staple sector for its survival. In short, this type of dependent development also means extremely vulnerable development. The Science Council of Canada, disbanded by the Mulroney government, concluded that the country's industrial structure had been "truncated" due to its over-dependence upon natural resource-based economic activity (Watkins 1997:20).

Economist Mel Watkins argues, in fact, that staples-led development produces a "staples trap" (1967) for countries such as Canada. According to Michael Howlett and M. Ramesh:

> This form of economic life could provide relatively high standards of living to citizens of exporting countries, but only as long as domestic resource supplies and world demand remained constant or increased. Any declines in demand or increases in supplies would have drastic consequences for the domestic political economy, which would be poorly placed to respond to the challenge of finding a new economic base (1992:96).

Staples theorists have tended to be pessimistic about Canada's future economic health (Howlett and Ramesh 1992:96) and have seen the only possibility of escape from the "staples trap" as a forceful economic nationalism (Watkins 1967).

A staples-dominated economy has also played a role in the creation of public debt. Energy megaprojects such as Hibernia, Arctic oil and gas development, and heavy oil upgrades in Alberta have drained about $13 billion annually from government just to cover the interest payment on loans for these projects. Furthermore, the Canadian state has also assumed significant infrastructure costs, such as the construction of transportation lines, pipelines and hydro development, much of it financed through increased debt to facilitate staple export-led growth. Such staples development dependence can result in a "staples debt trap." Thus, the resource character of Canadian economic development may lead to a more compelling explanation of Canada's debt problems rather than "social programs," which the corporate sector prefers to blame (Clement and Williams 1997:51).

Staples theory is hence quite useful in identifying the vulnerability of the domestic economy to changes in demand for natural resource products (witness the fate of the NEP) and to the distortions caused by massive amounts of direct foreign investment. But staples theory can also be too deterministic in its prognosis. The modern Canadian economy performs far more than the simple task of "hewer of wood and drawer of water." Furthermore, it is not difficult to envision, under the direction of a national policy, the use of the staples trade to prime the industrial pump of the domestic economy rather than just those of core capitalist states.

One factor indicating a weakness in the staples theory was a change in the pattern of foreign ownership in Canada that became evident by the 1980s. For instance:

> The level of foreign control of nonfinancial Canadian corporate assets fell from 35.3 percent in 1968 to 23.8 percent in 1984, manufacturing declined from 58 to 44.1 percent, mining and smelting from 65 to 35 percent, oil and gas from 64 to 57 percent, rubber products from 95 to 92 percent, and petroleum from 99 to 59 percent. (Bell 1992:139-40)

The explanation for this transformation, according to Joel Bell, rests with both the "economic maturation" of Canadian capitalism and the economic nationalism of the Third National Policy (Bell 1992:139).[13] This was demonstrated not just by the greater control of Canadian business over the local economy but also by its increasing presence in global markets. For example, Canadians had become one of the largest foreign investors in the United States, and the enhanced economic power of the nation was formally recognized by its inclusion in the G-7 group of countries in 1987 (Resnick 1990:187, 190–91, 199).[14] These developments were made possible, in part, by the decline in U.S. power. By the 1970s the U.S. GNP had slipped from about 40 percent of the OECD total to just over a third. What this revealed was "a dispersal of economic power in the capitalist world from which Canada, no less than Europe and Japan, could benefit" (Resnick 1982:15). Canada's ability to take advantage of this situation was in large measure made possible by the use of the state to actively promote Canadian capital; in Canada the state has played the role of "the mid-wife of economic development" (Resnick 1982:12). Free trade threatens to undo the role of the state, thus jeopardizing the process of the maturing of Canadian capitalism.

Rather than a "staples trap," resource-driven development may be viewed as a rational developmental strategy for Canadian capital (see Carroll 1986:204–06). Such a development strategy would need to be founded upon more than simply exporting relatively unprocessed natural resources. It would need to promote an indigenous industrial base around, and developing out of, staples products and it would require a leading role for the state.[15] The relatively small size and the staples character of a large sector of the economy would still entail vulnerability to fluctuations in the world economy, but such an economic strategy could set the country on the path to a far less dependent development than the one produced by the free-market policies of neo-liberal governments.

Where does Canada fit into the global capitalist system? The high standards of living enjoyed by Canadians, along with the advanced social and economic structure of the nation, clearly locate the country among the most advanced Western nations. But while Canada is a significant international economic actor, its power in the realms of economic, political, and military relations pale by comparison to the five largest Western nations. Moreover, Canada depends heavily on an export trade based primarily on natural resources, and its industrial structure is much more truncated and foreign-controlled than is the case for the largest capitalist economies. Canada's status might best be described as a "perimeter of the core" within the capitalist world system. This designation highlights the capitalist core-like features of Canadian development while correctly situating the country "at the perimeter of the grouping of core states" (Resnick 1990:181). This designation escapes the placement of the dependency and staples theories, which have Canada as part of the peripheral or underdeveloped states within the global capitalist system, yet it also serves to indicate the challenge that context or environment poses to Canadian decision-makers. It also helps us in highlighting the vulnerability of such economies to the loss of public policy control that free trade deals entail for Canada.

The Ideology of Comparative Advantage
The Mulroney government responded to this challenge by negotiating free-trade agreements with the United States and Mexico. Free-trade doctrine is constructed upon David Ricardo's classical economic theory of comparative advantage, a theory contending that trade results because of specialization—that there are certain products that every nation is able to produce more efficiently than others. If all nations were to specialize in the production of the products in which they possess a comparative advantage and engage in trade of those goods while importing other commodities, "an optimal allocation of world resources would result. The welfare of each individual country, as well as the world as a whole, would be maximized with perfectly free trade" (Kuttner 1991:116). The theory holds that, if the principles of comparative advantage are practiced, a natural international division of labour, beneficial to all nations, will emerge. Ricardo illustrated the mutual benefits to be derived from free trade by pointing to the example of the nineteenth-century trade between Portugal, specializing in wine, and Britain specializing in textiles. Economics textbooks continue to use this example to support the free-trade doctrine. The difficulty, of course, is the uncomfortable fact that Britain went on to become the workshop of the world and to prosper "while Portugal remained poor and was rendered marginal" (Watkins 1992:93).

In earlier periods of capitalism nations engaged in an international trade involving the exchange of "different goods with different peoples." The nature of modern trade, however, has altered significantly. Robert Chodos et al. put it plainly:

The problem with world trade now is that everybody—or almost everybody—makes and attempts to sell the same things. Where once no one would ever attempt to carry coals to Newcastle, the Japanese not only carry cars to Detroit but actually make thousands there for export back to Japan. Exotic cargoes from the Orient are now more likely to be computer chips and high-tech components of every description. (1993:1)

Trade in the new world economy produces a dynamic that can make it more cutthroat for the living standards of average workers.

Moreover, the doctrine of free trade assumes, wrongly, that the international division of labour, rationalized by the doctrine of comparative advantage, developed as a "natural" process. The international "free" market and the global division of labour it fostered were never the sole product of *laissez-faire* forces but have been imposed in large measure "by the substantial exercise of political and military force" (Frank 1979:94–95). The nineteenth- and twentieth-century practices of colonialism and neo-colonialism are a vivid reminder of this fact.

The nineteenth-century German political economist Frederick List also pointed out that Britain waited until 1846, after it had become the most advanced industrial nation in the world, to embrace a free-trade policy. British industrialization was achieved behind high tariff walls that nurtured infant manufacturing. Tariffs were the key to the initial success of British industry; only after success was achieved did free trade become acceptable. "Free" markets were not generated spontaneously. The hallmarks of the contemporary neo-liberal economic doctrine—*laissez-faire* as domestic policy and international "free" trade—were planned; it took active and centrally-organized states to create them (Drache and Gertler 1991b:xv; Watkins 1992:93). Only the most advanced and economically powerful countries enjoy a comparative or unequal advantage over other nations in a free-trade environment. Thus free trade has always been "the natural economic policy for the most powerful capitalist countries" (Warnock 1988:78).

Free trade should be viewed in terms of ideology and interests. This point is clearly put forward by Christopher Merrett:

> Free trade can be a form of economic nationalism as Britain used it against Portugal in the eighteenth century. It can also be a form of anti-nationalism as it is used by Canadian supporters of free trade in the twentieth century. Free trade is not a universal economic theory but a foreign policy that is promoted by different groups of people in different places and different times. (1996:19)

Another difficulty with the neo-classical approach to free trade is that it "tends to conceptualize comparative advantages in largely static terms" (Wolfe 1992:22). One of the implicit assumptions behind the theory of comparative advantage is that capital and labour are nation-bound. Domestic capital and workers displaced by the competition from newly-imported goods simply redeploy themselves to the export sector of the economy. This assumption, while it has never been entirely accurate, is clearly unfounded today. The nature of capital has always allowed it to be far more mobile than labour, and increasingly this is so.

With the rise of multinational corporations and international finance, capital has increased its ability to shift investment and production within the world economy. Consequently, the opening up of the home market to free trade can well result in the loss of employment and the export of domestic capital to foreign sources. In short, a country may well discover that on balance free trade brings more economic disadvantages than benefits.[16]

As well, the faith in the advantages of unfettered markets, as espoused by neo-classical liberal economics, fails to provide an explanation for the dramatic industrial performance of countries that are guided by a significant degree of state planning. Examples in the post-war period include Japan, Germany, France, and Sweden. These countries outperformed the United States and Britain in research and development (R&D) growth, which as a result provided an important spur to their general economic performance. Massive state support for R&D is a major feature of the industrial strategies of Japan, Germany, France, and Sweden (Bell 1992:128–29).

Free trade is in fact an ideology. The doctrine of free trade obscures the role that the state has played in providing core capitalist nations with a competitive advantage over other less economically-advanced countries. The ideology of comparative advantage obscures the process of uneven economic development and unequal exchange between nations and regions. The idea of free trade also promotes the false notion that all nations progress naturally through a set pattern of stages of growth on their way to economic maturity. The politics of the economic domination of the weak by the powerful is hidden beneath the doctrine of free trade.

Global Capitalism and the New World Order
The United States and Britain began to promote freer world trade during the Second World War. The Atlantic Charter pledged these countries to "endeavor . . . to further the enjoyment by all States, great and small, victor and vanquished, of access, on equal terms, to trade and to the raw materials of the world which are needed for their economic prosperity" (quoted in Harrison and Bluestone 1988:191). In 1948 the General Agreement on Tariffs and Trade (GATT) attempted to operationalize the principle of freer trade. It established the framework within which the modern international capitalist economy would develop (Harrison and Bluestone 1988:191). GATT's assigned role was to liberalize the international trading environment by reducing quotas and "tariffs on a specific set of internationally traded goods" (Shniad 1992:22). The organization's guiding principle was that of "nondiscrimination." Member states were bound by Article I of GATT's rules, which required "that any member country

must give all other members the same privileges regarding tariffs or other commercial policy measures that it gives to the most favoured nation with which it negotiates—the most-favoured-nation principle" (Wilkinson 1996).

GATT was successful in realizing its initial goals: "Today, the industrial tariffs of the developed market economies are probably lower than at any time since the late 1870s and substantially lower than during the 1930s" (Canada 1985a, vol. 1:280). By the mid-1980s the tariffs on manufactured goods had been reduced to average levels of 5.2 percent in Canada, 5 percent in Sweden and 4.3 percent in the United States, with many goods being traded duty free (Copeland 1992:181). By contrast, in the 1930s the average tariff in the United States stood at 50 percent (Canada 1985a, vol. 1:280).

Moreover, the amount of trade between nations expanded dramatically. Over the last four decades international trade flows expanded by fifteen-fold reaching some $6,000 billion in 1995. Over this same period production expanded only six-fold. Foreign direct investment (FDI) has grown at an even faster rate than international trade. Between 1986 and 1996 FDI "easily quadrupled, from around $60 billion to almost $300 billion per annum" (Ruggiero 1996:2). Multinationals have increasingly moved to a strategy of dispersing their physical assets.[17] This manoeuvre is designed, in part, to protect the multinationals from the rise of regional protective trading blocks. Even if such blocks solidify, the multinationals will be in a position to "use their investment networks to continue the process of international commerce" (Morici 1992:8). This development has also enhanced the globalization of capital. Globalization may be best viewed as "the systematic extension of corporate capitalism across borders in search of markets, raw materials, and lower cost labor" (Herman 1997:8).

The enhanced pace of globalization has not led to increased international economic harmony: "Contrary to widespread expectations, sources of tension among the leading capitalist powers have increased side by side with their growing interdependence" (Magdoff 1992:45). The tensions and struggles that surrounded GATT provide a clear indication of this.

> Because the GATT process has been so successful in achieving negotiated reductions in overt forms of protection, the world economy has become more integrated. When overt trade barriers are high, the economies of different countries tend to be insulated from one another, and hence the spillover effects of domestic policies are muted. However, as the economies become more integrated, the spillover effects of domestic policies increase in intensity, and thus become more of a candidate for international conflict. (Copeland 1992:189).

Increasingly, national policies dealing with social welfare, environmental, and labour market questions are being viewed as non-tariff trade barriers and have become the sources of international trade irritants. Moreover, as borders between nation-states have become ever more permeable, economic trouble in one country is often rapidly transferred to others creating instability and greater risk of crises (Albo and Jenson 1997:217).

The Uruguay round of GATT negotiations involved a much more complex and difficult set of issues than earlier rounds. With the successful completion of the Uruguay negotiations, GATT rules were extended to a series of nationally-sensitive goods not previously covered, including agriculture, textiles, and trade in services. Moreover, this round worked towards "the removal of what the corporate sector refers to as technical barriers to trade—national laws and regulations that are deemed to impede corporate behaviour" (Shniad 1992:22). The economic and policy areas that were subject to trade liberalization were those that have been central to the Keynesian demand-management of national economies. The policy capacity of the state is being eroded by such international agreements that compromise national democratic processes to the advantage of a neo-liberal corporate agenda (Evans, McBride and Shields 1997). Managing economic and social well-being has become a far more precarious task in the new global order.

U.S. dominance in manufacturing has been overtaken by the Japanese and Europeans. However, the United States still enjoys enormous "strength in the areas of data processing, banking, insurance, advertising, engineering and telecommunications" (Shniad 1992:22). The Americans were the prime movers in aggressively pressing for the further liberalization of GATT in their areas of strength and have been largely successful in this effort.

Even with the completion of the Uruguary GATT round in 1994 trade tensions and disputes are unlikely to disappear, especially in the context of global economic restructuring and the continuation of a "jobless recovery."[18] For example in Canada the agreement has raised significant tensions among farmers. Under GATT, border quotas on agricultural products, a structure that long allowed farmers to operate a supply-management system, must be replaced with a system of tariffs that will be eliminated over the next number of years, a process further speeded by NAFTA requirements (Fagan 1993:A1; Meilke 1995).

A new international trade body, the World Trade Organization (WTO), was established 1 January, 1995 to succeed GATT and implement the Uruguay agreement. The WTO has a broader scope than GATT, which focused on trade in merchandise goods. The WTO is presiding over the deregulating of trade in services and agriculture, and protecting intellectual property rights. Moreover, the WTO is a more formally-structured organization than GATT and possesses trade dispute and policing mechanisms to legally bind member states to its rules. In this sense the WTO represents an evolution of the GATT secretariat into a fully-developed permanent international organization on par with the World Bank and the International Monetary Fund (IMF). The WTO is designed to deepen global trade (World Trade Organization n.d.; Pitroda 1995:46–47): "The agreements that the WTO will administer are expected to increase annual world trade by at least $750 billion by the year 2002" (Microsoft 1996).

Globalization has imposed contradictory pressures upon the state. On the one hand, the state is pushed to provide protection to workers and industries threatened by external free-market forces. This is much in evidence around the battle to liberalize trade in agriculture, services, and textiles. On the other hand, the state is pressed in the direction of facilitating economic adjustment and restructuring to better position the nation in a more competitive world: "The economic imperative may be to adjust, but the political process often favours protection" (Simeon 1991:50). Whether bodies like GATT and the WTO can keep up with an increasingly globalized world (Winham 1992:115) or whether the contradictory pressures of globalization will result in a wave of national-based or regional-based protectionism is an open question.

The emerging new world economic order is also posing difficulties for the established world trading system. The U.S. economic hegemony firmly established after the Second World War has been undermined. In the 1980s this trend produced a notable shift in U.S. trade policy. The U.S. state resorted to "the more frequent use of nontariff trade barriers such as voluntary restraint agreements, aggressive pursuit of antidumping and countervailing duty actions, and unilateral measures mandated by Congress in the Super 301 and Special 301 provisions of the Omnibus Trade and Competitiveness Act" (McKinney et al. 1992b:x). Even under the Free Trade Agreement (FTA) Canada has been victimized by these kinds of U.S. protectionist measures. The trade responses reflect a U.S. reaction to its relative loss of economic power.

In part the current difficulties in multilateral trade relations stem from different visions of capitalism held by the Americans on one side and the Europeans and Japanese on the other. The United States endorses a view of capitalism that asserts a minimalist role for the state in the market: "In the American mind, large concentrations of business and government support for their collective actions are *prima facie,* market distorting, inefficient, welfare reducing. The Japanese and Europeans just do not see the world this way" (Morici 1992:5). Trade tensions are a natural end result of such contradictory positions.

The movement towards European economic and political union has established another economic force "to countervail U.S. hegemony" (Itoh 1992:199). The European Community (EC) represents a massive effort "to synergize European forces" to meet global competitive challenges. In part, this entails the construction of a supranational European state structure to help consolidate, coordinate, and project European economic and political power and influence (Gill 1992:164–65).

Thus a tripolar world economy is beginning to emerge. The three significant economic blocs, namely the EC, North America (centred on the United States), and the Asian Pacific Rim (centred on Japan), are not designed to operate "as autarkic economic entities, but as large liberalized trading spheres which will serve as launching pads for intensified competition in world markets. The trend towards trade blocs thus embodies elements of both internationalism and protectionism" (McNally 1991:237).

The effect of the multilateral trade framework established in the post-Second World War era was, ironically, to make Canada more dependent upon the U.S (Howlett and Ramesh 1992:146). Since 1945 Canada has become more integrated with the United States economy. The integration has, as staples theory warned, been established on unequal terms. Canadian trade patterns continued to be heavily weighted to staples exports, and the country's industrial structure remained truncated. In the present economic environment Canada is not in a particularly good position:

> Exports of natural resource-intensive goods are by no means undesirable. However, a high proportion of exports of unprocessed resources makes Canada sensitive to commodity price shifts, technological substitution, and the emergence of lower cost competitors. The problem is made more acute by the fact that technological change is reducing resource intensity in advanced economies, and that unprocessed resource industries are especially accessible by developing countries. . . . They also suggest that Canadian industry has failed to upgrade or extend its competitive advantages in processing technology and marketing and support of more processing goods. Canada's relative weakness in process technology . . . is evident. (Porter et al. 1991:22)

In this context, embracing a free-market approach to the new international political economy becomes doubly problematic. First, if we understand the lessons of Europe and Japan correctly, the pursuit of strictly *laissez-faire* responses to trade and investments in a highly competitive new world order is unlikely to make our industries more competitive internationally. Second, in the context of Canada's position within North America (that is, the economic dominance of the United States), the adoption of a free-market solution will only further Canada's dependence on U.S. markets and reinforce our position as a resource supplier. In fact as the economic hegemony of the United States has waned globally the American state "has moved to increase its hegemony continentally and now hemispherically" (Watkins 1997:34).

Within Canada the struggle between continentalist free traders and state interventionist nationalists had been engaged for some years. The failures of the NEP, however, opened up a strategic opportunity for large corporate interests. In the words of Glen Williams:

> The continentalists were determined to seize the opportunity presented by the policy reversals of their foes [the failure of the NEP] and the economic distemper of the early 1980s to press home a Canada–U.S.

free trade agreement that would consolidate and institutionalize their hegemony (1994:156).

Chapter 8 will examine these developments at length.

Notes

1. For Naylor, commercial capitalists in Canada played a similar role to that played by the so-called "comprador bourgeoisie" in Latin America and other underdeveloped nations. According to dependency theorists the comprador bourgeoisie forged economic links to industrially advanced countries in a fashion that perpetuated unequal development. The industrial-centre economies remained dominant while the comprador bourgeoisie's home nations became industrially underdeveloped and economically tied to and dependent upon the centre economies. The comprador bourgeoisie directed its resources and interest to trade in primary products, leaving the industrial structure of their own nations to be dominated by foreign interests. Such economies would remain economically backward and vulnerable to the demands of imperial economies (see, for instance, Amin 1976).

2. U.S. investment in Canada did not overtake British investment until the mid-1920s. By 1914 U.S. branch plants constituted only about 10 percent of the total capital in Canada, although this investment was concentrated in the high-growth industries (Hutcheson 1978:95).

3. Roger Gibbins argues for the existence in British North America by the 1860s of a "'national dream' of a new transcontinental state stretching from sea to sea . . . across the northern half of the continent" (1985:19). This was a dream, Gibbins reminds us, nurtured by an elite.

    Admittedly, the territorial expansion embodied in the national dream was championed primarily by the banking, transportation and manufacturing interests of central Canada who stood to gain most from the creation of new hinterlands to the east and west, and who sought a firmer governmental base to support the massive debt engendered by territorial expansion. There was, however, a grander vision than commercial exploitation, a vision bordering on imperialism. (1985:19)

4. Policy centralization at the federal level, which characterized much of the twentieth century, did not create overwhelming problems in the province of Québec, in the words of J.R. Mallory, "as long as the province was seeking to contract out of the twentieth century." However, with the quiet revolution of the 1960s in Québec, federal–provincial relations altered for ever.

    Québecers now wanted a state that had the full range of powers to create opportunities for Francophones. The managers of the new society set their sights on transforming Québec society through the most innovative use of Keynesian kinds of measures that the country had ever witnessed. (Drache 1995:34-35)

5. The Conservative Party and anti-free-trade advocates made the theme "No truck or trade with the Yankees" a rallying call against the pro-reciprocity forces (Granatstein and Hillmer 1991:53).

6. Lorraine Eden and Mareen Apple Molot (1993) outline a somewhat different categorization of national policies in Canada. They identify three such policies,

namely: i) defensive expansionism (1867–1940); ii) compensatory liberalism (1941–1981); and iii) market liberalism (1982–present). For a revealing critical commentary on their model see Tupper (1993).

7. Doern and Phidd (1992) contend that Canada never completely embraced Keynesian policy prescriptions. Rather, Keynesianism was significantly modified to fit into the framework of the National Policy of 1879. As they observe:

> Keynesian fiscal policy has never been fully practiced in Canada. . . . Moreover, other than the new array of social welfare programs launched in the post-World War II period (family allowances, expanded old age security programs, etc.), the core of Canada's economic policies during this period were not forged by a Keynesian Department of Finance, but rather by a Department of Reconstruction, Defence Production, and later Trade and Commerce headed by C.D. Howe. Howe's policies were essentially to use tariff and tax policies to encourage foreign equity investment in Canada. The result was to produce continued prosperity until the late 1950s, but also to reinforce the age-old pattern of Canada's truncated industrial structure first put in place by MacDonald's National Policy. But by the end of the 1950s it was dominated by foreign ownership. (1992:138)

On the incomplete implementation of Keynesianism in Canada see also Campbell (1987) and Drache and Glasbeek (1992:17–22).

8. This social policy railway had significant economic dimensions. Social policy has been important both to stabilize (legitimate) the capitalist system and, from a Keynesian perspective, social programs perform the important role of automatic stabilizers—they help maintain the levels of consumer demand in a slumping economy.

9. Donald Smiley, writing in 1975 about Liberal government initiatives like FIRA but before the emergence of the NEP, was already willing to identify the emergence of what he termed a "new national policy" centred around gaining Canadian control of the national economy especially in the areas of key natural resources, secondary manufacturing, and businesses featured by technological innovation. Once again the federal government would be reserved a central role in economic development (1975:55–59).

10. For instance, the Liberal government's 1975 Anti-Inflation Program (AIP), which imposed strict wage controls on the economy, was an important part of its industrial strategy. The AIP was a much more ambitious project for controlling inflation than had been tried in other liberal democracies (Russell 1991a:32).

11. "Export staples can be identified as industries based on agricultural and extractive resources, not requiring elaborate processing and finding a large portion of their market in international trade" (Bertram 1967:75).

12. The staples theory bears similarities to dependency theory. A fruitful examination of much of Canada's economic history could be undertaken by taking as a point of departure Dos Santos's definition of dependency as "a situation in which a certain group of countries have their economy conditioned by the development and expansion of another economy, to which their own is subjected" (quoted in Roxborough 1981:66).

But the temptation to blindly equate Canadian economic relationships with those of Third World economies must be resisted. Staples theory is not "a general theory about the growth of export-oriented economies," but rather applies to the special case of new countries (white settler colonies) or, as Watkins (1980b) refers to them, "staples societies." These "staple societies" from the beginning had the social relations of production transferred to them from the centre, but because their growth was dependent on staples exports they, from the outset, developed dependency characteristics similar to those of an underdeveloped country (Watkins 1980b:1). They were societies born rich, with inherited Western political and social institutions. Characterized today by their liberal-democratic and welfare state political systems and high-wage labour forces, they possess the political and social class structures and historical and cultural traditions of core countries.

13. Resnick (1982:15) agrees with this assessment, suggesting that by the 1980s "Canadian capital had come of age."

14. Resnick adds a qualification:

> By this, I do not want to claim that Canada had been promoted to the ranks of a major economic power comparable to the United States, Japan, or the main European states, or that the Canadian economy had ceased to be resource-oriented in exports and correspondingly weaker in the high technology and manufacturing fields. Still, something had changed during the decade, with Canadian-based capital becoming a significant participant in the international capitalist economy. (1982:15)

15. An industrial strategy developing out of staples products would require that staples commodities undergo extensive processing domestically before being exported. And further, it would need to ensure that the economic growth and profits generated out of staples-related businesses be invested in the formation of new enterprises independent of the staples industries. As for the leading role for the state, James Laxer sets out one example of how such a new economic strategy might be constructed. (1984:120–39)

16. Further to the point, Robert Bleckner offers a critique of the standard theory of comparative advantage for the static manner in which it deals with trade; the theory falsely "assumes that trade is balanced and that there is full employment in all countries," ignoring the reality that some countries enjoy absolute competitive advantages over others (1987:225).

17. Direct foreign-investment flows between 1985 and 1989 grew at twice the rate of trade flows. By 1989 multinationals from Japan, Western Europe, and North America had accumulated a trillion dollars of assets outside their home markets (Morici 1992:8).

Magdoff (1992) cites data indicating that, at the end of 1990, the value of foreign direct investment worldwide rested at the level of at least $1.5 trillion. Moreover, he found that in the final three years of the 1980s direct foreign-investment flows in 1980 dollars had reached over $100 billion a year, a rate ten times higher than in the first three years of the 1970s (1992:44, 50).

18. For a discussion of differing views on the future of the world trading system see *The Economist* (1993:23–26). On the potential threats posed for OECD countries due to increased levels of social and economic exclusion see Organization for Economic Cooperation and Development (OECD) (1996:vii–xii).

Chapter 8

Embracing Free Trade: Embedding Neo-Liberalism

The most fundamental aspect of the neo-liberal assault on the traditional Canadian polity is represented by the Free Trade Agreement (FTA) and the North American Free Trade Agreement (NAFTA). These agreements have already had a negative impact on the economic structure of Canada; for example they have promoted significant levels of de-industrialization in central Canada. But their importance goes far beyond their economic impact. The agreements work to limit the ability of governments, present and future, to moderate or escape from the free-market principles upon which they are based. Further restrictions on government's ability to control or regulate the market will be implemented if the Multilateral Agreement on Investment (MAI), currently under negotiation at the OECD, or another version, the Multilateral Investment Agreement (MIA) under discussion at the WTO, are signed. As well as tightening the prohibitions against interventionist governments that are already part of NAFTA, the draft MAI would seek to make these irreversible in effect. To be precise, a government would have to give five years notice of its intention to withdraw and any investments made while MAI was in operation would be "grandfathered" for a further fifteen years. A *Globe and Mail* article on the cultural impact of the MAI concluded: "the most far-reaching effect of the MAI could be to weaken the already strained bonds holding the country together. . . . MAI would enforce its rules at the provincial level as well as the federal. Should the deal go through with a weak or subvertible cultural exception, Québec would have all the more reason to question its future in confederation" (Everett-Green 1997) .

In this chapter we seek to assess both the socio-economic and "quasi-constitutional" impact of the free-trade agreements that are already in effect, especially NAFTA.

Free Trade: The Corporate Constitution
Free trade has been variously described as the economic constitution of Canada and as a "Corporate Charter of Rights and Freedoms" (Barlow 1992a:A23; see also Clarkson 1993:3–20). In fact Ronald Reagan referred to the Canada–U.S. free-trade deal as "an economic constitution for North America" (quoted in

Laxer1992:209). While neither the Canada–U.S. Free Trade Agreement (FTA) nor the North American Free Trade Agreement (NAFTA) enjoys formal constitutional status, their impact is such that they extend wide-ranging protection to corporate property rights and freedoms from governmental interference.[1] Such corporate rights can be counterposed both to Canadian political sovereignty and popular democracy (see Laxer 1993 and Robinson 1993). Continental free trade is the centrepiece of Canadian neo-liberal policy:

> The free-trade agreement is the bedrock of the Conservative/corporate agenda to reshape Canada as part of a new continental order. This new order is about shifting power from governments to corporations. It is about limiting the capacity of Canadian governments, present and future, to actively determine the course of economic development. It is about breaking down the structures of the national economy and preventing Canada from establishing an activist policy, ever. (Barlow and Campbell 1991:21)

This agenda initially proved difficult to pursue and implement because of the constraints of domestic politics. But by pursuing continental free-trade agreements, the logic of the "free" market has been embedded into Canadian public policy, greatly constraining governmental options and evading domestic obstacles such as those imposed by Canadian political culture and attitudes. Like constitutional documents, international trade deals such as the FTA and NAFTA formally obligate governments to abide strictly by their terms.[2] Although the agreements have been negotiated solely by the federal government, most observers see them as binding the hands of provincial governments as well. Thus the difficulties posed by the federal–provincial division of powers can be sidestepped. The effect, however, is not to maximize federal power but rather to privilege corporate rights over those of governments. In the case of NAFTA in particular, freedom of corporate decision-making takes precedence over various forms of activist state policy. In the meantime, more than any other neo-liberal policy initiative, free trade imposes significant restraints on progressive public policy; and in the longer term it is a key part of the package that threatens to dismantle the nation.

FTA and NAFTA: Trading Away Our Sovereignty

Canadian business and government circles came to accept a made-in-America "free-trade solution" to problems of economic development and growth for a number of reasons. In part, free trade with the United States was an attempt to find an alternative economic model to the Keynesian policy paradigm. Canada–U.S. free trade was also a response to the perceived economic failure and political defeat of the NEP, the Third National Policy. Moreover, there was a growing fear in Canada of U.S. protectionism in reaction to the decline of U.S. economic hegemony and the development of regional trading blocks elsewhere.[3]

Corporate policy think-tanks conferred increased legitimacy on a Canada–U.S. free-trade pact. One of the most important of these was the C.D. Howe Institute, which moved towards neo-liberalism and endorsing free trade in the early 1980s (Ernst 1992:109–40).[4] Such "corporate funded think-tanks," Ernst notes, "have been important in providing the ideological framework for the restructuring of the global economy" (1992:110).

The Royal Commission on the Economic Union and Development Prospects for Canada (Macdonald Commission) played a pivotal role in placing the free-trade option at the centre of the Canadian political agenda when it recommended that Canada take a "leap of faith" and adopt free trade with the United States (Doern and Tomlin 1991:24; see also Inwood 1997; Laxer 1986; McQueen 1985). The Macdonald Commission was among the largest royal commissions in Canadian history and paralleled in significance the Rowell-Sirois Commission of 1937. Such commissions serve an explicit political purpose:

> Since royal commissions are perceived to operate impartially, they are the ideal instruments of brokerage politics. In contrast to the theoretical purpose of *producing* a consensus through the formal process of fact-finding, the job of a royal commission is to *appear* to have produced a consensus.
>
> A royal commission can change not only the focus of public discourse but also conventional wisdom, by generating an "expert" body of knowledge. (Drache and Cameron 1985b:xi)

The Macdonald Commission helped to foster an elite consensus around free trade and to confer considerable public legitimacy on the continentalist option as well.[5]

For the leading sectors of the Canadian business community, Canada–U.S. free trade, and later NAFTA, became a logical policy stance to endorse. For the most influential Canadian business lobby, the Business Council on National Issues (BCNI), Canada–U.S. and North American free trade represented a significant advance and victory over economic nationalists (BCNI 1987b:2–3; see also BCNI 1985, 1987a, 1988, 1990a, 1990b, 1990c). Ideologically, free trade served corporate interests, primarily by helping to redefine the role of the Canadian state (Rocher 1991:142).[6]

Initially free trade was not at the head of the Conservative government's policy agenda. Prime Minister Mulroney had publicly opposed the idea of Canada–U.S. free trade during the Conservative leadership debates (Barlow 1991:25).[7] However, free trade did fit very nicely with the policies for "economic renewal" promoted by the Tories. The Conservatives "were determined to create a more open market within which business could operate with greater efficiency. A climate had to be created that would encourage firms to adapt to market conditions and invest for expansion" (Doern and Tomlin 1991:30, 30–35). Given these circumstances the Tories became easy converts to the doctrine of free trade. Canada–U.S. and North American free trade had both great ideological and practical value for the neo-liberal agenda.

The Free Trade Agreement between Canada and the United States was enacted into law in 1988 and came into effect on 1 January, 1989.[8] The North American Free Trade Agreement was reached in 1992, was ratified by the legislatures of Canada, Mexico, and the United States, and came into effect in 1994. For our purposes there were a number of key themes: i) free trade and national unity; ii) the implications for social policy; iii) free trade's economic impact: goals, claims and record; iv) the case of energy, natural resources, and foreign investment; and v) NAFTA: revealing the U.S. agenda.

i) Free Trade and National Unity

The Macdonald Report asserted: "It is probable that the most significant and long-term effect of free trade would be the strengthening of national unity and the removal of one of the most persistent and corrosive sources of regional alienation in Canada's political history" (Canada 1985a, vol. 1:357). Historically the source of regional tension this refers to involved the issue of free trade versus protectionism. High tariffs had fostered considerable resentment in the west and east. Those regions saw tariffs as working to support central Canadian manufacturing through forcing local consumers to pay artificially high prices on manufactured goods while being "required to sell their natural resources in volatile, unprotected world markets." Such a national policy, it was asserted, worked to the decided benefit of "the centre at the expense of the hinterland" (Simeon 1987b:84). The adoption of the FTA, the Conservative government and Canadian business argued, would eliminate one of the primary sources of regional tension in Canada, and have a healing effect on the economy (Doern and Tomlin 1991:31–32; d'Aquino and Bulloch 1986:5; Canada 1985a, vol. 1:357).[9]

There is also an unstated premise behind the optimistic regional scenario of free-trade proponents: that market forces, if left to operate freely, will bring about more even regional economic development and thus reduce regional tensions. Staples theory suggests that this is an unwarranted "leap of logic." The profound economic inequalities between countries globally, and the glaringly uneven economic development within them, seriously call into question this supposition (see, for instance, Mandel 1973).

The National Policy of 1879 was founded upon an assumption that nation-building required a national economy constructed on an east-west axis and geared to enhancing the commercial linkages within the country. For the nation to survive politically, a solid economic basis of trade had to be maintained. Free trade embraces a different logic. The doctrine asserts the separation of political unity and economic unity. Trade must be allowed to follow its "natural" market course, which is north-south (Simeon 1987b:93). Political unity is, for the free traders, a state of mind. They argue that by adopting free trade Canadians will finally demonstrate that they have shed their colonial psychological status: "It seems probable that a free-trade arrangement would actually strengthen our national assurance by providing clear evidence that Canadians can prosper in a highly competitive market, without the aid of artificial protection" (Canada 1985a, vol. 1:354).

Critics argue that trade carries with it cultural values, interpersonal linkages, interregional communications, and so forth; and that weakening trade within the country will also weaken these other national values and connections: "We run the risk of reducing the capacity to build national support across regions for common national purposes" (Simeon 1987b:93; see also McDougall 1991). In fact, the national value system is in a period of flux as core values are re-evaluated (see Peters 1995). These value transitions have been brought on in large measure by the forces of free trade/globalization and the movement to a more socially and economically polarized society. As the state increasingly sheds itself of its social responsibilities the nation-building/sustaining role of Canada's "social policy railway" has become compromised.

Canadian identity has also been closely linked to culture. The pervasiveness of American cultural influence through print and broadcast media has been especially threatening to the survival and nurturing of a distinct English Canadian culture. Historically, the state, through various protective measures, has sought to promote Canadian cultural industries as a core part of the nation-building project. While certain NAFTA articles appear to exclude cultural industries from "free trade" rules, other sections of the agreement leave openings for U.S. countervail in the case of protectionism. Part of the problem is that the Americans have tended to define culture extremely narrowly, viewing most of what is produced in the print, image, film, music and broadcast media not as culture but as commercial activities encompassed broadly by the title, the entertainment industry. This has resulted in U.S. charges of unfair trade practices being brought against Canada (Barlow 1996:A17). The opening up of the cultural industries in Canada to free-trade forces represents a profound threat to Canadian national cultural integrity.

Arguably free trade also presents important challenges to regional development policies since those policies that use loans, grants, and subsidies aimed directly at specific industries or sectors run the risk of being considered non-tariff barriers. More importantly, the market pressures created by free trade in the longer term will force the federal government to reconsider its role in regional development and equalization. This role is not confined to explicitly regional measures, but also includes general social programs that have a regionally redistributive impact. The logic of this change was spelled out in advance by Simeon:

> Even if explicit regional development policy survives, the logic of free trade could undermine it. The big claim for free trade is that it will

promote efficiency through forcing Canadian industry to become more competitive by responding to market signals. There are strong pressures in this direction . . . that Canadian economic policy generally must look more to efficiency and aggregate growth and less to redistributive policies. Free trade would massively strengthen that argument. Mobility—moving people to jobs—would become more important; the traditional Canadian commitment to preservation of less economically vigorous regions would be harder to sustain. (1987b:94)

In contrast to Ottawa's traditional role, free trade "tends to undermine the political consensus around regional redistribution and development—which is a constitutionally vital function of the federal government" (Doern and Purchase 1991b:15).

Moreover, tariffs, while continuing to symbolize regional and, especially Western Canadian discontent, have long since ceased to be a major source of economic disadvantage for the "peripheral" provinces (Stevenson 1988:139). The GATT has effectively reduced the level of tariffs on most goods to minor significance. However, by forcing governments to abdicate interventionism in favour of market forces, free trade will impose limits on the provinces' ability to use non-tariff barriers. This will reduce "their freedom of political and governmental manoeuvre" (Canada 1985a, vol. 1:364). The provinces have used many non-tariff barriers (loan guarantees, subsidies, tax incentives, and the like) to foster local economic development, and these barriers involve sensitive areas such as agriculture. Free trade will constrain the ability of the provincial state to promote local development. Once again free trade will more likely increase federal–provincial strains rather than weaken them. So far the only definitive attempt to eliminate provincial trade barriers has been the Agreement on Internal Trade (AIT). It has been widely criticized by the corporate sector, which would prefer a more rigorous and enforceable agreement, as an ineffective instrument.

Daniel Latouche maintains that the Québec government's support for free trade was predicated upon the belief that the policy would have a decentralizing effect on federalism. Policies that are alternatives to free trade tend to promote a pan-Canadian economic nationalism, which is anathema to the province (Gold and Leyton-Brown 1988:132). For Québec separatists, free trade, "with its promise of access to the large U.S. market, represents a bedrock of Québecers' confidence in the economic feasibility of a separate Québec state. In effect, closer economic integration with the United States has lowered the perceived costs of the political disintegration of the current Canadian federation" (Banting 1992:164; also see Watkins 1997:34). Drache has set forth the case as follows:

> Among Québec's elites, the FTA and NAFTA are perceived as a way to achieve more control for the province in a globalized setting. These agreements are used as "nation-restricting devices" against Ottawa

because they give Québecers something that no provincially-elected government has ever been able to achieve. They set limits on the way Canada's national government can use its power for national ends. . . .

These strictures fit Québec's constitutional agenda to a "t." What Québec wants in this era of constitutional change are fewer national programs, an economy less anchored in national needs and more opportunity to assert provincial paramountcy. (1995:41)

Thus free trade has worked to strengthen the forces of Québec separatism as well as regionalism with English Canada.

Free trade was sold as measure that would reduce regional strains, but it is a strategy that, in fact, "is inherently one of disengagement, not of developing stronger links." Free trade has fostered decentralization, not national unity (Simeon 1991:53). The reality is:

> that continentalism undermines the very *raison d'etre* of the Canadian federal government. A central government that exercises only minimal powers over the economy may not be controversial, but it runs the more serious risk of being irrelevant. . . . To the extent that the federal government is unable to pursue such policies, Canadians will increasingly consider that the governments most relevant to their welfare are those in the provincial capitals and in Washington. (Stevenson 1988:140)

More generally, the role that free trade plays in handcuffing the work of government at both the federal and provincial levels reveals that the FTA and NAFTA will operate as the neo-liberal economic constitution of the nation.

ii) The Implications for Social Policy

Advocates of free trade have argued that there is nothing in the FTA, or for that matter in NAFTA, that prevents Canadian governments from pursuing the type of universal social policies they deem appropriate. Free trade, for supporters, is an economic arrangement that has no direct social policy implications. In fact, they contend, social policies in Canada will be enhanced by free trade because the economic growth nurtured by free trade agreements will increase government revenues and make it easier to finance such programs (Doern and Tomlin 1991:261).

At the same time free traders and their corporate supporters have argued that globalization demands a shifting of public policy-making priorities away from social policy towards economic, trade, and labour-market policies. For them the interests of international competitiveness demand that deficits be brought under control, taxes cut, and impediments to businesses removed (Doern, Pal and Tomlin 1996:24). Given the realities of globalization and technological change, they argue, policy-makers have no choice but to restructure social programs to meet the new competitive reality (Lipsey 1996; Courchene 1995)—i.e., social programs must be restrained and drastically trimmed back.

Critics, for the most part, concede that existing Canadian social security programs, because they are made generally available and are "broadly based efforts to alleviate poverty and redistribute income," are unlikely to be classified as subsidies under the free trade agreements, although the "status of income maintenance programs for the so-called working poor" remains unclear (Doern and Tomlin 1991b:265). The service chapters of the FTA and NAFTA do open up management services to "national treatment" rights, although the direct provision of health, education, and social services is exempt from this directive. National treatment means that rules governing such management services cannot discriminate against U.S. or Mexican firms. The danger is that this "may open the door to greater pressure to privatize social services, beginning with their management, and then . . . extending to the provision of social services themselves" (Doern and Tomlin 1991:263–64).

In the case of the creation of new public services, such as child care or auto insurance, under both FTA and NAFTA, foreign corporations have the right to claim compensation for loss of potential earnings. If the claim is held to be valid, and not acted on, retaliatory trade measures can be invoked (Sanger 1993:16). The rules governing the creation of "legitimate" new public sector monopolies are stringent (see Drache 1988:83). The existence of such threats may already have restrained Canadian and provincial governments from enhancing the public sector, as with the case of public auto insurance in Ontario. Canadian sovereignty is clearly compromised.

However, the most substantial threat to social policy results from pressures within the country for a "level playing field." Because Canada is more dependent upon the U.S. economy than the United States is on it, and because public intervention in the economy is higher north of the border, the pressure to harmonize is upon Canada to move closer to the underdeveloped U.S. model (Smiley 1988:443–44). The addition of Mexico to the free-trade equation only works to increase downward pressures on social welfare policies in Canada.

Policy harmonization between countries has increased significantly with globalization (Teeple 1995). Regional free trade will place even greater pressures on states to resist deviating from minimal social standards. Neo-liberals view free trade as a great benefit for these reasons. It intensifies the disciplinary effects of raw market forces, restraining the ability to use the state as a social policy instrument (Simeon 1991:49). The Canadian Manufacturers' Association understood clearly that free trade would lead to policy harmonization. Its former president, J. Laurent Thibault, observed:

> As we remove trade restrictions and move more and more towards an open flow of goods, it is obvious that we reduce the degree of political independence in Canada. There is nothing sinister in that. It is simply

a fact that, as we ask our industries to compete toe to toe with American industry under a full free product flow basis, we in Canada are obviously forced to create the same conditions in Canada that exist in the US whether it is the unemployment insurance scheme, Workmen's Compensation, the cost of government, the level of taxation, or whatever. The whole socioeconomic policy environment would have to be reasonably comparable with that of the US in order to give Canadian industry a reasonable chance to manufacture at a competitive cost, and that means that we would have less freedom to create in Canada an environment that is very much different from that which exists in the United States. Basically, I think that is what we are really talking about, ultimately, as a country when we talk about free trade. (quoted in Rocher 1991:143)

Free trade lends "enormous symbolic value" to neo-liberal governments and employers in their struggle to slash wages and business taxes (CCPA 1992:89; also see Albo and Jenson 1997). This not only reduces income security for many Canadians but also places fiscal pressure on public budgets. "The FTA's promise to create a level playing field," Isabella Bakker contends, "raises questions about the viability of differential tax and benefit levels on different sides of the border" (CCPA 1991:282). If there will be negative effects on the social security system in the shift to a more regressive tax system, free trade releases a political and economic dynamic that will further intensify the problem.

Critics of free trade have raised the issue of "social dumping." Social dumping is not simply the result of lower wage rates between nations or regions. Lower wage rates are generally expected to rise with increased levels of productivity. If low wage rates are accompanied by low productivity they pose no serious threat to high wage economies. Social dumping occurs when wage rates, labour, social and environmental standards are deliberately and artificially repressed (Stanford, Elwell and Sinclair 1993:1).

The southern and southwestern United States and Mexico have used low wages combined with high productivity to gain significant cost advantages over those jurisdictions with more advanced labour and social protection:

> There is no evidence that North American wage differentials are narrowing as productivity increases in low-standards jurisdictions. Rather they are widening. While average real wages declined in all three countries between 1980 and 1991, they fell furthest in Mexico despite huge productivity gains. (Stanford, Elwell and Sinclair 1993:1)

In Mexico basic commitments to democracy and the rule of law are minimal (see Warnock 1993:6–10; Zinser 1993:205–216). Free collective bargaining is denied and labour repression is the norm. In the U.S. many states demonstrate an active disregard for minimum wage laws, employment standards, health and safety, and collective bargaining rights (Stanford, Elwell and Sinclair 1993:43–54). The evidence suggests that social and worker protection has been suppressed in Mexico and American "right to work" states as a strategy to gain competitive economic advantage over higher standard jurisdictions.

Some of the concerns with social dumping were voiced in the U.S. Congress. The Clinton administration's response, supported by the Chrétien Liberal government in Ottawa, was to work out side deals on labour and the environment. While the side deals provide a measure of protection against extremely poor environmental and labour standards, they offer little opportunity for upward harmonization of continental norms. The deals are extremely narrow in scope. The labour side deal, for example, does not cover collective bargaining rights. Only health and safety, child labour, and minimum wage laws are within its reach. The length of time that must elapse from the raising of an issue to a penalty assessment is very long, set at between two and a half to three years. Moreover, the maximum penalty, at $20 million, is low. The side deals will not be able to address the fundamental problem of eroding social and environmental standards (see, for example, Rae 1996).

There is some evidence of pressures to lower social, labour, and environmental standards in Canada (Banting 1997 and Myles 1996). With respect to workers' rights, U.S. evidence demonstrates that corporations have been using threats of plant movement to Mexico to defeat unionization drives. This practice is widespread and, in many instances, a successful unionization effort is indeed followed by a shutdown of the operation and its transfer to Mexico (Bronfenbrenner 1997). No similar systematic study has been conducted in Canada but it is likely that such corporate threats are also in use here. Such tactics cannot help but have a chilling effect on labour relations, further weakening the position of workers.

Health care offers an interesting example of the types of market pressures that free trade imposes on social services. Before the FTA, health care had not been considered a "for profit" commercial service. The FTA and NAFTA open the door to privatizing the health care services by opening up to the market "managerial services for hospitals, nursing homes, and other health care facilities, as well as ambulance services, medical laboratories and blood banks" (CCPA 1992:93).

Another effect of the free-trade negotiations was to guarantee greater protection for intellectual property rights. The FTA in the end did not include a formal intellectual property code, and NAFTA incorporates GATT provisions on this matter. However, informally, the United States was able to get a commitment from the Conservative government to extend patent protection rights. Under pressure from the United States and multinational drug companies, the Tories passed Bill C-91, extending patents on brand-name drugs to twenty years. Only a few years earlier the time limit had been four years. This move has damaged the viability of generic drug producers in Canada and means that hundreds of millions of more dollars have to be added to the health bill to cover the added cost for prescription drugs (CCPA 1992:93–94; also see Diebel 1993). Under free trade, the effects of Bill C-91, as researcher John Dillon observes, are profound.

> Bill C-91, which amends Canada's patent law to give a full 20 years of monopoly protection to pharmaceutical patents, ends the practice of licensing generic copies of new patent medicines.
>
> The availability of less expensive generic copies of brand name drugs now saves Canadians over $500 million a year. The Ontario government estimates that the elimination of compulsory licensing will increase that province's drug plan costs by $80 to $100 million a year.
>
> The NAFTA text would prevent any future Canadian government from reversing Bill C-91 and restoring the right to issue licenses for generic copies of patent medicines. (1993a:12)

The fiscal pressures coming from an increasingly market-driven health care system will tend to erode the quality of and commitment to publicly-funded health care in Canada. The continued fiscal restraint enacted by the federal Liberal government, even though one of its 1993 election promises was to protect medicare, provides ample evidence of this erosion (Weller 1996). NAFTA, again, serves to restrain the state in a constitution-like manner.

The Macdonald Commission recognized that free trade would cause a difficult period of transition for many Canadians and recommended that individuals and communities be protected through adjustments in unemployment insurance and job training. Additionally, it proposed a guaranteed annual income program be established to ensure income security protection for the working poor (Doern and Tomlin 1991:266). The Conservative and Liberal governments have failed to adopt these recommendations.

iii) Free Trade's Economic Impact: Goals, Claims, and Record
The FTA was intended to realize a number of stated goals. One was to secure access for Canadian goods in the U.S. market. Another was to expand access to the U.S., which would enable Canadian industry to achieve economies of scale. This would lead to industrial restructuring and adjustment, making Canadian industry more competitive within North America and abroad. A third goal was to achieve a more ordered and predictable framework "for managing the trade relationship and resolving disputes" (Howlett and Ramesh 1992:148).

With respect to NAFTA the Mulroney government first attempted to play down the importance of the deal on the grounds that Canada's economic trade with Mexico was insignificant. The government later changed its public stance because of the unpopularity of free trade in Canada. The Tory Finance Minister Michael Wilson maintained that NAFTA would fix problems with the FTA, serve to advance and strengthen the free-trade process in Canada (Barlow 1992b:A15), and maintain "Canada as a place for foreign investors seeking continental-wide markets" (Saunders 1992:B5).

The FTA agreement established the basis for a free-trade area between the United States and Canada by the end of 1998. The trade relationship would be based upon many of the principles incorporated in GATT, but it would also push beyond GATT in liberalizing trade in services—long a U.S. goal in GATT negotiations. For the Americans the example of North American free trade was used as a standard for further trade liberalization under GATT.

Under FTA all tariffs between the countries would be eliminated over a ten year period, and export subsidies would be prohibited along with the use of many non-tariff barriers. Rights to investment and the free flow of energy resources between the countries would be secured. Additionally, institutions were established to oversee the agreement and manage the trade relationship (Hart 1992:71). NAFTA incorporated the major provisions of the FTA with some changes and extended the free-trade area to include Mexico (CCPA 1992:1).

Free-trade advocates argued that while the FTA and NAFTA would mean adjustment and some industries would be losers, in general the economic benefits of free trade would far outweigh the negatives (see, for instance, Courchene 1988a:36–44). For example, it was initially claimed that the Gross Domestic Product (GDP) would increase under free trade by between 3 and 8 percent (d'Aquino and Bulloch 1986:3), a projection supported by the Macdonald Commission. Interestingly, as the deal got closer, the estimated economic benefits of the FTA diminished. By 1988 the standard projection by trade supporters was a GDP increase over a ten-year period of only 2.5 percent. The modesty of these figures is revealing if we compare them with actual growth figures in the decades between 1951 and 1981, when Canada's average real GDP increase was 33 percent per decade (Howlett and Ramesh 1992:153).

It is instructive to observe the rather contradictory approaches that free trade proponents adopted to argue the validity of their position. On the one hand, they presented the case for free trade as one rooted in "economic science" and "irrefutable laws." Opponents, by contrast, were most often caste as operating by an "entirely different logic based on ethical issues such as the public good, national interest, and the social responsibilities of corporations" (Merrett 1996:43). On the other hand, the Macdonald Commission asserted that Canadian policymakers needed to take a "leap of faith" and go for free trade. The clear implication is that the free trade advocates' empirical "evidence" as to the beneficial implications of free trade was weak (Merrett 1996:83).

The Mulroney government continued to assert that the FTA had been a great success and that NAFTA would consolidate and extend the economic gains (see Canada 1992f). The Conservatives cited a 10 percent increase in exports to the U.S. in the first three years of FTA's operation. Critics, however, pointed to the fact that the government's numbers failed to take into account either inflation or the Canadian dollar's exchange rate: a high Canadian dollar meant that Canadian goods were worth more in U.S. dollars. With these factors included, the Canadian balance of trade with the United States was in fact down by some $4 billion over this three-year period (Winsor 1992:A6; see also *The Globe and Mail*, October 16, 1992:B4). Statistics Canada data revealed an interesting pattern in exports and imports in goods and services which betrayed the Mulroney government's optimistic report. The numbers indicated that Canadian trade moved from a situation of advantage to a deficit—a process that began around 1989, when the FTA was enacted (*The Daily,* June 22, 1992:4).

In its merchandise trade Canada has long held a surplus and continued to do so after the FTA and NAFTA . However, that surplus declined by more than 26 percent in the first three years after the FTA, compared to the three years before. In the same timeframe Canada's surplus merchandising with the United States declined by $6 billion (Hurtig 1992:50).[10] These balances did not begin to move in Canada's favour again until after 1994, spurred on by the devaluation of the Canadian dollar (see Merrett 1996:114–118).

Prior to the passage of the FTA the Americans expressed concerned about the future value of the Canadian dollar. For the United States the danger was that the Canadian government could use a devalued dollar, achieved easily enough by lowering the Bank of Canada rate, as a way of lowering the price of Canada's goods and thus gaining a trade advantage (Laxer 1987:64). No formal deal about controlling the value of the dollar was reached under either the FTA or NAFTA. However, there has been a great deal of suspicion that a private deal was cut, a position supported by former Conservative Cabinet Minister Sinclair Stevens. Whatever the truth of this, it is certain that after the FTA there was a sharp rise in interest rates and the value of the Canadian dollar. The high-interest-rate policy of the Canadian government, which has forced the dollar up, has been responsible for many job losses (Doern and Tomlin 1991:292). Only in 1994 did the Canadian dollar significantly fall against the American currency (Merrett 1996:47).

The Economic Council of Canada (1988) predicted that the FTA would create 251,000 jobs. The reality has been that from 1989 to mid-1992 Canada experienced a loss of 511,000 manufacturing jobs and nearly a million service sector jobs (Winsor 1992:A6). It is not easy to determine how much of the job loss is a result of the FTA and how much is simply the effect of the recession Canada entered at the end of 1989. It is worth noting, though, that the economic downturn hit Canada before it did most other Western countries. In fact the federal government's policies, including high interest rates, support for a high dollar, and, presumably, free trade, helped produce the first "made in Canada" recession this country had ever experienced. Of course, "Canada's recession" of the early 1990s was followed quickly by a global downturn, which exacerbated the nation's economic difficulties. Still, job losses were about four times higher than those experienced in the United States (Winsor 1992:A6).

The case of Ontario, Canada's industrial heartland, offers a more specific reading of the costs of free trade. For Ontario the 1990s recession, as was the case for most of the other provinces, was the deepest and longest since the depression of the 1930s. The decline in real Ontario Gross Domestic Product between 1989 and 1991 was -7.8 percent, far exceeding the average post-war recession drop of -2.4 percent (Ontario Ministry of Treasury and Economics 1992:35). The depth of the downturn can be explained by the fundamental structural alterations still underway in the Ontario, and more generically in the Canadian economies.

By the end of 1992 Ontario's unemployment rate stood at 11 percent. Historically, Ontario's unemployment rate has been lower than the national average—in recent years it had been on average about 3 percent lower—but the current economic restructuring meant that by 1992–93 Ontario was tracking national unemployment levels. Most of the job losses were accounted for in lost manufacturing employment. Between September 1989 and August 1992 about 18 percent of the province's manufacturing jobs disappeared—a loss of about 189,000 positions (Freeman 1992b:A1). One calculation placed Ontario's job losses over the initial years of the 1990s at nearly 500 jobs a day, the result of a daily average of one plant closure (Spratt 1992:8).

A comparison of the early 1990s job losses in Ontario with those lost in the previous recession in 1982 indicates the extent of deindustrialization that occurred in the industrial centre of Canada. In 1991, 61.3 percent of total layoffs were due to complete or partial plant closures. By contrast in 1982, only 24.2 percent of job losses fell into these categories. In 1982, 74.8 percent of layoffs were due to reduced operations—a situation in which workers had a reasonable chance of recall. Moreover, in the recession of the early 1990s, in contrast to that of the early 1980s, the average length of time a person remained unemployed was substantially longer, and unemployment was much more heavily concentrated among prime-age workers (Ontario Ministry of Labour 1992:10, 14). The marked increase in structural unemployment (unemployment accounted for by complete or partial closures) became especially prominent after 1988 (Office of Labour Adjustment 1992:2). The economic transformations that confronted Ontario by the early 1990s have been characterized as "the most dramatic change in the recent history of the Canadian labour market" (Statistics Canada 1993).

This profile of Ontario unemployment history suggests that free trade has had a negative effect on employment. Most of the job losses in the 1990s recession were permanent, with manufacturing operations being the hardest hit.

Since the end of the early 1990s recession economic growth in Canada has been characterized by its polarized character. There has been a "jobless recovery" with official unemployment levels stuck at over 9 percent. The jobs that have been generated have tended to be low-waged service sector employment, much of it contingent in nature, and income earnings have become increasingly polarized. Economic insecurity, especially among the so-called middle classes, abounds (see Betcherman and Lowe 1997; Shields 1996). There has also been a considerable degree of corporate concentration, especially in the form of American-based multinationals buying up smaller Canadian companies. This is a trend that has accelerated since the signing of the FTA (Merrett 1996:94). There is an important jobs dimension to this development. As Merrett observes:

> takeovers translate into job loss for Canadian workers. For every billion
> dollars of profit made by Canadian firms in Canada, 765 jobs are
> created. For every billion dollars of profit made by American firms
> operating in Canada, 17 jobs are created. An American takeover of a
> Canadian firm can therefore be considered as an indirect job loss of 748
> jobs for every Can$1 billion in American profits from Canadian
> subsidiaries. (1996:95)

The contemporary economic reality betrays the promise of the free-trade
advocates.

The Fraser Institute's Michael Walker has provided a contrary view: that the
loss of manufacturing jobs, even if accelerated by the FTA, is not a bad thing; the
process is a natural one and will mean greater prosperity in the future (1993:16–
18). Walker's dismissive approach to the deindustrialization of Canada, like that
of much of the business community, tends to be self-serving. The brighter future
predicted by corporate interests neglects the reality of the emerging labour
force—one in which there is an increasing polarization of income, fewer good
jobs, and more poorly paid and uncertain employment (see Shields and Russell
1994; Economic Council of Canada 1990) and enormous insecurity for youth
(see Rehnby and McBride 1997). For capital, this type of flexible just-in-time
labour force can be viewed as a benefit.

More questions must be raised about the anticipated gains of free trade. It is
true that Canada is a trade-reliant nation and was, before the FTA, the only
advanced industrial country except Japan and the United States not to be part of
a trading bloc. Japan, of course, has access to a domestic market of over 100
million people (Lipsey 1988:67). Under NAFTA, North America forms the world's
largest free-trade zone, with a population of 360 million. Moreover, Canada's
trade dependence on the United States—well over 70 percent of Canadian
exports are to its neighbour (Hart 1992:19)—is well-known. The question to be
posed is whether Canada gained secure access to the U.S. market as a result of
the FTA. While Canadian trade with the United States is "enormous," most of that
trade is centred in "a relatively small range of products" going "to a regionally
specific market, highly concentrated in the American mid-west and mid Atlantic
states. Much of the trade is a function of the intra-firm transfers of American-
owned corporations back and forth across the frontier" (Laxer 1987:57). The
bulk of this trade consists of auto parts, covered by the 1965 Auto Pact agreement,
and resources and semiprocessed inputs destined for final manufacture in the
United States. For the most part the threat of U.S. protectionist pressures against
these exports is low (Laxer 1987:57–59), and for those products that are vulnerable (like steel and softwood lumber), there is serious reason to believe that the
FTA and NAFTA have failed to protect them from U.S. trade sanctions.

A second anticipated result of free trade was the creation of the economies of scale necessary to help Canadian industry rationalize its production and become more competitive. Notwithstanding trends to greater Canadian ownership in the early 1980s, this argument failed to take into account the foreign ownership (mostly U.S.) of much of the Canadian-based industry. This was especially true in manufacturing and other leading sectors of the economy: "It is . . . Alice-in-Wonderland economics to expect branch plants in Canada to compete with their parent companies on their home ground in the United States. Indeed, the reverse phenomenon is more likely: free trade will encourage the dismantling of Canadian branch plants and the Canadian market will be served . . . from the United States" (Canadian Institute for Economic Policy 1985:132).[11] The Ontario employment data suggests that this is just what is happening.

Stephen Clarkson makes a telling observation: "The price of admission to the American market would be economic policies needed to put Canadian industry in a position to compete there" (quoted in Watkins 1992:86). But the Conservative government was not prepared, practically or ideologically, to enact policies that required the active use of the state. And the FTA and NAFTA will ensure the impossibility of the state enacting such a national strategy in future. The subsequent Liberal government's failure to articulate an alternative industrial strategy, along with their adoption of NAFTA despite being unable to win concessions from the U.S. government, reinforces the point. Neo-liberal economic management comes to be enshrined under these free-trade terms. The economic policies necessary to ensure competitiveness are rendered more difficult by the terms of the agreements themselves.

The final expectation was that free trade would ensure orderly and predictable trade and establish mechanisms to head off and solve trade disputes. One of the primary reasons for negotiating the FTA, according to the Mulroney government, was to establish a set of desirable rules to govern trade, most importantly common rules governing the use of antidumping and countervailing sanctions. One of the difficulties facing Canadian trade with the United States was the increasing use of U.S. trade law and its "unilateral U.S. definition of what is unfair, instead of applying an international standard and using an international mechanism to settle disputes" (Lipsey 1987:40).

In the end no binding "supreme court of trade" was agreed to under the FTA (Doern and Tomlin 1991:251). Instead the countries could refer disputes to a panel that could issue only declaratory opinions. Moreover, it was U.S. trade laws that were to prevail in conflicts under the FTA (a provision carried forward under NAFTA as well). Both the FTA and NAFTA reserve "the right of each country to apply its antidumping and countervailing duty laws" (CCPA 1992:84). The Americans refused to give up their sovereignty on the application of U.S. "fair trade" laws. One important difficulty with this provision is that if the trade panel begins to make rulings against the United States, there is nothing to prevent the U.S. Congress from unilaterally changing its trade laws in a direction that would ensure a more favourable outcome (CCPA 1992:84–86). In fact this was the reaction of the U.S. in the recent softwood lumber dispute—a response that forced Canada into making concessions (Barlow 1996:A17).

The FTA bound the two countries to continue negotiations with the purpose of developing rules in both countries to control dumping and countervailing duties. Unless a new regime of rules were agreed to within five to seven years, either party was to have the right to abrogate the FTA. NAFTA retreats on this provision by eliminating any deadlines for reaching new rules (CCPA 1992:84). The Chrétien Liberal government was able to secure a verbal commitment from the Clinton administration to reach agreements on rules within a two-year period. However, this commitment was not a formal part of NAFTA and consequently holds no legal force. Two years have long since passed with no resolution. Given the protectionist inclinations of the American Congress, agreeing to satisfactory rules is proving to be a daunting and perhaps unachievable task.

Bruce Doern and Brian Tomlin argue that:

> The real test of this key element of the FTA [and by extension NAFTA] will be in its effects on U.S. behaviour. In the case of American producers, the question is whether the existence of a review process in which other nationals are involved will reduce the number of countervail actions that are even attempted. (1991:251)

On this score the free trade disputes-settlement provisions appear to have been a failure. U.S. trade actions against Canadian exports, including actions against softwood lumber, Canadian-made Honda Civics, beer, fish, durum wheat, Canadian cultural products and steel, have continued apace (see Anderson 1995). Fred Telmer, chairman of Canada's largest steel company, Stelco Inc., has been very critical of NAFTA on this score. His charge is that the Americans ignore the dispute panels and engage in harassment of Canadian producers until they achieve their desired concessions. In Telmer's words: "Free trade is the name that's attached to it, but it doesn't really have any relevance" (Israelson 1996:B1).

Supporters of free trade argued that one of the most important sources of new investment in Canada would be non-North American companies that, under the FTA, would be guaranteed access to the U.S. market. In fact U.S. trade harassment of Honda and other companies has served seriously to tarnish "Canada's carefully cultivated image abroad as a gateway to North America." These aggressive trade tactics send a clear signal to foreign investors that if they want assured access to the U.S. market they would be better advised to invest in the United States. Foreign investors continue to see the United States and Canada as separate markets in spite of the free-trade pact (Drohan and Terry 1992:B1-B9).

The consequences of the unequal power relations under "free" trade place Canada in a weak and dependent position:

After the countries become locked into a free trade area, their economies become much more integrated, and the costs of getting out of a deal can be high. This means that power relations between countries are altered after a free trade area is formed, and there may be incentives for relatively more powerful countries to behave opportunistically. (Copeland 1992:192)

U.S. trade harassment actions should be viewed in this light.

Disputes over "rules of origin" of products have been a major source of trade conflict under the FTA. The sections in the free-trade agreements dealing with rules of origin are among the most important because they determine which "goods are to be considered eligible for duty-free access to the markets of Canada, the United States and Mexico" (Cameron 1993:16). The FTA established a 50 percent local-content rule for U.S.–Canadian goods. Under the FTA, however, the rules for deciding how to define local content were left imprecise and the United States has tended to use them in a protectionist manner (CCPA 1992:52). NAFTA does set out a clearer method of calculating "rules of origin," although there is still considerable room for interpretation: "NAFTA will give too much discretion to Customs Service employees who have injected protectionist intention into previous trade laws" (Bovard 1992:B3). Moreover, NAFTA increased the local-content levels for many goods, including autos, clothing, and televisions. This was done at the insistence of the United States. NAFTA rules with respect to autos provide a revealing case.

The former Tory government viewed foreign-transplant automakers as the best source of new investment in Canada. One of the Canadian goals in NAFTA was to ensure that Canada would remain a major site for new foreign investors seeking access to the North American market. Yet the Japanese view NAFTA as a significant setback. Under NAFTA the rules of origin for cars have been increased from 50 to 62.5 percent. Many Japanese automakers believe that they were lured to Canada by the prospect of access to the broader North American market, and then abandoned. The new content rules mean that non-North American auto manufacturers will have to invest in manufacturing engines and transmissions in North America, because these add high value to a car (Pritchard 1992:B1–B2). This is causing non-North American foreign manufacturers to rethink their investment intentions in Canada. The provision may lead to greater regional protectionism in the world economy: "Such strict rules may also discourage investment in Mexico and Canada if foreign investors balk at meeting such stringent requirements" (Cameron 1993:17). Again, one of the free-trade goals of neo-liberal government has been met in an unsatisfactory way.

In the final analysis the free-trade deals have served to make Canada even more dependent and thus increasingly vulnerable to the forces of the U.S. economy and state. Revealingly, the regional impact of globalization in this case has resulted not in a greater diversification of Canada's international trade patterns but rather a significant narrowing of its economic relationships. Canada's exports to the nations of the European Union and Pacific Rim countries in 1988 accounted for 9 and 17 percent of total sales. However, today those figures have shrunk to 6 and 12 percent respectively. In 1980 about 64 percent of our trade was with the U.S. Free trade has worked to increase this level to near 80 percent (Campbell 1977).

iv) The Case of Energy, Natural Resources, and Foreign Investment

In pursuing the FTA, a major U.S. objective was to guarantee secure access to Canadian natural resources and energy. With NAFTA, the Americans aimed to extend that goal to Mexican resources.

Energy accounts for about 14 percent of total Canadian investment and about 10 percent of total exports. The United States is the world's largest energy consumer and importer, with Canada being its largest supplier. Energy for the purposes of the FTA and NAFTA includes oil, natural gas, light petroleum gas, coal, uranium, and electricity. The agreements remove virtually all barriers to trade in these resources (Howlett and Ramesh 1992:149).

Both the FTA and NAFTA bind the Canadian government into sharing its energy resources with the United States. The proportional-sharing clauses, as they are called, "oblige Canada to continue exporting the same proportion of its supply of non-renewable resources as were sold over the previous 36 months, even in the case of national shortage" (CCPA 1992:21). Mexico insisted that agreeing to such a provision would be against its constitution and compromise its sovereignty, and it was able to achieve an exemption. The trade deals forbid the use of differential pricing of energy, which would give domestic consumers a price advantage. They also forbid export taxes to cover the replacement costs of resources. However, governments are permitted to subsidize the exploration and development of oil and gas. In other words, governments can subsidize the energy industry through taxpayers' dollars but are not allowed to provide subsidies to domestic consumers:

> As net petroleum exporters, continental energy sharing has very different consequences for Canada and Mexico than it has for the U.S., a major petroleum importer. Integration of the energy sector means that both Canada and Mexico face the premature depletion of their non-renewable petroleum resources. Selling conventional oil and gas reserves at prices far below their replacement costs subsidizes U.S. consumers. These lower-cost, more accessible and more environmentally benign conventional reserves will have to be replaced with more costly offshore and frontier resources. (CCPA 1992:25)

The Tories and their business allies wanted to ensure that nationalist policies like the National Energy Policy could never again be implemented. They wished to place such policy instruments out of the reach of future governments. For the Conservatives, the energy provisions of the free-trade agreements were "a desirable loss of sovereignty" (Doern and Tomlin 1991:258).

Under NAFTA and the FTA other natural resources, including water, are treated as tradable goods: "Generally, the rights and obligations pertaining to energy will also apply to natural resources" (Sinclair 1993:15). Continental norms will now govern the access to all natural resource stocks.

The agreements significantly liberalize cross-border barriers to investment, although NAFTA goes further down this road than the FTA. The continental free-trade agreement requires that Canada accord national treatment to U.S. and Mexican firms. This means that U.S. or Mexican investors "must be treated no less favourably than domestic" investors (Sinclair 1993:14). The FTA and NAFTA also place a host of prohibitions on performance requirements such as minimal levels of Canadian ownership, purchasing from local suppliers, or repatriation of profits. Public corporations are also strictly limited in their ability to regulate investments. NAFTA stipulates that the public monopoly must "act solely with commercial considerations in the purchase or sale of that monopoly good"—a provision that negates the reason for establishing many Crown corporations in the first place (CCPA 1992:12–13). Further:

> Governments (provincial and federal) are greatly restricted from active industrial policies which regulate investment in order to influence to what sectors or regions of the economy it is channeled and ensure that its citizens get a share of the employment and other benefits. Thus industrial policies to promote balanced economic development—industrial diversification, adding domestic value to resources, regional development, knowledge-intensive production—are severely curtailed. (CCPA 1992:13)

Free trade will thus make state-directed Canadianization policies like FIRA or rhe NEP impossible to pursue. The state is compromising sovereignty in the interests of "free" markets and corporate rights.

During the 1993 federal election campaign Chrétien promised that a Liberal government would not approve NAFTA unless the energy provisions were changed to make them consistent with the terms governing Mexico. The Americans refused but the Liberals nevertheless approved NAFTA. The Liberal government issued a declaration stating that Canada retains sovereignty over the control of its energy resources. Its status as a unilateral declaration, and its absence from the text of the agreement, makes its enforceability highly problematic. Once again the Liberal record is one marked by meaningless rhetoric while a neo-liberal agenda is advanced.

Free trade was sold as an industrial strategy for an era of globalization. But as the energy and foreign investment provisions of the deals reveal, it will likely do more to entrench the role of staples within the Canadian economy: "The removal of barriers to trade permits each country to pursue more fully its comparative advantage. For Canada, already strong sectors (such as staples) grow further, while weak sectors (such as secondary manufacturing) shrink" (Watkins 1997:33).

v) NAFTA: Revealing the U.S. Agenda

In recent decades, the United States has become increasingly dependent upon the world economy. This has occurred in the context of a growing challenge to its economic hegemony, especially from Japan and Europe. North American free trade opens up an avenue by which the United States may be able to regain some of its lost economic influence and competitive edge. The strategy also poses the possibility that intensified economic rivalries might result from the development of regional economic trading blocs (Brunelle and Deblock 1992:119). Within the U.S. trading bloc the United States would be guaranteed hegemony, consolidating its hold over the Americas. NAFTA will also serve to "lock Canada and Mexico into the American model of development, on terms set by capital (Cameron 1993:9).

A "hub-and-spoke" economic relationship has long existed between the United States and Canada and Mexico. The United States serves as the economic hub, and Canada and Mexico function as economic spokes linked to that hub. The FTA and NAFTA intensify and institutionalize this form of economic relationship (Eden and Appel Molot 1992:67). The reality is that Canada and Mexico are far more economically dependent on the United States than the United States is on them. Over 70 percent of Canadian exports are to the United States, while Canada accounts for only about 22 percent of U.S. exports. About 67 percent of Mexican exports are to the United States. By contrast, only about 6.5 percent of U.S. total exports are Mexico-bound (Cameron, Eden and Appel Molot 1992:176). Moreover, trade between Canada and Mexico is slight. In 1991 Canada exported only $543 million in goods to Mexico, while Mexican trade to Canada accounted for only $2.6 billion (Fagan and Saunders 1992:B1). Since the passage of NAFTA, trade between Canada and Mexico has grown but it remains modest, with Mexico enjoying a decided balance of trade advantage. NAFTA alone will be insufficient to significantly deepen the trade relationship between these two countries (Stevenson 1995). The figures reveal the "hub-and-spoke" relationship—Canada and Mexico are heavily dependent upon the United States but enjoy limited economic ties to each other.

Multinational corporate executives did perceive:

> strategic advantage to the FTA industries in transferring some of their labour-intensive production to a low wage Third World country like Mexico rather than to a NIC [newly industrialized country]. This was because the FTA capital controlled, and would therefore directly benefit from, most of the backward and forward economic linkages within an

expanding Mexican industrial structure, while a NIC had the potential to grow into an economic competitor. Put crudely, capital's objective has been to constitute Mexico as sort of a low-wage Bantustan within the continental economy where labour can be annexed at Third World rates for specific parts of the continental production process. (Williams 1994:179, 182).

In this way North American capital sought to enhance its international competitiveness.

NAFTA is not a genuinely trilateral relationship, because trade between Canada and Mexico is so meagre. The North American free-trade arrangement is also asymmetrical to the extent that one of the parties to the deal is a developing nation while another "sees itself as a world power whose responsibilities and hegemonic pretensions far exceed those of any members of the other two blocs [Europe and Japan]" (Brunelle and Deblock 1992:124–25)

Mexico has, however, emerged as a manufacturing centre. Until the early 1980s petroleum was Mexico's major export to the United States: now its major export is manufactured goods (Eden and Appel Molot 1992:68–69). Mexico exports more fully-manufactured goods to Canada—nearly 70 percent of its Canadian-bound exports—than Canada exports to Mexico—less than 25 percent (Cameron, Eden and Appel Molot 1992:176).

The rise of Mexico's manufacturing capacity is directly linked to the establishment of the maquiladoras—free-trade exporting zones. These were established in 1965 and opened Mexico for the first time to massive levels of direct foreign investment (Eden and Appel Molot 1992:71; Kopinak 1993). U.S. multinationals have predominately established manufacturing operations in the maquiladoras. The use of low-cost Mexican labour from these zones "has become critical to the competitiveness of U.S. manufacturing firms." Because there were no duties on goods entering the United States from the maquiladoras the FTA had already established a kind of free trade between the United States, Canada, and Mexico (Cameron, Eden and Appel Molot 1992:178–79).

Japanese direct investment in Mexico has also been high, in fact outpacing Japanese investment in Canada. Japanese businesses view the maquiladoras as offering the attractive features of low wages and proximity to the U.S. market (Cameron, Eden and Appel Molot 1992:179). This may serve to undermine the Canadian free traders' arguments about the FTA and NAFTA establishing Canada as the logical location for Japanese investments.

For over a decade the Mexican government has been pursuing an agenda of freer trade, reversing former nationalistic policies (Teichman 1993). The impact upon the country's poor has been less than favourable. In agriculture it has resulted in land-ownership concentration that has forced more and more peasants off the land and into the cities. NAFTA will further accelerate this trend and contribute to overturning agrarian reform. Also, since 1982 higher-paying industrial jobs have been disappearing, and there has been a deindustrialization of Mexico proper. Industrial operations have increasingly set up shop in the maquiladoras close to the U.S. border, where the average wage is the equivalent of only sixty-eight Canadian cents an hour (Morley 1992:A15). Mexican society is becoming even more polarized under the impact of the new strategy.

By far more closely linking a developing nation's economy with their own more mature developed economies, NAFTA poses enhanced risks to both Canada and the U.S. Soon after entering into NAFTA Mexico experienced its worst recession in sixty years (*The Globe and Mail*, December 14, 1995:B10). The most obvious manifestation of difficulties in the Mexican economy was the "peso crisis" of 1994–95. In a two-week period in December 1994 the peso was devalued by 35 percent, resulting in an estimated $10 billion loss in foreign investment. An $18 billion international bailout package, of which Ottawa contributed $1.5 billion, was quickly arranged to shore-up the faltering Mexican economy. In fact, under the terms of NAFTA member states are obligated to come to the financial aid of a partner confronting a currency crisis (McDonald 1996).

The Mexican economic crisis was further marked by a steep decline in Mexico's annual GDP, rampant inflation, the loss of more than a million jobs between 1994–1995, an average wage decline of 25 percent over this same period, and plunging living standards for the country's emerging middle class (*The Globe and Mail*, December 20, 1995:B7). The causes of the crisis are multifaceted, including difficulties in rapidly adjusting the Mexican economy to neo-liberal policy, widespread political corruption and scandal, and intensified social and political instability, illustrated by a Zapatistas-led rebellion in the southern state of Chiapas (see Barry 1995). All of this highlights the inherent instability of the Mexican economy and society and the hazards for Canada and the U.S. in more closely integrating their production machines to this developing region.

The size of the Mexican economy is just under 40 percent of that of the Canadian economy, but its potential is much larger. It is projected that Mexico's economy will overtake Canada's in the early part of the next century, if stability can be maintained. This means that in the relatively near future the Mexican economy could become more important to the United States than Canada's (Crane 1992b:H4).

Canada entered the trilateral NAFTA negotiations for defensive purposes. Rather than for the purpose of pursuing new markets, Canada "needed" to be at the table to ensure that its trade opportunities in the U.S. market were not undermined (Cameron, Eden and Appel Molot 1992:180). On a number of fronts, and from Canada's perspective, the NAFTA agreement weakened the FTA.

An important component of NAFTA is its accession clause, which opens up the opportunity for other countries to join the free-trade arrangement. Canada and Mexico will have a say in future additions to free trade, but there is no veto right and there is nothing in NAFTA that prevents the original agreement from being rewritten when others join. As new countries will be joining to secure access to U.S. markets, Canada and Mexico will be in a weak bargaining position compared to the United States (CCPA 1992:97). To a significant extent Canada has been "carried along as a 'captive rider' on the American train in the expansion of the free trade agreement to include Mexico and, subsequently, other Latin American countries" (Crane 1992a:F2). Other countries will most likely also enter the trade agreements with little bargaining power. Before they are even eligible to negotiate entrance they must have first liberalized trade and investment laws and implemented protection of intellectual property provisions consistent with NAFTA (CCPA 1992:98; Schott 1995).

Canada, since NAFTA's passage, has negotiated a separate free-trade arrangement with Chile. However, Canada's current and prospective trade with Chile is meagre. The U.S. failure to join this initiative at this time is an indication of its determination to strike deals exclusively on its own terms.

The future expansion of the free-trade arrangement is consistent with the Enterprise for the Americas Initiative (EAI) announced by the Bush administration in June 1990. Bush launched the EAI under the slogan "trade, not aid" and "drew on the traditional bulwarks of U.S. foreign economic policy—trade liberalization abroad and active encouragement of private investment" (Randall et al. 1992:3; Dillon 1993b). The EAI contained three major elements: 1) the goal of establishing a hemispheric free-trade zone; 2) the vigorous promotion of foreign investment; and 3) proposals for foreign-debt repayment for Latin American countries. In Latin America the EAI would extend the pattern of export-led growth, with much of the wealth generation being skimmed off to pay North American creditors (CCPA 1992:98; see also Braga 1992).

In pursuing NAFTA and the Enterprise for the Americas Initiatives, the United States seeks to realize three primary objectives. First, these measures would provide U.S. multinationals with a larger market and allow them the opportunity to take advantage of Mexican and Canadian comparative advantages in cheap labour and natural resources: "What is at stake is the creation of a regional economic space which would allow American firms to improve their competitiveness, and thereby regain their lost share of international markets" (Brunelle and Deblock 1992:129). Second, Canadian and Mexican economic nationalism would be neutralized. Continental free trade would serve to integrate "conflicting economic policies into one vision of America"—a "continental" vision dominated by a U.S. economic and political policy. And third, the FTA and NAFTA have been strategically used by the United States in GATT negotiations to successfully press for a further liberalization of trade in its areas of prime concern, namely investments, services, intellectual property, and agriculture (Brunelle and Deblock 1992:129–30). The free-trade agreements will be presented as models for imitation.

Locking in the State
To break the pattern of economic dependence upon the United States, develop national policies that truly benefit "ordinary" Canadians, and make Canadian industry truly competitive internationally would require the Canadian state to play a much more active role in the economy and society. The adoption of continental free trade will guarantee the opposite pattern of development. The Canadian state will be locked into the terms of the free-trade agreements. Continental free trade "will result in a loss of Canadian sovereignty, understood as the practical ability to chart a course independent of the United States" (Gold and Leyton-Brown 1988:375). Free trade embeds a market-led neo-liberal ideology and seriously limits the Canadian state's room for policy manoeuvre.

> For Canada and Mexico NAFTA has become the law of the land. But this is not the case for the United States. The U.S. negotiated NAFTA, as it did the Canada–U.S. trade deal, under the so-called fast track authority. This allows the president to enact NAFTA as an executive agreement with Canada and Mexico, if a simple majority of both the Senate and the House of Representatives agrees to pass enabling legislation. An international treaty requires two-thirds support of the Senate and becomes the law of the land, standing above domestic legislation. Under an executive agreement, it is the enabling legislation that gives the treaty effect and it is subject to the general legislative practice of Congress, meaning it can be overridden by any subsequent law passed by Congress. (Cameron 1993:9)

Clearly NAFTA has become an economic constitution for Canada and Mexico, subjecting these countries' governments to significant legislative restraints that will not necessarily apply to the U.S. state. North American free trade means that Canadian sovereignty is compromised, continental integration under U.S. hegemony secured, and a neo-liberal policy paradigm advanced.

Notes
1.   Michael Walker of the neo-conservative think-tank, the Fraser Institute, has noted that the free-trade deal "limits the extent to which the U.S. or other signatory governments may respond to pressure from their citizens" (quoted in Shniad 1992:21).
2.   It is important to note that the provinces were formally excluded from the free-trade negotiating table between Canada and the United States (see Doern and Tomlin 1991:126–51). Nonetheless they are tied to the agreements signed by the government of Canada. Perhaps the most important tie is not purely legal but comes in the form of negative economic consequences likely to be imposed by the United States should the terms of the deal be broken. It has been suggested that this was one of the primary motivations that prompted the former Ontario's NDP government to back away from its promise to embrace publicly-owned auto insurance (Shniad 1992:26–27).
      There is a lively debate over the question of whether, legally speaking, the

provinces are subject to obey the terms of FTA (see Gold and Leyton-Brown 1988:ch. 4, 5). For those who question the federal government's legal ability to impose international treaties in provincial areas of jurisdiction, the Labour Conventions Case of 1937 is the point of reference. In this case the Judicial Committee of the Privy Council "refused to accept the treaty implementation power as a constitutional support for interfering in provincial powers. However, this case directly conflicts with another court ruling, the Radio Case of 1932, which did seem to give the federal authorities such powers for the purposes of international treaties (Russell, Knopff and Morton 1989:104–10). The legal ground rules are cloudy. It is significant, however, that none of the provinces have attempted to challenge the federal government's position with respect to the FTA by referring the matter to the Supreme Court of Canada (Stevenson 1988:136).

Clarkson argues that the establishment, under FTA, of the Canada-United States Trade Commission will force provinces into compliance with the terms of FTA (1988:160–67). And Andrew Petter argues:

What the FTA does is add a major new variable to federal–provincial relations in this country. It brings to the federal–provincial bargaining table a third party—the United States—with authority to demand legal remedies to problems of concern to both levels of government. In doing so, it seeks not only to curtail the regulatory activities of federal and provincial governments; it places strong political pressure on the federal government to revive and expand its supervisory powers to force provinces into line with the FTA. Indeed, evidence of this pressure may already be found in Prime Minister Mulroney's statements that the federal government possesses full power to enforce the treaty, and in his assurances to U.S. politicians that his government will ensure that the treaty is "respected" by the provinces. (1988:145–46)

Significantly, Article 105 of NAFTA commits the federal government to take "all necessary measures" to ensure that provinces comply with the terms of the agreement (CCPA 1992:2).

FTA and NAFTA will significantly constrain the actions of all levels of government in Canada in favour of free-market forces, and thus it becomes rather a moot point as to whether free trade will place more of a limit on federal or provincial powers.

3. Following a similar line of thought, Brodie has argued that free trade became attractive as a development strategy because:

First, the Trudeau government's abortive attempt at a resource-led interventionist industrial strategy which collapsed under the shock of declining oil prices and a capital strike in the resource sector as well as the recession of 1981–82, served to discredit the neo-interventionist position. . . . Second, Canada became a net capital exporter and many political elites, especially at the provincial level, became convinced that Canada should once again seek out foreign capital to promote domestic growth. Third, and relatedly, Canadian capital began to invest abroad, often in the United States, as a response to global economic restructuring. By the early 1980s, both resource based as well as industrial and financial capitalists tied Canada's economic future to market-driven continentalist design. (1989:177–78)

4. Other policy think-tanks to endorse Canada–U.S. free trade include the Economic Council of Canada and the Fraser Institute (Ernst 1992:110).

5. On the important role which Royal Commissions play in the Canadian public policy process see Bradford (1994) and Jenson (1994).

6. The support of Canadian business for free trade with the United States was overwhelming. Rocher captures the essence of this state of affairs.

    Free trade proponents clearly dominated the public debate. They imposed themselves within the main business associations, getting even the support of those who, while liable to lose from free trade, nevertheless sided with them as they saw an opportunity to reduce state intervention and encourage entrepreneurship. As for the Canadian heads of U.S. subsidiaries, even if their operations could be negatively affected by the lowering of tariff barriers, they remained silent following the implicit or explicit directives of American head offices, which always believed they would gain from trade liberalization. (1991:151–52)

    With regard to NAFTA, Canadian business appeared to be rather lukewarm to the agreement. There seems to be a couple of main reasons for this: 1) NAFTA is not seen to affect Canada as much as FTA, because our trade with Mexico is small; and 2) the Canadian economy was performing so poorly that it was difficult to generate much enthusiasm among businesses. Big business in Canada came out firmly behind the NAFTA deal but smaller business was split. For instance, the 83,000-member Canadian Federation of Independent Business reported that a survey revealed their membership to be nearly evenly divided on the question of whether NAFTA was a good or bad thing (Freeman 1992a:A1–AI).

7. Other leading Conservatives also rejected free trade as a policy in the early 1980s. Joe Clark argued that it would result in the loss of thousands of jobs, and Michael Wilson suggested that free trade was a simplistic solution to Canada's economic problems and that it would hinder the country's ability to compete (Barlow 1991:25).

8. For an indepth account of the FTA negotiations see Hart, Dymond and Robertson (1994).

9. For the Conservative government, it was hoped that adopting FTA would bring the added advantage of helping to solidify its political base in Western Canada and Québec. Québec had reversed its historical position in favour of protectionism to become an enthusiastic supporter of free trade (Doern and Tomlin 1991:32). Of course, in the end this was a failed strategy as the federal Progressive Conservative Party support dissolved in the 1993 election.

10. Barlow, using Statistics Canada figures, indicates that in constant 1986 dollars, Canadian bilateral trade with the United States declined by more than $4 billion, with imports outpacing export growth by greater than 50 percent. Moreover, an April 1992 U.S. Department of Commerce report asserted that the United States was a net gainer under FTA—"boasting that the U.S. trade balance with Canada has improved by $6 billion in five years" (1992b:A15).

11. For the classic study on the nature and effects of the Canadian branch-plant economy, see Levitt 1970. The branch-plan character of much of the Canadian economy has also placed it in a poor position to compete on an equal footing with the United States. In part this is because Canada has a poor record in research and development, which has made much of Canadian industries "innovative backwaters" (Britton and Gilmour 1978:104). A highly state interventionist industrial strategy would probably be needed to correct this situation, but this approach would probably run afoul of the FTA and NAFTA.

Chapter 9

Conclusions and Alternatives

The comparative analysis of political economies anticipates both similarities and variations between national cases. In focusing on the Canadian example it has become apparent that Canada's political economy is both similar to and different from the political economies of the other advanced industrial economies.

An example of similarity would be the construction, in the post-war era, of a Keynesian welfare state, and the subsequent challenge to that state by advocates of neo-liberal economic doctrines. The driving force behind the establishment of neo-liberal hegemony has been the corporate sector. Neo-liberalism is the preferred ideology of capital in the late twentieth century. For this reason we have summarized the implementation of neo-liberalism by the Canadian state in the book's subtitle as "the transition to corporate rule."

Most Western nations have experienced comparable developments. All of them, Canada included, were actors in one sort of international political economy that existed from the immediate post-war years until the mid-1970s. And Canada, like the others, must now adjust to the new sort of international political economy that is conveniently summarized in the term "globalization." Yet, as we have noted at various points, adjustments to globalization have not been structurally determined. In common with other countries Canada has helped shape the content of globalization through its participation in international trade agreements—a process that is far from finished as the unfolding story of the negotiations on a Multilateral Agreement on Investment (MAI) indicates. The content of these agreements is thoroughly neo-liberal and their provisions have diminished the capacity of nation-states to interfere with the operations of capital—another indication that we are in transition to corporate rule. The Canadian state has thus been actively complicit in its own dismantling, a process that can best be explained by the dominance of capital in the political process of the country.

In many of these respects Canada is a typical advanced industrial country, experiencing ideological and structural trends that are characteristic of other nations. However, recognition of the commonalities needs to be tempered by an understanding of Canadian distinctiveness. Some aspects of Canada's political economy, in the context of neo-liberal globalization, bring the very survival of the country into question. No one can deny that many political systems are being changed and transformed as a result of these processes. Few of the other advanced industrial countries appear to be in danger of disintegrating or disappearing entirely; yet this is a real possibility for Canada.

The fact that Canada is a political "nation" containing more than one sociological nation is well-known and has often been viewed as a source of potential disintegration. But, while this is an important factor in the Canadian experience, the tensions associated with these cleavages have proved capable of being contained within the political arrangements constructed in 1867. The margin by which this has been achieved, however, has become very narrow, as the 1995 Québec referendum shows all too clearly.

The question now is whether these arrangements can withstand the predominantly economic pressures flowing from a "globalized" international political economy that has been shaped by neo-liberalism. Both structural and ideological pressures challenge the central role of the state in modern societies. Given Canada's fragile national identity, the result of linguistic and community cleavages, the state's nation-building role has been more important than in most comparable societies. Consequently the challenge to its central role threatens to melt the glue that has served to bond together the disparate entities.

The state played an intimate role in founding and nurturing the Canadian polity. Canada has been tellingly described as a "political nationality" (Smiley 1967). A good deal of the state's early role was concerned with promoting capital accumulation in a staples economy; but central to this project was an association with nation-building through a series of "national policies." The first of these, initiated by John A. Macdonald, was predominantly economic in orientation; the second, influenced by Keynes's ideas, included both economic accumulation and social legitimation. The component of social legitimation was largely an attempt to regulate class conflicts that had intensified during the Second World War. It was also, because it came to incorporate regional policy as well, an attempt to respond to cleavages based on territory and community. Canada's Second National Policy, involving state activism in both the economic and social dimensions, extended the "statist legacy" that had been established almost from the country's inception. This legacy forms a distinct part of the Canadian identity, especially in comparison to the United States.

Since the mid-1970s, economic difficulties everywhere and the development of neo-liberal opposition to the interventionist state have led to an assault upon the state's role in both economic and social spheres. Canada experienced an interregnum between roughly 1975 and 1984 in which advocates of enhanced state interventionism joined but ultimately lost a political battle with the pro-market neo-liberals. Since 1984 the record of the Mulroney and Chrétien governments has consistently expressed the ideology of neo-liberalism, modified occasionally by electorally-induced trimming. This has been apparent, as we have seen, in the application of neo-liberal thinking to various spheres of government activity—the erosion of the components of public policy character-

istic of the Keynesian era: abandoning full employment, deactivating government, cutting social provision, deregulation and privatization, restriction of trade
union rights, and so on.

The Mulroney government made efforts to take advantage of the "openness"
of Canada's constitutional arrangements, largely the result of territorial and
national cleavages, to constitutionalize neo-liberal principles concerning the
respective spheres of governments and markets. The apparent failure of these
efforts may be less of a setback to the neo-liberal project than appearances
suggest, because much the same ends may prove to have been achieved by ad hoc
quasi-constitutional measures adopted by the Chrétien government. More importantly, they may also have been indirectly enacted by the free-trade agreements of the late 1980s and early 1990s.

The policy conclusions of neo-liberalism are strikingly reminiscent of
nineteenth-century liberalism: a small state—though in certain narrowly-defined
areas, a strong one too—is essential to maximize freedom, not least for corporations. Classical liberalism was the ideology of the "age of capital" in the
nineteenth century. A confined state posture enhances the role of markets in the
economy and thus enhances the role of individual choice, competition, and
freedom, and stresses the role of individual or private responsibility in the social
area. One of the assets held by neo-liberal politicians in other countries was their
ability to combine appeals to the free market *and* to the strong state. They tied the
idea of the strong state to nationalism, often through military policy. Thus neo-
liberalism and a version of nationalism went hand-in-hand, each drawing
sustenance from the other. Canada had difficulty pursuing this strategy because
as a secondary power it tends to play a loyal supporting role to U.S. foreign policy
initiatives. To say the least this sends mixed messages and cannot trigger the
proper identification of neo-liberal government with a sense of nation, as seen in
Britain and the United States. Similarly, the impact of Canada's binational or
trinational composition has made the appeal to nationalism an awkward construction for Canadian neo-liberalism. In this country nationalist symbols have
been most readily manipulated by interventionist governments engaged in the
simultaneous orchestration of tangible benefits for classes, regions, or communities. For a government supervising the reduction or dismantling of those same
tangible benefits and negotiating an increasingly subordinate relationship with
the United States, the opportunities for playing the nationalist card were few.

In Canadian politics, with its statist legacy and, later, the expanded state role
implied by even the tepid adoption of the Keynesian paradigm, public policy
initiatives had eased class, community, and regional tensions. Not surprisingly,
the neo-liberal assault on the Keynesian formula had the effect of increasing
social tensions. The line-up of interest groups waiting to contest an increasing
number of policy issues has come to resemble a class-politics model of policy-
making. Yet this development has not spilled over into party politics, which has
become increasingly fragmented on regional rather than class lines. In the 1997

election the great majority of the Canadian electorate supported regionally-divisive yet programmatically-neo-liberal parties even as opinion polls continued to show attachment to many of the policies and programs established in the Keynesian era. In this situation opposition to neo-liberalism has largely been ineffective. The reduction of social rights in Canada has therefore occurred without major political crisis over that issue. However, the degree to which social rights had become a source of *national* identity, no doubt more important in this country because other sources of national identification were unavailable, or divisive, may have contributed to the increasing fragmentation on regional lines.

Neo-liberal ideas have had their impact in a number of policy areas. Under Chrétien the process of erosion initiated by Mulroney has accelerated and many elements of the Keynesian welfare state, for instance the unemployment insurance system, have been transformed radically. Neo-liberal initiatives encountered considerable resistance: from Canadian political culture and attitudes, which in many respects continue to favour collectivist or statist solutions to problems; from the makeup of the federal system itself, which served to slow the construction of the welfare state and may, in turn, be slowing its destruction; and from the mobilization of class and other interests in defence of particular programs. But despite this considerable opposition, the neo-liberal agenda has largely been implemented. In macroeconomic policy the full-employment commitment is long gone, high interest rates and tax changes have served to redistribute income in an upward direction, and the successful ideological crusade to define the deficit as the leading economic problem has had a deadening effect on any proposals for increased state activity. All of this was accompanied by cautious moves towards deregulation and privatization of the Canadian economy. But the caution was in effect restricted to domestic politics—when the anticipated impact of the free-trade agreements is factored into the equation the neo-liberal record becomes much more radical.

The developments in macroeconomic policy found their parallels in other policy areas. In social policy the Mulroney and Chrétien governments terminated some universal programs and made other programs subject to incremental erosion. They followed the same pattern in the cultural, labour-market, and regional development areas, where restraint and retrenchment best describe its activities. In industrial relations too the extension of collective bargaining rights to trade unions was subject to restriction and erosion.

Even in areas where less evidence of transient ideological impulses like neo-liberalism might be expected there has been a consistent effort to shape the polity into a favoured mould. Canada's constitutional arrangements have been in flux largely because of national and territorial cleavages; and as an agenda item the constitution has been driven by the traditional issues of relations between French and English, among regions, and, increasingly, between aboriginal peoples and more recent settlers. Even in this area neo-liberal ideology has strongly influenced developments.

There was clear evidence of a neo-liberal approach to constitutional questions in the federal government's proposals of September 1991. Indeed, this initiative was an attempt to make neo-liberal policy changes permanent by entrenching them in the constitution itself. The groundwork for these proposals, which involved adjusting the powers of the provincial and federal governments and subordinating both levels to market forces, was laid by the Macdonald Commission and reinforced, as with so much else in the neo-liberal agenda, by support and pressure from the business community. Restructuring Canada's political institutions was explicitly linked, in business and government rhetoric, to economic restructuring and the imperative to become competitive in the new global economy. Much of the neo-liberal constitutional agenda was gutted in the run-up to the Charlottetown Accord, and the defeat of the accord in the October 1992 referendum simply confirmed the defeat of the government's original proposals. The combination of the institutional obstacle of the federal system and the stubborn resistance of Canadian political culture to the pure-market vision enthusiastically promoted by the federal government turned out to be too much for the neo-liberal constitutional agenda. That victory proved to have been a Pyrrhic one: the imposition of the discipline of market forces on governments was the central feature of the Mulroney administration's trade agreements. Thus, if the constitution did not serve to entrench neo-liberal policies, the same end was achieved through the vehicle of international treaty obligations. Should the current negotiations on a Multilateral Agreement on Investment (MAI) come to fruition the restrictions on the role of the state will be still more encompassing. Other aspects of the neo-liberal constitutional agenda have been implemented administratively under the Chrétien government.

Although Canada's statist legacy had not historically prevented an advanced degree of economic integration between Canada and the United States—a situation that amounted to economic dependency—the free-trade agreements represented a dramatic departure in Canadian public policy. This is because Canadian governments had always before retained considerable theoretical freedom to modify the terms of Canada's dependency. If they did not always make maximum use of their freedom, there were still at least occasions for exercising that freedom. The most recent and most dramatic example of this was the policies of the 1980–84 Trudeau government. Although that effort was not successful, this was largely because circumstances became highly and unexpectedly adverse when falling energy prices undercut the logic of the policy. Still, the episode stands as an example of how a government can intervene to modify the relationship with the United States and multinational capital. Under the terms of the free-trade agreements such initiatives, and much lesser ones, will be beyond the capacity of Canadian governments. The trade agreements serve as an economic constitution for Canada. They impose major restrictions on governments and give significant rights to corporations. In their pronouncements on the de facto role of governments they realize the constitutional goals of neo-liberalism.

There seems little doubt that the effect of the policy package implemented by the Mulroney government and continued by its Liberal successor have seriously undermined the foundations of Canadian nationhood. Canada is a political nationality, and the state and its policies have played a key role in maintaining it. The chief goal of neo-liberalism is to reduce the state's role as drastically as politics permit and to replace the state with the dominance of markets and private enterprise. This dominance removes the prop that has sustained the Canadian nation. The other props that maintain other nations— common ethnicity, language, history, ideology—are not available in Canada. Thus the logic of neo-liberalism—if its prescribed changes prove permanent— leads to the dismantling of the nation. Whether this will transpire in the formal sense, or how soon, depends upon the interplay of domestic political forces and international structural pressures. What is certain is that the legacy of neo-liberalism, and particularly the trade agreements negotiated by the Mulroney government, will make it very difficult for subsequent governments to restore Canada's traditional statism, or even maintain existing state initiatives. At the provincial level the effect of federal neo-liberal policies, especially cuts to transfer grants, has moved the governments, even social democratic ones, onto a decidedly right-wing policy course of deficit reduction.

Neo-liberal thinking in Canada may not have captured the hearts and minds of the populace, but popular opposition to it has been unable to crystallize around any viable political vehicle. Neo-liberalism remains the preferred approach of powerful interests—this means, especially, Canada's business community. The conversion of Canada's business community to neo-liberal principles has been well-documented (Ornstein 1986; Langille 1987; Williams 1989; Ernst 1992). There seems little doubt that the representations of business played a role in bringing the state elite to similar conclusions. On the odd occasion where the business sector's political allies seemed as though they might be unable to deliver the goods, as in the free-trade election of 1988, business intervened directly and massively to save its agenda (Watkins 1992:113). Given the business sector's structural power, international links, control over most of the means of ideological production, and ties to the major political parties, its support for neo-liberalism can only act as a powerful deterrent to any future government that might wish to deviate from that agenda. On current evidence no such government is likely. One of the arguments marshalled by business spokespersons in defence of its program is that structural factors such as globalization make it necessary to take apart the Keynesian state and perhaps the nation-state itself. The bottom line for this point of view seems to be that while governments continue to be organized on a territorial basis and to express national values and priorities, "markets have become global, regional and local, i.e., everything but national" (Hart 1993:5). Because, for true believers, markets reflect consumer sovereignty, any diminution of democracy or the ability of people to make choices through their governments is only apparent. For critics, however, it seems remarkable to "espouse choice at the microeconomic level but want to hinder it at the societal level" (Grinspun 1993:18). And, as we saw in Chapter 8, the free-trade agreements are precisely about restricting or eliminating choice at the societal level.

The perception that choices do and ought to remain possible has fueled the formation of an impressive coalition of labour and social action groups. The coalition has rallied in opposition to the free-trade agreements and in defence of many of the ingredients of Canada's national identity that have been under attack in the neo-liberal era. The Action Canada Network, for example, is composed of almost fifty organizations—labour, cultural, women's, seniors', farmers', and social action groups (see Clarke 1992); the Council of Canadians has roughly 70,000 members; and there is an impressive range of social movement activity. Just as business is at the centre of those favouring the neo-liberal version of globalization, so too is labour at the centre of those proposing an alternative. Since at least the 1988 election the interest group scene has been dominated by class politics. Although the policy victories have gone to business and its allies, those sectors have failed to implant their arguments completely in the consciousness of the Canadian public, and many of the neo-liberal initiatives are deeply unpopular.

The policy victories of the neo-liberals have been important ones—and none more so than the free-trade agreements. Their significance has little to do with free trade *per se*. Rather, their importance lies in the limitations they place on future governments and the future democratic majorities that stand behind them:

> In the past when things went wrong, governments could try new policies. The tragedy now is that governments' ability to act appropriately when the economy deteriorates has been abdicated by almost total reliance on market forces, a turn of events that reflects not simply the political whim of the current government, but that has been codified in international trade law. (Cohen 1992:15)

Any opportunities for reversing the neo-liberal trend that might be permitted by Canada's political constitution have now been obstructed by our economic constitution—the market principles "codified" in the free-trade agreements. The effect is surely to make the political playing field a lot less level than it was in the past. Having achieved political dominance in the 1980s the Mulroney government and its business supporters sought to insulate their achievements from future modification by the democratic process.

This constitutes the political legacy of Canadian neo-liberalism, and it is one that it will be extraordinarily difficult to escape. But the stakes are high. For the logic of neo-liberalism has served to dismantle Canada. Unless ways are found to roll back at least part of that legacy, dissolution into smaller units or integration into a continental state under U.S. hegemony will eventually occur. It is difficult to imagine that either of these eventualities would increase the sum of human happiness. Neither represents a preferable alternative to the imperfect but nevertheless solid historical achievements of the Canadian people and their state. The results of the 1997 election indicate that the process of dismantling a nation is likely to continue. Avoiding such a regression remains the challenge of Canadian politics.

Bibliography

Abele, Frances (ed.). 1991. *How Ottawa Spends 1991–92: The Politics of Fragmentation.* Ottawa: Carleton University Press.

———— (ed.). 1992a. *How Ottawa Spends: The Politics of Competitiveness 1992–93.* Ottawa: Carleton University Press.

————. 1992b. "The Politics of Competitiveness." In Abele 1992a.

Aitken, H.G.J. 1967. "Defensive Expansionism: The State and Economic Growth in Canada." In Easterbrook and Watkins 1967.

Albo, Gregory. 1994. "'Competitive Austerity' and the Impasse of Capitalist Employment Policy." In Miliband and Panitch 1994.

Albo, Gregory, and Jane Jenson. 1997. "Remapping Canada: The State in the Era of Globalization." In Clement 1997.

Allen, Robert C., and Gideon Rosenbluth (eds.). 1992. *False Promises: The Failure of Conservative Economics.* Vancouver: New Star.

Anderson, A.D.M. 1995. *Seeking Common Ground: Canada-U.S. Trade Dispute Settlement Policies in the Nineties.* Boulder: Westview.

Amin, Samir. 1976. *Unequal Development: An Essay on the Social Formations of Peripheral Capitalism.* New York: Monthly Review.

Armit, Amerita, and Jacques Bourgeault (eds.). 1996. *Hard Choices or No Choices: Assessing Program Review.* Toronto: Institute of Public Administration of Canada.

Appel Molot, Maureen. 1990. "State Enterprise in Canada: Nationalization vs. Privatization." In Gagnon and Bickerton 1990.

Argue, Robert, Charlene Gannagé, and David Livingstone (eds.). 1987. *Working People and Hard Times.* Toronto: Garamond.

Axworthy, Lloyd. 1994a. *Creating Opportunity . . . Through Social Security Reform.* Notes for an Address. Mimeo. Ottawa.

————. 1994b. *Proposed Changes to the Unemployment Insurance System.* Ottawa: HRDC.

Axworthy, Thomas S., and Pierre Elliot Trudeau. 1992a. *Towards a Just Society.* Toronto: Penguin.

————. 1992b. "The Tempest Bursting: Canada in 1992." In Axworthy and Trudeau 1992a.

Bakan, Joel. 1992. "Against Constitutional Property Rights." In Cameron and Smith 1992.

Bakker, Isabella. 1990. "The Size and Scope of Government: Robin Hood Sent Packing?" In Whittington and Williams 1990.

————. 1991. "Canada's Social Wage in an Open Economy, 1970–1983." In Drache and

Gertler 1991a.

Bakvis, Herman. 1997. "Federalism, New Public Management, and Labour Market Development." In Fafard and Brown 1997.

Banting, Keith G. 1982. *The Welfare State and Canadian Federalism*. Montreal and Kingston: McGill-Queen's University Press.

——— (ed.). 1986a. *State and Society: Canada in Comparative Perspective*. Toronto: University of Toronto Press.

———. 1986b. "Images of the Modern State: An Introduction." In Banting 1986a.

———. 1987. *The Welfare State and Canadian Federalism*. Second edition. Montreal and Kingston: McGill-Queen's University Press.

———. 1988. "Federalism, Social Reform and the Spending Power." *Canadian Public Policy*, 14 (Supplement).

———. 1992. "If Quebec Separates: Restructuring Northern North America." In Weaver 1992.

———. 1996. "Social Policy." In Doern et al. 1996a.

Banting, Keith, George Hoberg, and Richard Simeon (eds.). 1997. *Degrees of Freedom: Canada and the United States in a Changing World*. Montreal: McGill-Queen's University Press.

Barlow, Maude. 1991. *Parcel of Rogues: How Free Trade is Failing Canada*. Toronto: Key Porter.

———. 1992a. "NAFTA: 'A Corporate Charter of Rights and Freedoms.'" *The Toronto Star*, August 13, A23.

———. 1992b. "Assessing the Price of Free Trade Part II." *The Globe and Mail*, June 29.

———. 1996. "Why is Canada still a signatory to NAFTA?" *The Globe and Mail*, March 4.

Barlow, Maude, and Bruce Campbell. 1991. *Take Back the Nation*. Toronto: Key Porter.

Barry, Norman. 1990. *Welfare*. Minneapolis: University of Minnesota Press.

Barry, T. 1995. *Zapata's Revenge: Free Trade and the Farm Crisis in Mexico*. Boston: South End Press.

Bartlett, Bruce R. 1982. *Reaganomics: Supply-Side Economics in Action*. New York: Quill.

Battle, Ken, and Sherri Torjman. 1996. "Desperately Seeking Substance: A Commentary on the Social Security Review." In Pulkingham and Ternowetsky 1996.

Baxter-Moore, N.J. 1991. "Ideology or Pragmatism? The Politics and Management of the Mulroney Government's Privatization Program." Paper presented at the Annual Conference of the British Association for Canadian Studies, University of Nottingham, April 12–14.

Beaudoin, Gérald A., and Dorothy Dobbie. 1992. *Report of the Special Joint Committee on a Renewed Canada*. Ottawa: Minister of Supply and Services.

Behiels, Michael D. (ed.). 1989. *The Meech Lake Primer: Conflicting Views on the 1987 Constitutional Accord*. Ottawa: University of Ottawa Press.

Bell, Daniel, and Irving Kristol (eds.). 1981. *The Crisis in Economic Theory*. New York: Basic.

Bell, Joel. 1992. "Canadian Industrial Policy in a Changing World." In Axworthy and Trudeau 1992a.

Bellon, Bertrand, and Jorge Niosi. 1988. *The Decline of the American Economy*. Montreal: Black Rose.

Bertram, G.W. 1967. "Economic Growth in Canadian Industry, 1870–1915: The Staple

Model." In Easterbrook and Watkins 1967.

Betcherman, Gordon, and Graham S. Lowe. 1997. *The Future of Work in Canada: A Synthesis Report.* Ottawa: Canadian Policy Research Networks.

Bickerton, James. 1994. "Regional Development Policy and the Labour Market in Atlantic Canada." In Johnson, McBride and Smith 1994.

Blais, André, and François Vaillancourt. 1986. "The Federal Corporate Income Tax: Tax Expenditures and Tax Discrimination." *Canadian Tax Journal* 34, 4.

Bleckner, Robert A. 1987. "International Competition, Economic Growth, and the Political Economy of the U.S. Trade Deficit." In Cherry et al. 1987.

Block, Fred, Richard A. Cloward, Barbara Ehrenreich, and Frances Fox Piven (eds.). 1987. *The Mean Season: The Attack on the Welfare State.* New York: Pantheon.

Bluestone, Barry, and Bennett Harrison. 1982. *The Deindustrialization of America.* New York: Basic.

Boadway, Robin. 1992. *The Constitutional Division of Powers: An Economic Perspective.* Ottawa: Economic Council of Canada.

Bogdanor, Vernon. 1983. "Of Lions and Ostriches: The Meaning of Mrs. Thatcher's Victory." *Encounter*, September/October.

Bolaria, B. Singh (ed.). 1991. *Social Issues and Contradictions in Canadian Society.* Toronto: Harcourt Brace Jovanovich.

Bovard, James. 1992. "Pandering to Protectionists Clogging Free-Trade Arteries." *The Globe and Mail*, August 1.

Bowker, Marjorie. 1990. *The Meech Lake Accord.* Hull, Que.: Voyageur.

Bradford, Neil. 1994. *Creation and Constraint: Economic Ideas and Politics in Canada.* Unpublished PhD dissertation, Department of Political Science, Carleton University, Ottawa.

Braga, Carlos Alberto Primo. 1992. "NAFTA and the Rest of the World." In Lustig, Bosworth and Lawrence 1992.

Britton, John, and James Gilmour. 1978. *The Weakest Link.* Ottawa: Science Council of Canada.

Brodie, Janine. 1989. "The 'Free Trade' Election." *Studies in Political Economy: A Socialist Review* 28 (Spring).

———. 1990. *The Political Economy of Canadian Regionalism.* Toronto: Harcourt Brace Jovanovich.

Brodie, Janine, and Jane Jenson. 1988. *Crisis, Challenge and Change: Party and Class in Canada Revisited.* Ottawa: Carleton University Press.

Bronfenbrenner, Kate. 1997. "The Effects of Plant Closing or Threat of Plant Closing on the Right of Workers to Organize." Submitted to the Labor Secretariat of the North American Commission for Labor Cooperation. Available from Labor-Rap@csf.colorado.edu.

Brooks, Neil. 1990. *Paying for Civilized Society: The Need for Fair and Responsible Tax Reform.* Ottawa: Canadian Centre for Policy Alternatives.

Brooks, Stephen. 1996. "Federal–Provincial Relations: The Decline of the New Centralism." In Johnson and Stritch 1996a.

Brooks, Stephen, and Andrew Stritch. 1991. *Business and Government in Canada.* Scarborough, Ont.: Prentice-Hall Canada.

Brunell, Dorval, and Christian Deblock. 1992. "Economic Blocs and the Challenge of the North American Free Trade Agreement." In Randall et al. 1992.

Buchanan, James M., and Richard E. Wagner. 1977. *Democracy in Deficit: The Political*

Legacy of Lord Keynes. New York: Academic Press.

Buchholz, Todd G. 1989. *New Ideas From Dead Economists: An Introduction to Modern Economic Thought.* New York: Plume.

Business Council on National Issues (BCNI). 1983. *National Priorities.* Ottawa: BCNI.

———. 1985. "Canadian Trade, Competitiveness and Sovereignty: The Prospect of New Trade Agreements with the United States." Mimeo. Ottawa.

———. 1987a. "The Canada-United States Free Trade Agreement." Submission to the House Standing Committee on External Affairs and International Trade. November 5. Ottawa: BCNI.

———. 1987b. "The Draft Canada–United States Free Trade Agreement." Mimeo. Toronto: BCNI.

———. 1988. "The Canada–United States Free Trade Agreement." Submission to the Ontario Select Committee on Economic Affairs. January 28. Toronto: BCNI.

———. 1990a. *The Meech Lake Accord and Constitutional Renewal.* Ottawa: BCNI.

———. 1990b. *Canada's Constitutional Options.* Ottawa: BCNI.

———. 1990c. "Canada–Mexico–United States Free Trade: A Canadian Business Perspective." Submission to the House of Commons Standing Committee on External Affairs and International Trade. September 27. Ottawa: BCNI.

———. 1991. *Canada and the 21st Century: Towards a More Effective Federalism and a Stronger Economy.* Ottawa: BCNI.

———. 1992. *Canada's Economic Union.* Ottawa: BCNI.

Cairns, Alan C. 1991. *Disruptions: Constitutional Struggles, from the Charter to Meech Lake.* Toronto: McClelland and Stewart.

———. 1995. *Reconfigurations: Canadian Citizenship and Constitutional Change.* Toronto: McClelland and Stewart.

Cameron, Duncan. 1992. "Introduction." In Cameron and Smith 1992.

———. 1993. "One America." *The Canadian Forum,* January-February.

Cameron, Duncan, and Miriam Smith (eds.). 1992. *Constitutional Politics: The Canadian Forum Book on the Federal Constitutional Proposals.* Toronto: James Lorimer.

Cameron, Duncan, and Mel Watkins (eds.). 1993. *Canada Under Free Trade.* Toronto: James Lorimer.

Cameron, Max. 1993. "Developing a Bloc Mentality." *The Canadian Forum,* January-February.

Cameron, Maxwell A., Lorraine Eden, and Maureen Appel Molot. 1992. "North American Free Trade: Co-operation and Conflict in Canada–Mexico Relations." In Hampson and Maule 1992.

Campbell, Murray. 1977. "Nationalism dips at dawn of global era" *The Globe and Mail,* July 1.

Campbell, Robert M. 1987. *Grand Illusions: The Politics of the Keynesian Experience in Canada, 1945–75.* Peterborough, Ont.: Broadview Press.

———. 1991. *The Full-Employment Objective in Canada, 1945–85.* Ottawa: Economic Council of Canada.

Canada. 1945. Department of Reconstruction. *Employment and Income with Special Reference to the Initial Period of Reconstruction.* Ottawa: Queen's Printer.

———. 1979. Task Force on Canadian Unity. *A Future Together.* Ottawa: Minister of Supply and Services.

———. 1981. Task Force on Unemployment Insurance. *Unemployment Insurance in the 1980s.* Ottawa: Employment and Immigration Canada.

———. 1985a. *Report: Royal Commission on the Economic Union and Development Prospects for Canada.* 3 vols. Ottawa: Minister of Supply and Services.

———. 1985b. Department of Finance. *Account of the Cost of Selective Tax Measures.* Ottawa: Department of Finance.

———. 1991a. *Shaping Canada's Future Together: Proposals.* Ottawa: Minister of Supply and Services.

———. 1991b. *Canadian Federalism and Economic Union: Partnership for Prosperity.* Ottawa: Minister of Supply and Services.

———. 1992a. *Renewal of Canada Conferences, Compendium of Reports: Economic Union Conference.* Ottawa: Minister of Supply and Services.

———. 1992b. *Renewal of Canada Conferences, Compendium of Reports: Institutional Reform Conference.* Ottawa: Minister of Supply and Services.

———. 1992c. *Renewal of Canada Conferences, Compendium of Reports: Identity, Rights and Values Conference.* Ottawa: Minister of Supply and Services.

———. 1992d. *Renewal of Canada Conferences, Compendium of Reports: Division of Powers Conference.* Ottawa: Minister of Supply and Services.

———. 1992e. "Canadian Objectives Met in North American Free Trade Agreement." *News Release* 165 (August 12). Ottawa: Minister of Supply and Services.

———. 1992f. *The Global Trade Challenge.* Special Tabloid Supplement. Ottawa: Minister of Supply and Services.

———. 1994. *Agenda: Jobs and Growth, Improving Social Security in Canada: A Discussion Paper.* Ottawa: HRDC.

Canadian Centre for Policy Alternatives (CCPA). 1996. *Monitor,* June. Ottawa: CCPA.

Canadian Centre for Policy Alternatives (CCPA). 1992. *Which Way For the Americas: Analysis of NAFTA Proposals and the Impact on Canada.* Ottawa: CCPA.

Canadian Council on Social Development. 1990. *Canada's Social Programs Are in Trouble.* Ottawa: CCSD.

Canadian Institute for Economic Policy. 1985. "The Pitfalls of Free Trade." In Drache and Cameron 1985a.

Carmichael, E.A., W. Dobson, and R.G. Lipsey. 1980. "The Macdonald Report: Signpost or Shopping Basket." *Canadian Public Policy* 12 (Supplement).

Carroll, William K. 1986. *Corporate Power and Canadian Capitalism.* Vancouver: University of British Columbia Press.

——— (ed.). 1997. *Organizing Dissent: Contemporary Social Movements in Theory and Practice.* Second edition. Toronto: Garamond.

Chandler, Marsha A., and William A. Chandler. 1979. *Public Policy and Provincial Politics.* Toronto: McGraw-Hill Ryerson.

Chernomas, Bob. 1983. "Keynesianism, Monetarism and Post-Keynesian Policy: A Marxist Analysis." *Studies in Political Economy: A Socialist Review* 10.

Cherry, R.C. D'Onofrio, C. Kurdas, T. Michl, F. Moseley, and M. Naples (eds.). 1987. *The Imperiled Economy: Macroeconomics from a Left Perspective.* New York: The Union for Radical Political Economics (URPE).

Chodos, Robert, Rae Murphy, and Eric Hamovitch. 1993. *Canada and the Global Economy: Alternatives to the Corporate Strategy for Globalization.* Toronto: James Lormier.

Chorney, Harold. 1988. *Sound Finance and Other Delusions: Deficit and Debt Management in the Age of Neo-Liberal Economics.* Montreal: Concordia University.

Chorney, Harold, and Andrew Molloy. 1988. "The Myth of Tax Reform: The Mulroney

Government's Tax Changes." In Gollner and Salée 1988.

Chrétien, Jean. 1980. *Securing the Economic Union in the Constitution*. Ottawa: Minister of Supply and Services.

Clarke, Tony. 1997. *Silent Coup: Confronting the Big Business Takeover of Canada*. Toronto: Canadian Centre for Policy Alternatives and James Lorimer.

———. 1992. "Fighting Free Trade, Canadian Style." In Sinclair 1992.

Clarkson, Stephen. 1988. "The Canada–United States Trade Commission: The Political Implications of CUSTER." In Gold and Leyton-Brown 1988.

———. 1991. "Disjunctions: Free Trade and the Paradox of Canadian Development." In Drache and Gertler 1991a.

———. 1992. "Trade Treaties and Constitution Making: Canada's Experience as a Post-National State." Paper presented at Universidad Nacional Autonoma de Mexico. November.

———. 1993. "Constitutionalizing the Canadian–American Relationship." In Cameron and Watkins 1993.

———. 1996. "Continentalism." *The Canadian Encyclopedia Plus*. Toronto: McClelland and Stewart.

Clement, Wallace. 1975. *The Canadian Corporate Elite: An Analysis of Economic Power*. Toronto: McClelland and Stewart.

——— (ed.). 1997. *Understanding Canada: Building on the New Canadian Political Economy*. Montreal: McGill-Queen's University Press.

Clement, Wallace, and Glen Williams. 1997. "Resources and Manufacturing in Canada's Political Economy." In Clement 1997.

Clement, W., and D. Drache (eds.). 1978. *A Practical Guide to Canadian Political Economy*. Toronto: James Lorimer.

Coburn, D. (ed.). 1987. *Health and Canadian Society*. Second edition. Markham: Fitzhenry and Whiteside.

Cohen, Marjorie Griffin. 1992. "The Lunacy of Free Trade." In Sinclair 1992.

Cooper, Barry, Allan Kornberg, and William Mishler (eds.). 1988a. *The Resurgence of Conservatism in Anglo-American Democracies*. Durham, N.C.: Duke University Press.

———. 1988b. "The Resurgence of Conservatism in Britain, Canada and the United States: An Overview." In Cooper, Kornberg and Mishler 1988a.

Copeland, Brian R. 1992. "Regional Trading Blocs and Canadian Trade Policy." In Allen and Rosenbluth 1992.

Corcoran, Terence. 1992. "How They Eviscerated the Common Market." *The Globe and Mail*, July 10, B2.

Corry, J.A. 1939. *The Growth of Government Activities Since Confederation*. Ottawa: Report of the Royal Commission on Dominion–Provincial Relations.

Courchene, Thomas J. 1986. *Economic Management and the Division of Powers*. Studies of the Royal Commission on the Economic Union and Development Prospects for Canada, Vol. 67. Toronto: University of Toronto Press.

———. 1988a. "The Canada–U.S. Free Trade Agreement: Selected Political and Economic Perspectives." In Gold and Leyton-Brown 1988.

———. 1988b. "Meech Lake and Socio-Economic Policy." *Canadian Public Policy* 14 (Supplement).

———. 1992. "What Does It Mean?" *The Globe and Mail*, October 27.

———. 1995. *Celebrating Flexibility: An Interpretive Essay on the Evolution of Cana-*

dian Federalism. Toronto: C.D. Howe Institute.

——. 1996. *Access: A Convention on the Canadian Economic and Social Systems*. Toronto: Ministry of Intergovernmental Affairs.

Coyne, Deborah. 1989. "The Meech Lake Accord and the Spending Power Proposals: Fundamentally Flawed." In Behiels 1989.

Crane, David (ed.). 1981a. *Beyond the Monetarists: Post-Keynesian Alternatives to Rampant Inflation, Low Growth and High Employment*. Toronto: James Lorimer.

——. 1981b. "Stagflation and Economic Crisis." In Crane 1981a.

——. 1992a. "Economic Ties with U.S. Will Have Political Impact." *The Toronto Star*, July 16.

——. 1992b. "Mexico Will Loom Large for Us with or without Trade Pact." *The Toronto Star*, August 19.

Cross, Michael S., and Gregory S. Kealey (eds.). 1984. *Modern Canada 1930–1980s*. Toronto: McClelland and Stewart.

Crozier, Michel, Samuel P. Huntington, and Joji Watanuki. 1975. *The Crisis of Democracy: Report on the Governability of Democracies to the Trilateral Commission*. New York: New York University Press.

d'Aquino, Thomas, and John Bulloch. 1986. "The Canada–United States Trade Initiative." Mimeo. June 26. Ottawa: Business Council on National Issues and the Canadian Federation of Independent Business.

Diebel, Linda. 1993. "How Trade Deals Work for U.S. Corporations: The Case of Patents and Pharmaceutical Drugs." In Cameron and Watkins 1993.

Dillon, John. 1993a. "Intellectual Property." *The Canadian Forum*, January-February.

——. 1993b. "The Enterprise for the Americas." In Cameron and Watkins 1993.

Djao, A.W. 1983. *Inequality and Social Policy: The Sociology of Welfare*. Toronto: John Wiley and Sons.

Dobbin, Murray. 1991. *Preston Manning and the Reform Party*. Toronto: James Lorimer.

Doern, G. Bruce (ed.). 1981. *How Ottawa Spends Your Tax Dollars: Federal Priorities 1981*. Toronto: James Lorimer.

—— (ed.). 1982. *How Ottawa Spends*. Toronto: Methuen.

——, research co-ordinator. 1986. *The Politics of Economic Policy*. Royal Commission on the Economic Union and Development Prospects for Canada, Vol. 40. Toronto: University of Toronto Press.

Doern, G. Bruce, Allan M. Maslove, and Michael J. Prince. 1988. *Public Budgeting in Canada: Politics, Economics and Management*. Ottawa: Carleton University Press.

Doern, G. Bruce, and Bryne B. Purchase (eds.). 1991a. *Canada at Risk? Canadian Public Policy in the 1990's*. Toronto: C.D. Howe Institute.

——. 1991b. "Whither Ottawa?" In Doern and Purchase 1991a.

Doern, G. Bruce, and Richard W. Phidd. 1992. *Canadian Public Policy: Ideas, Structure, Process*. Second edition. Scarborough, Ont.: Nelson Canada.

Doern, G. Bruce, and Brian W. Tomlin. 1991. *Faith and Fear: The Free Trade Story*. Toronto: Stoddart.

Doern, G. Bruce, Leslie A. Pal, and Brian W. Tomlin (eds.). 1996a. *Border Crossings: The Internationalization of Canadian Public Policy*. Toronto: Oxford University Press.

Doern, G. Bruce, Leslie A. Pal, and Brian W. Tomlin. 1996b. "The Internationalization of Canadian Public Policy." In Doern et al. 1996a.

Donner, Arthur W., and Douglas D. Peters. 1979. *The Monetarist Counter-Revolution: A Critique of Canadian Monetary Policy 1975–1979*. Toronto: James Lorimer.

Drache, Daniel. 1978. "Rediscovering Canadian Political Economy." In Clement and Drache 1978.

———. 1982. "Harold Innis and Canadian Capitalist Development." *Canadian Journal of Political and Social Theory* 6 (1–2).

———. 1988. "The Mulroney–Reagan Accord: The Economics of Continental Power." In Gold and Leyton-Brown 1988.

——— (ed.). 1992. *Getting on Track: Social Democratic Strategies for Ontario.* Montreal and Kingston: McGill-Queen's University Press.

———. 1995. "The Eye of the Hurricane: Globalization and Social Security Reform." In Drache and Ranachan 1995.

Drache, Daniel, and Andrew Ranachan (eds.). 1995. *Warm Heart, Cold Country: Fiscal and Social Policy Reform in Canada.* Ottawa: Caledon Institute of Social Policy.

Drache, Daniel, and Duncan Cameron (eds.). 1985a. *The Other Macdonald Report.* Toronto: James Lorimer.

———. 1985b. "Introduction." In Drache and Cameron 1985a.

Drache, Daniel, and Meric S. Gertler (eds.). 1991a. *The New Era of Global Competition: State Policy and Market Power.* Montreal and Kingston: McGill-Queen's University Press.

———. 1991b. "Preface." In Drache and Gertler 1991a.

Drache, Daniel, and Harry Glasbeek. 1992. *The Changing Workplace: Reshaping Canada's Industrial Relations System.* Toronto: James Lorimer.

Drohan, Madelaine, and Edith Terry. 1992. "U.S. Trade Tactics Tarnish Canada's 'Gateway' Image." *The Globe and Mail*, July 27.

Dunk, Thomas, Stephen McBride, and Randle Nelsen. 1996. *The Training Trap: Ideology, Training and the Labour Market.* Halifax: Fernwood.

Dunsmuir, Mollie. 1990. *Mobility-Rights, The Economic Union and the Constitution.* Ottawa: Library of Parliament Research Branch.

Dupré, Stefan. 1989. "Section 106A and Federal–Provincial Fiscal Relations." In Behiels 1989.

Easterbrook, W.T., and Hugh G.J. Aitken. 1956. *Canadian Economic History.* Reprinted with corrections, 1963. Toronto: Macmillan.

Easterbrook, W.T., and M.H. Watkins (eds.). 1967. *Approaches to Canadian Economic History.* Toronto: McClelland and Stewart.

Economic Council of Canada. 1984a. *Steering the Course.* 21st Annual Review. Ottawa: Minister of Supply and Services.

———. 1984b. *Western Transition.* Ottawa: Minister of Supply and Services.

———. 1990. *Good Jobs, Bad Jobs: Employment in the Service Economy.* Ottawa: Minister of Supply and Services.

———. 1988. *Venturing Forth.* Ottawa: Minister of Supply and Services.

Economist, The. 1993. "The eleventh hour," December 4.

Ecumenical Coalition for Economic Justice. 1996. *Economic Justice Report* 7, 4 (December).

Eden, Lorraine, and Maureen Appel Molot. 1992. "The View from the Spokes: Canada and Mexico Face the United States." In Randall et al. 1992.

Eden, Lorraine, and Mareen Apple Molot. 1993. "Canada's National Policies: Reflections on 125 Years," *Canadian Public Policy* 19 (3).

Ehrenreich, Barbara. 1987. "The New Right Attack on Social Welfare." In Block et al. 1987.

Elliott, Larry. 1995. "New Initiatives on Jobs in Short Supply." *Manchester Guardian Weekly*, 25 June.

Employment and Immigration Canada. 1985. *The Canadian Jobs Strategy*. Ottawa: Employment and Immigration Canada.

Erickson, Lynda. 1995. "The October 1993 Election and the Canadian Party System." *Party Politics* 1(1).

Ernst, Alan. 1992. "From Liberal Continentalism to Neoconservatism: North American Free Trade and the Politics of the C.D. Howe Institute." *Studies in Political Economy: A Socialist Review* 39 (Autumn).

Esping-Andersen, Gosta. 1983. "After the Welfare State." *Public Welfare* (Winter).

———— ed. 1996. *Welfare States in Transition: National Adaptations in Global Economies*. London: Sage.

Evans, Bryan, and John Shields. Forthcoming. *Reinventing the Canadian State: Globalization, Governance and the Political Economy of Public Administrative Reform*. Halifax: Fernwood.

Evans, Bryan, Stephen McBride, and John Shields. 1997. "Globalization and the Challenge to National Governance: Canada and the New World Order." Unpublished paper, Ryerson Polytechnic University, Montreal.

Everett-Green, Robert. 1997. "Culture Talks Present New Risk" *Globe and Mail*, May 29.

Fafard, Patrick C. 1997. "Of Chess and Heart Attacks: The State of the Federation 1996." In Fafard and Brown 1997.

Fafard, Patrick C., and Douglas M. Brown (eds.). 1997. *Canada: The State of Federation 1996*. Kingston, Ont.: Institute of Intergovernmental Relations.

Fagan, Drew, and John Saunders. 1992. "Ottawa Says It Will Walk Out If NAFTA Deal Not Palatable." *The Globe and Mail*, July 16.

Fagan, Drew. 1993. "Tariffs must go by 1998, U.S. says," *The Globe and Mail*, December 18.

The Financial Post Outlook '88. 1987–88. "Report on the Nation." Winter.

Finkel, Alvin, Margaret Conrad with Veronica Strong-Boag. 1993. *History of the Canadian Peoples. Vol. 2. 1867 to the Present*. Toronto: Copp Clark Pitman.

Flora, Peter, and Arnold J. Heidenheimer (eds.). 1981. *The Development of Welfare States in Europe and North America*. New Brunswick, N.J.: Transaction.

Forget, Claude. 1986. *Report of the Commission of Inquiry on Unemployment Insurance*. Ottawa: Employment and Immigration Canada.

Fortin, Pierre. 1991. "Exclusive Focus on Zero Inflation: A Dangerous Proposal." *The Network*, November-December.

Fowke, V.C. 1967. "The National Policy—Old and New." In Easterbrook and Watkins 1967.

Frank, André Gunder. 1979. *Dependent Accumulation and Underdevelopment*. New York: Monthly Review Press.

Fraser, Graham. 1983. "Widening split along class lines revealed by proposed U.I. changes." *The Globe and Mail*, February 3.

Freeman, Richard B., and James L. Medoff. 1984. *What Do Unions Do?* New York: Basic.

Freeman, Alan. 1992a. "Business Blasé about NAFTA." *The Globe and Mail*, August 17.

————. 1992b. "Jobless Rate in Ontario Hits 9-Year High." *The Globe and Mail*, September 5.

Friedman, Milton. 1989. "Economists and Economic Policy." In McCullough 1989.

————. 1982. *Capitalism and Freedom*. Chicago: University of Chicago Press.

Fuller, Colleen. 1996. "Doctoring to NAFTA." *The Canadian Forum*, June.

Furlong, Kieran, and Douglas Moggach. 1990. "Efficiency, Competition and Full-Employment in the Canadian Free Trade Literature." *Studies in Political Economy: A Socialist Review* 33 (Autumn).

Fusfeld, Daniel R. 1990. *The Age of the Economist*. Sixth edition. Glenview, Ill.: Scott, Foresman.

Gagnon, Alain G. 1991. "The Dynamics of Federal Inter-governmental Relations: Delivery of Regional Development Programmes in Canada." *Regional Politics and Policy* 1(1).

——— (ed.). 1993. *Quebec: State and Society*. Second edition. Scarborough, Ont.: Nelson Canada.

Gagnon, Alain G., and James P. Bickerton (eds.). 1990. *Canadian Politics: An Introduction to the Discipline*. Peterborough, Ont.: Broadview Press.

Galipeau, Claude, and Andrew F. Johnson. 1990. "The Old Right, the New Right and the State: An Introduction." *Journal of History and Politics* 8.

Gamble, Andrew. 1988. *The Free Economy and the Strong State*. London: Macmillan.

Gibbins, Roger. 1985. *Conflict and Unity: An Introduction to Canadian Political Life*. Toronto: Methuen.

———. 1997. *Time Out: Assessing Incremental Strategies for Enhancing the Canadian Political Union*. Toronto: C.D. Howe Institute.

Gilder, George. 1981. *Wealth and Poverty*. Toronto: Bantam.

Gill, Stephen. 1992. "The Emerging World Order and European Change: The Political Economy of European Union." In Miliband and Panitch 1992.

Ginsburg, Helen. 1983. *Full Employment and Public Policy: The United States and Sweden*. Lexington, Mass.: Lexington.

The Globe and Mail. 1992. "Free-Trade Claims Challenged." October 16.

Gold, Marc, and David Leyton-Brown (eds.). 1988. *Trade-Offs on Free Trade: The Canada–U.S. Free Trade Agreement*. Toronto: Carswell.

Gollner, Andrew, and Daniel Salée (eds.). 1988. *Canada Under Mulroney: An End-of-Term Report*. Montreal: Véhicule Press.

Gonick, Cy. 1987. *The Great Economic Debate*. Toronto: James Lorimer.

Gonick, Cy, and Paul Phillips. 1996. *Labour Gains, Labour Pains: 50 Years of PC 1003*. Halifax: Fernwood.

Gough, Ian. 1981. *The Political Economy of the Welfare State*. London: Macmillan.

———. 1980. "Thatcherism and the Welfare State." *Marxism Today*, July.

Graham, Katherine A. (ed.). 1990. *How Ottawa Spends*. Ottawa: Carleton University Press.

Graham, Ron. 1986. *One-Eyed Kings*. Toronto: Collins.

Gramsci, Antonio. 1971. *Selections From the Prison Notebooks*. Quintin Hoare and Geoffrey Nowell (eds.). New York: International.

Granatstein, J.L., and Norman Hillmer. 1991. *For Better or for Worse: Canada and the United States to the 1990s*. Toronto: Copp Clark Pitman.

Grant, George. 1965. *Lament for a Nation*. Toronto: McClelland and Stewart.

Grayson, J. Paul (ed.). 1980. *Class, State, Ideology and Change: Marxist Perspectives on Canada*. Toronto: Holt, Rinehart and Winston.

Green, David G. 1987. *The New Right: The Counter Revolution in Political, Economic, and Social Thought*. Brighton, Sussex: Wheatsheaf.

Grinspun, Ricardo. 1993. "Do the FTA's Help Us Live a Better Life?" *Policy Options*,

January-February.

Grinspun, Ricardo, and Maxwell A. Cameron (eds.). 1993. *The Political Economy of North American Free Trade*. Montreal: McGill-Queen's University Press.

Gregg, Allan R. 1996. "Can Canada Survive?" *Maclean's*, December 25, 1995–January 1, 1996.

Grosscup, Beau. 1982. "The Neo-conservative State and the Politics of Terrorism." *New Political Science* (Spring).

Guest, Dennis. 1985. *The Emergence of Social Security in Canada*. Second edition. Vancouver: University of British Columbia Press.

———. 1987. "World War II and the Welfare State in Canada." In Moscovitch and Albert 1987.

Gwyn, Richard. 1995. *Nationalism Without Walls: The Unbearable Lightness of Being Canadian*. Toronto: McClelland and Stewart.

Haiven, Larry, Stephen McBride, and John Shields (eds.). 1991. *Regulating Labour: The State, Neo-Conservatism and Industrial Relations*. Toronto: Garamond.

Hall, Stuart, and Martin Jacques (eds). 1983. *The Politics of Thatcherism*. London: Lawrence and Wishart.

Hampson, Fred Osler, and Christopher J. Maule (eds.). 1992. *A New World Order? Canada Among Nations 1992–93*. Ottawa: Carleton University Press.

Hardin, H. 1974. *A Nation Unaware: The Canadian Economic Culture*. Vancouver: J.J. Douglas.

———. 1989. *The Privatization Putsch*. Halifax: Institute for Research on Public Policy.

Hardina, Donna. 1997. "Workfare in the U.S.: Empirically-Tested Programs or Ideological Quagmire?" In Shragge 1997.

Harrison, Bennett, and Barry Bluestone. 1988. *The Great U-Turn: Corporate Restructuring and the Polarization of America*. New York: Basic.

Hart, Michael. 1990. *A North American Free Trade Agreement: The Strategic Implications for Canada*. Ottawa: Centre for Trade Policy and Law and the Institute for Research on Public Policy.

———. 1992. *Trade—Why Bother?* Ottawa: Centre for Trade Policy and Law.

———. 1993. "Canadian Trade Policy and Globalization." *Policy Options*, January-February.

Hart, Michael with Bill Dymond and Colin Robertson. 1994. *Decision at Midnight: Inside the Canada–U.S. Free Trade Negotiations*. Vancouver: University of British Columbia Press.

Hayek, F.A. 1960. *The Constitution of Liberty*. London: Routledge and Kegan Paul.

Heap, Shaun Hargreaves. 1980/81. "World Profitability Crisis in the 1970s: Some Empirical Evidence." *Capital and Class* 12.

Heilbroner, Robert, and Lester Thurow. 1986. *Economics Explained*. New York: Touchstone.

Held, David. 1987. *Models of Democracy*. Stanford: Stanford University Press.

Henderson, Michael D. (ed.). 1987. *The Future on the Table: Canada and the Free Trade Issue*. North York, Ont.: Masterpress, York University.

Herman, Edward S. 1997. "Globalization in Question?" *Z Magazine*, April.

Himmelstein, Jerome L. 1983. "The New Right." In Wuthnow 1983.

Hobsbawm, Eric. 1995. *Age of Extremes: The Short Twentieth Century 1914–1991*. London: Abacus.

Hoover, Kenneth, and Raymond Plant. 1989. *Conservative Capitalism in Britain and the*

United States. London: Routledge.

Hoskins, Colin, and Stuart McFadyen. 1992. "The Mandate, Structure and Financing of the CBC." *Canadian Public Policy* 18.

Houle, François. 1990. "Economic Renewal and Social Policy." In Gagnon and Bickerton 1990.

Howe, Irving. 1983. "From Roosevelt to Reagan." *Dissent* 30(1).

Howlett, Michael, and M. Ramesh. 1992. *The Political Economy of Canada: An Introduction.* Toronto: McClelland and Stewart.

Howse, Robert. 1991. "Economic Integration or Political Fragmentation?" *The Network,* October.

———. 1996. *Securing the Canadian Economic Union: Legal and Constitutional Options for the Federal Government.* Toronto: C.D. Howe Institute.

Human Resources Development Canada. 1995. *Media Package.* December 1. Ottawa: HRDC.

———. 1996a. *Government of Canada Offers Provinces and Territories Responsibility for Active Employment Measures.* News release. 30 May. Ottawa: HRDC.

———. 1996b. *Getting Canadians Back to Work.* 30 May. Otttawa: HRDC.

Hueglin, Thomas O. 1990. *A Political Economy of Federalism: In Search of a New Comparative Perspective with Critical Intent Throughout.* Kingston, Ont.: Institute of Intergovernmental Relations.

Hurtig, Mel. 1991. *The Betrayal of Canada.* Toronto: Stoddart.

———. 1992. *The Betrayal of Canada.* Second edition. Toronto: Stoddart.

Hutcheson, John. 1978. *Dominance and Dependency: Liberalism and National Policies in the North Atlantic Triangle.* Toronto: McClelland and Stewart.

Innis, Harold A. 1975. *The Fur Trade in Canada: An Introduction to Canadian Economic History.* Revised edition. Toronto: University of Toronto Press.

International Labout Organization. 1996. *World Employment 1996/97: National Policies in a Global Context.* Geneva: International Labout Organization.

Inwood, Gregory J. 1997. *Nationalism Versus Continentalism: Ideology in the Mirror of the Macdonald Royal Commission.* Unpublished Ph.D. dissertation, Department of Political Science, University of Toronto, Toronto.

Ismael, Jacqueline S. (ed.). 1987. *The Canadian Welfare State: Evolution and Transition.* Edmonton: University of Alberta Press.

Israelson, David. 1996. "The free trade lie." *The Toronto Star,* April 21.

Itoh, Makoto. 1992. "Japan in a New World Order." In Miliband and Panitch 1992.

Jackson, Andrew. 1992. "The Economic Union." In Cameron and Smith 1992.

Jenson, Jane. 1989. "'Different' But Not 'Exceptional': Canada's Permeable Fordism." *Canadian Review of Sociology and Anthropology* 26.

———. 1990. "Representations in Crisis: The Roots of Canada's Permeable Fordism." *Canadian Journal of Political Science* 23.

———. 1994. "Commissioning Ideas: Representation and Royal Commissions." In Philips 1994.

Jessop, Bob, Kevin Bonnett, Simon Bromley, and Tom Ling. 1988. *Thatcherism: A Tale of Two Nations.* Oxford: Polity Press.

Johnson, Andrew F. 1981. "A Minister as an Agent of Policy Change: The Case of Unemployment Insurance in the Seventies." *Canadian Public Administration* 24 (4).

———. 1988. "Canadian Social Services Beyond 1984: A Neo-Liberal Agenda." In Gollner and Salée 1988.

Johnson, Andrew F., Stephen McBride, and Patrick J. Smith (eds.). 1994. *Continuities and Discontinuities: The Political Economy of Social Welfare and Labour Market Policy in Canada.* Toronto: University of Toronto Press.

Johnson, Andrew, and Andrew Stritch. 1996a. *Canadian Public Policy: Globalization and Political Parties.* Toronto: Copp Clark.

————. 1996b. "Epilogue: Globalization and Canadian Public Policy at the End of the Twentieth Century." In Johnson and Stritch 1996a.

Johnson, A.W. 1992. "A National Government in a Federal State." In Cameron and Smith 1992.

Jones, L.R. 1986. "Financial Restraint Management and Budget Control in Canadian Provincial Governments." *Canadian Public Administration* 29 (2).

Justice, Department of. 1997. *Reference to the Supreme Court of Canada: Summary of the Government of Canada's Position.* Ottawa: Department of Justice.

Keane, John. 1988. *Democracy and Civil Society.* London: Verso.

Kennett, Steven A. 1995. "The Environmental Management Framework Agreement: Reforming Federalism in Post-Referendum Canada." *Resources: The Newsletter of the Canadian Institute of Resources Law* 52 (Fall).

Kernaghan, Kenneth, and David Siegel. 1991. *Public Administration in Canada.* Second edition. Scarborough, Ont.: Nelson Canada.

Keynes, John M. 1936. *The General Theory of Employment, Interest and Money.* New York: Harcourt, Brace and World.

King, Desmond S. 1987. *The New Right: Politics, Markets and Citizenship.* Chicago: Dorsey Press.

Klein, Naomi. 1997. "The Secret Treaty the Government Doesn't Want You to Know About." *This Magazine*, May/June.

Klein, Seth. 1996. "Good Sense Versus Common Sense: Canada's Debt Debate and Competing Hegemonic Projects." Unpublished M.A. thesis, Department of Political Science, Simon Fraser University, Vancouver.

Kopinak, Kathryn. 1993. "The Maquiladorization of the Mexican Economy." In Grinspun and Cameron 1993.

Krehm, William. 1993. *A Power Unto Itself: The Bank of Canada.* Toronto: Stoddart.

Kristol, Irving. 1978. *Two Cheers for Capitalism.* New York: Basic.

Kroeger, Arthur. 1996. "Changing Course: The Federal Government's Program Review of 1994–95." In Armit and Bourgeault 1996.

Kudrle, Robert T., and Theodore R. Marmor. 1981. "The Development of Welfare States in North America." In Flora and Heidenheimer 1981.

Kuttner, Robert. 1991. *The End of Laissez-Faire: National Purpose and the Global Economy After the Cold War.* Philadelphia: University of Pennsylvania Press.

Lachapelle, Guy. 1988. "Between Income Security and Family Equalization." In Gollner and Salée 1988.

Laforest, Guy. 1995. *Trudeau and the End of a Canadian Dream.* Montreal: McGill-Queen's University Press.

Lalonde, Marc. 1992. "Riding the Storm: Energy Policy, 1968–1984." In Axworthy and Trudeau 1992a.

Langille, David. 1987. "The Business Council on National Issues and the Canadian State." *Studies in Political Economy: A Socialist Review* (Autumn).

Laux, Jeanne Kirk. 1991. "Shaping or Serving Markets? Public Ownership after Privatization." In Drache and Gertler 1991a.

Laxer, Gordon. 1989. *Open For Business: The Roots of Foreign Ownership in Canada*. Toronto: Oxford University Press.

———. 1992. "Constitutional Crisis and Continentalism: Twin Threats to Canada's Continued Existence." *Canadian Journal of Sociology* 17(2).

Laxer, James. 1984. *Rethinking the Economy: The Laxer Report on Canadian Economic Problems and Policies*. Toronto: New Canada Press.

———. 1986. *Leap of Faith: Free Trade and the Future of Canada*. Edmonton: Hurtig.

———. 1987. "Free Trade and Canada's Choice of an Economic Model." In Henderson 1987.

———. 1993. *False God: How the Globalization Myth Has Impoverished Canada*. Toronto: Lester.

Laxer, Robert M. 1973. *Canada Ltd.: The Political Economy of Dependency*. Toronto: McClelland and Stewart.

Leslie, Peter M. 1987. *Federal State, National Economy*. Toronto: University of Toronto Press.

Levitt, Kari. 1970. *Silent Surrender: The Multinational Corporation in Canada*. Toronto: Macmillan.

Leys, Colin. 1980. "Neo-Conservatism and the Organic Crisis in Britain." *Studies in Political Economy: A Socialist Review* 4 (Autumn).

Liberal Party of Canada. 1993. *Creating Opportunity: The Liberal Plan for Canada* (Red Book). Ottawa: Liberal Party of Canada.

Lipsey, Richard G. 1988. "The Free Trade Agreement in Context." In Gold and Leyton-Brown 1988.

———. 1996. *Economic Growth, Technological Change, and Canadian Economic Policy*. Toronto: C.D. Howe Institute.

———. 1987. "The Economics of a Canadian–American Free Trade Association." In Henderson 1987.

Lipsey, Richard G., and Robert C. York. 1988. *Evaluating the Free Trade Deal: A Guided Tour Through the Canada–U.S. Agreement*. C.D. Howe Institute, Policy Study No. 6. Toronto: Prentice-Hall Canada.

Lithwick, Harvey. 1982. "Regional Policy: The Embodiment of Contradictions." In Doern 1982.

Livingstone, David. 1996. "Wasted Education and Withered Work: Reversing the 'Postindustrial' Education-Jobs Optic." In Dunk, McBride and Nelsen 1996.

Lustig, Nora, Barry P. Bosworth, and Robert Z. Lawrence (eds.). 1992. *North American Free Trade: Assessing the Impact*. Washington: Brookings Institution.

MacDonald, L.R. 1975. "Merchants Against Industry: An Idea and Its Origins." *The Canadian Historical Review* 56(3).

MacDonald, Martha. 1991. "Post-Fordism and the Flexibility Debate." *Studies in Political Economy: A Socialist Review* 36.

McDonald, Marci. 1996. "Mexico's Peso Crisis." *The Canadian Encyclopedia Plus*. Toronto: McClelland and Stewart.

MacDonald, Wendy. 1983. "Restraint and Retrenchment in Government: Policy and Practice in Canada, Britain, and the United States." M.Sc. essay, London School of Economics, London.

Macpherson, C.B. 1962. *The Political Theory of Possessive Individualism*. Oxford: Oxford University Press.

———. 1980. *Burke*. Oxford: Oxford University Press.

Magdoff, Harry. 1992. "Globalization—To What End?" In Miliband and Panitch 1992.

Mahon, Rianne. 1990. "Adjusting to Win? The New Tory Training Initiative." In Graham 1990.

Mallory, J.R. 1954. *Social Credit and the Federal Power in Canada.* Toronto: University of Toronto Press.

Mandel, Ernest. 1973. *Capitalism and Regional Disparities.* Toronto: New Hogtown Press.

Mandel, Michael. 1989. *The Charter of Rights and the Legalization of Politics in Canada.* Toronto: Wall and Thompson.

———. 1994. *The Charter of Rights and the Legalization of Politics in Canada.* Revised edition. Toronto: Wall and Thompson.

Manley, John, and Paul Martin. 1994. *Growing Small Business.* Ottawa: Departments of Finance and Industry.

Marchak, M. Patricia. 1981. *Ideological Perspectives on Canada.* Second edition. Toronto: McGraw-Hill Ryerson.

———. 1988. *Ideological Perspectives on Canada.* Third edition. Toronto: McGraw-Hill Ryerson.

———. 1991. *The Integrated Circus: The New Right and the Restructuring of Global Markets.* Montreal and Kingston: McGill-Queen's University Press.

Marr, William L., and Donald G. Paterson. 1980. *Canada: An Economic History.* Toronto: Gage.

Marsh, Leonard. 1943. *Report on Social Security for Canada.* Reprinted 1975. Toronto: University of Toronto Press.

Martin, Paul. 1994a. *Budget Speech.* Ottawa: Department of Finance.

———. 1994b. *Facing Choices Together: Response to Pre-Budget Consultations.* Ottawa: Department of Finance.

———. 1994c. *A New Framework for Economic Policy* (Purple Book). Ottawa: Department of Finance.

———. 1995. *Budget Speech.* Ottawa: Department of Finance.

———. 1996. *Budget Speech.* Ottawa: Department of Finance.

———. 1997. *Budget in Brief.* Ottawa: Department of Finance.

Maslove, Allan M. 1981. "Tax Expenditures, Tax Credits and Equity." In Doern 1981.

Maslove, Allan M., Michael J. Prince, and G. Bruce Doern. 1986. *Federal and Provincial Budgeting.* Toronto: University of Toronto Press.

McBride, Stephen. 1983. "Public Policy as a Determinant or Interest Gang Behaviour: The Canadian Labour Congress Corporatist Initiative, 1976–1978." *Canadian Journal of Political Science* 16.

———. 1985. "Corporatism, Public Policy and the Labour Movement." *Political Studies* 33.

———. 1986. "Mrs. Thatcher and the Postwar Consensus: The Case of Trade Union Policy." *Parliamentary Affairs* 39.

———. 1987. "Hard Times and the 'Rules of the Game': The Legislative Environment of Labour-Capital Conflict." In Argue, Gannagé and Livingstone 1987.

———. 1990. "The New Right's Political Economy: Ideology and Political Practice in Britain, Canada, and The United States." *Journal of History and Politics* 9.

———. 1991. "Authoritarianism Without Hegemony? The Politics of Industrial Relations in Britain." In Haiven, McBride and Shields 1991.

———. 1992. *Not Working: State, Unemployment, and Neo-Conservatism in Canada.*

Toronto: University of Toronto Press.

———. 1993. "Renewed Federalism as an Instrument of Competitiveness: Liberal Political Economy and the Canadian Constitution." *International Journal of Canadian Studies* 7–8 (Spring-Fall).

———. 1996a. "Coercion *and* Consent: The Recurring Temptation of Corporatism in Canadian Labour Relations." In Gonick and Phillips 1996.

———. 1996b. "The Continuity Crisis of Social Democracy: Ontario's Social Contract in Perspective." *Studies in Political Economy* 50.

McCarthy, Shawn. 1997. "Debt burden is next Liberal Target." *The Globe and Mail*, June 17.

McCullough, H.B. (ed.). 1989. *Political Ideologies and Political Philosophies*. Toronto: Wall and Thompson.

McDonald, Marcie. 1996. "Mexico's Peso Crisis." *The Canadian Encyclopedia Plus*. Toronto: McClelland and Stewart.

McDougall, John N. 1991. "North American Integration and Canadian Disunity." *Canadian Public Policy* 17(4).

McIlveen, Murray, and Hideo Mimoto. 1990. "The Federal Government Deficit, 1975–76 to 1988–89." Unpublished mimeograph. Ottawa: Statistics Canada.

McKay, David. 1989. *American Politics and Society*. Second edition. Oxford: Basil Blackwell.

McKinney, Joseph A., and M. Rebecca Sharpless (eds.). 1992a. *Implications of a North American Free Trade Region: Multidisciplinary Perspectives*. Ottawa: Carleton University Press.

———. 1992b. "Introduction." In McKinney and Sharpless 1992a.

McLellan, Anne. 1996. "Notes for a Speech to the Standing Committee on Natural Resources on the Main Estimates." 1 May 1996. Ottawa: Environment Canada.

McNally, David. 1981. "Staple Theory as Commodity Fetishism: Marx, Innis and Canadian Political Economy." *Studies in Political Economy: A Socialist Review* 6 (Autumn).

———. 1991. "Beyond Nationalism, Beyond Protectionism: Labour and the Canada–US Free Trade Agreement." *Capital and Class* 43 (Spring).

McNiven, Chris R. 1987. "Social Policy and Some Aspects of the Neoconservative Ideology in British Columbia." In Ismael 1987.

McQuaig, Linda. 1987. *Behind Closed Doors: How the Rich Won Control of Canada's Tax System*. Markham, Ont.: Viking.

———. 1995. *Shooting the Hippo*. Toronto: Viking.

McQueen, Rod (ed.). 1985. *Leap of Faith: The Macdonald Report*. Toronto: Cowan.

McRoberts, Kenneth. 1993. *Quebec: Social Change and Political Crisis*. Third edition. Toronto: McClelland and Stewart.

———. 1995. "Quebec: Province, Nation, or Distinct Society?" In Whittington and Williams 1995.

McRoberts, Kenneth, and Patrick Monahan (eds.). 1993. *The Charlottetown Accord, the Referendum and the Future of Canada*. Toronto: University of Toronto Press.

Meilke, Karl D. 1995. "Sizing Up the Canada–U.S. Dairy and Poultry Dispute." *Policy Options* 16(9).

Meltzer, Allan H. 1981. "Monetarism and the Crisis in Economics." In Bell and Kristol 1981.

Merrett, Christopher D. 1996. *Free Trade: Neither Free Nor About Trade*. Montreal:

Black Rose.

Microsoft. 1996. "World Trade Organization." *Microsoft Encarta 97 Encyclopedia.* New York: Microsoft Corporation.

Miliband, Ralph, and John Saville (eds.). 1980. *The Socialist Register 1980.* London: Merlin Press.

Miliband, Ralph, Leo Panitch and John Saville (eds.). 1987. *The Socialist Register 1987: Conservatism in Britain and America: Rhetoric and Reality.* London: Merlin Press.

Miliband, Ralph, and Leo Panitch (eds.). 1992. *Socialist Register 1992: New World Order?* London: Merlin Press.

————. 1994. *Socialist Register 1994: Between Globalism and Nationalism.* London: Merlin Press.

Miller, David (ed.). 1987. *The Blackwell Encyclopedia of Political Thought.* Oxford: Basil Blackwell.

Milne, David. 1991. *The Canadian Constitution.* Toronto: James Lorimer.

Milne, William J. 1996. *The McKenna Miracle: Myth or Reality?* Toronto: University of Toronto Faculty of Management Series on Public Policy and Administration.

Ministry of Finance. 1997. "Budget Chartbook" (http://www.fin.gc.ca), March.

Mishra, Ramesh. 1987. "Public Policy and Social Welfare: The Ideology and Practice of Restraint in Ontario." In Ismael 1987.

————. 1990. *The Welfare State in Capitalist Society: Policies of Retrenchment and Maintenance in Europe, North America and Australia.* Toronto: University of Toronto Press.

Mittelstaedt, Martin. 1991. "Property-rights Plan under Fire." *The Globe and Mail,* October 2.

Monahan, Patrick J. 1991. *Meech Lake: The Inside Story.* Toronto: University of Toronto Press.

Morici, Peter. 1992. "The Twilight of the General Agreement on Tariffs and Trade, a North American Free Trade Agreement, and U.S.–Canadian Relations." In McKinney and Sharpless 1992a.

Moniere, Denis. 1981. *Ideologies in Quebec.* Toronto: University of Toronto Press.

Morley, David. 1992. "More Hard Times for Mexico's Poor." *The Globe and Mail,* August 24.

Moscovitch, Allan. 1990. "'Slowing the Steamroller': The Federal Conservatives, The Social Sector and Child Benefits Reform." In Graham 1990.

Moscovitch, Allan. 1988. "The Canada Assistance Plan: A 20 Year Assessment, 1966– 1986." in Catherine A. Graham (ed.) *How Ottawa Spends 1988/89: The Conservatives Heading into the Stretch.* Ottawa: Carleton University Press.

Moscovitch, Allan, and Jim Albert (eds.). 1987. *The Benevolent State: The Growth of Welfare in Canada.* Toronto: Garamond.

Mullaly, Robert. 1994. "Social Welfare and the New Right: A Class Mobilization Perspective." In Johnson, McBride and Smith 1994.

————. 1997. "The Politics of Workfare: NB Works." In Shragge 1997.

Mulroney, Brian. 1993. "NAFTA Will Expand Free Trade Success." *Issues of the Day: Canadian Speeches* 6(10).

Munro, Gary. 1991. "The American Impact on Changes in Transportation Regulations in Canada." Paper presented at the Canadian Political Science Association Meetings, Queen's University, Kingston, Ontario.

Myles, John. 1996. "When Markets Fail: Social Welfare in Canada and the United States."

In Esping-Andersen 1996.

Naiman, Joanne. 1997. *How Societies Work: Class, Power and Change in Canadian Society*. Concord, Ontario: Irwin.

National Council of Welfare. 1991a. *The Canada Assistance Plan: No Time For Cuts*. Ottawa: National Council of Welfare.

————. 1991b. *Funding Health and Higher Education: Danger Looming*. Ottawa: National Council of Welfare.

————. 1994 *A Blueprint for Social Security Reform*. Ottawa: National Council of Welfare.

National Union of Public and General Employees. 1995. *Divided We Fall*. Ottawa: NUPGE.

————. 1996. *Employment Insurance Act 1995: Analysis of its Impacts*. Ottawa: NUPGE.

Naylor, Tom. 1975. *The History of Canadian Business, 1867–1914. Vol 1. The Banks and Finance Capital*. Toronto: James Lorimer.

————. 1973. "The History of Domestic and Foreign Capital in Canada." In Laxer 1973.

Network, The. Vol. 1, No. 4. University of Ottawa.

Norman, Wayne. 1991. "Network Seminar on Economics." In Network Seminar on the Constitution, *Taking Stock*. Ottawa.

Norrie, Kenneth, Richard Simeon, and Mark Krasnick. 1986. *Federalism and Economic Union in Canada*. Toronto: University of Toronto Press.

O'Connor, James. 1973. *The Fiscal Crisis of the State*. New York: St. Martin's Press.

————. 1986. *Accumulation Crisis*. Oxford: Basil Blackwell.

Offe, Claus. 1984a. *Contradictions of the Welfare State*. John Keane (ed). Cambridge, Mass.: MIT Press.

————. 1984b. "Competitive Party Democracy and the Keynesian Welfare State." In Offe 1984a.

————. 1984c. "Some Contradictions of the Modern Welfare State." In Offe 1984a.

Office of Labour Adjustment. 1992. *Report on Permanent and Indefinite Layoffs in Ontario*. DEcember. Toronto: Ontario Ministry of Labour.

Okun, Arthur M. 1970. *The Political Economy of Prosperity*. New York: W.W. Norton.

Ontario Federation of Labour. 1995. "Submission to the Ministry of Labour on Bill 7, The Labour Relations and Employment Statute Amendment Act 1995." Toronto: Ontario Federation of Labour.

Ontario, Government of. 1993a. *Ontario Budget 1993*. Toronto: Queen's Printer.

————. 1993b. *Jobs and Services: A Social Contract for the Ontario Public Sector*. Toronto: Queen's Printer.

Ontario Ministry of Intergovernmental Affairs. 1991. *A Canadian Social Charter: Making Our Shared Values Stronger*. Toronto: Queen's Printer.

Ontario Ministry of Labour. 1992. *Quarterly Report on Labour Market Developments in Ontario*. February. Toronto: Queen's Printer.

Ontario Ministry of Treasury and Economics. 1992. *Ontario Economic Outlook 1992-1996*. October. Toronto: Queen's Printer for Ontario.

Organization for Economic Development and Cooperation. 1996. *Employment Outlook, 1996*. Paris: Organization for Economic Development and Cooperation.

Ornstein, Michael. 1986. "The Political Ideology of the Canadian Capitalist Class." *Canadian Review of Sociology and Anthropology* 23.

O'Sullivan, Noel. 1987. "Conservatism." In Miller 1987.

Ouellet, André. 1983. *Labour and Labour Issues in the 1980's*. Ottawa: Labour Canada.

Pal, Leslie A. 1988. *State, Class and Bureaucracy: Canadian Unemployment Insurance and Public Policy*. Montreal and Kingston: McGill-Queen's University Press.

Palmer, John. 1980. "Economic Crisis." In Miliband and Saville 1980.

Panitch, Leo (ed.). 1977. *The Canadian State: Political Economy and Political Power*. Toronto: University of Toronto Press.

Panitch, Leo, and Don Swartz. 1988. *The Assault on Trade Union Freedoms: From Consent to Coercion Revisited*. Toronto: Garamond.

———. 1993. *The Assault on Trade Union Freedoms: From Wage Controls to Social Contract*. Toronto: Garamond.

Peters, Suzanne. 1995. *Exploring Canadian Values: Foundations for Well-Being*. CPRN Study No. F-01, Revised Version. Ottawa: Canadian Policy Research Networks.

Petter, Andrew. 1988. "Free Trade and the Provinces." In Gold and Leyton-Brown 1988.

Phillips, Susan D. (ed.). 1993. *How Ottawa Spends 1993–1994: A More Democratic Canada ...?* Ottawa: Carleton University Press.

———. 1994. *How Ottawa Spends 1994–1995: Making Change*. Ottawa: Carleton University Press.

Phillips, Paul. 1977. "Canadian Barons." *Canadian Dimension* 12(2).

Pitroda, Salil S. 1995. "From GATT to WTO: The Institutionalization of the World." *Harvard International Review* (Spring).

Piven, Frances Fox, and Richard E. Cloward. 1982. *The New Class War*. New York: Pantheon.

Porter, Michael E., and the Monitor Company. 1991. *Canada at the Crossroads: The Reality of a New Competitive Environment*. Toronto: Business Council on National Issues and Government of Canada.

Pratt, Larry. 1982. "Energy: The Roots of National Policy." *Studies in Political Economy: A Socialist Review* 7 (Winter).

Prince, Michael J. (ed.). 1987a. *How Ottawa Spends 1987–88: Restraining the State*. Toronto: Methuen.

———. 1987b. "Restraining the State: How Ottawa Shrinks." In Prince 1987a.

———. 1991. "From Meech Lake to Golden Pond: The Elderly, Pension Reform and Federalism in the 1990's." In Abele 1991.

Pritchard, Timothy. 1992. "Detroit's Big Three Take the Victory Lap." *The Globe and Mail*, August 15.

Pulkingham, Jane, and Gordon Ternowetsky (eds.). 1996. *Remaking Canadian Social Policy: Social Security in the Late 1990s*. Halifax: Fernwood.

Raboy, Marc. 1990. *Missed Opportunities: The Story of Canada's Broadcasting Policy*. Montreal and Kingston: McGill-Queen's University Press.

Rae, Bob. 1991. "Message From the Premier." In Ontario Ministry of Intergovernmental Affairs 1991.

———. 1993. *Statement to the Ontario Legislature Regarding the North American Free Trade Agreement*. October 13. Toronto: Queen's Printer.

Randall, Stephen J. et al. (eds.). 1992. *North America Without Borders*? Calgary: University of Calgary.

Rehnby, Nadene, and Stephen McBride. 1997. *Help Wanted: Economic Security for Youth*. Ottawa: Canadian Centre for Policy Alternatives.

Reeves, M.A., and W.A. Kerr. 1986. "Implications of the Increasing Emphasis on Monetary Policy for the Federal State: The Case of Canada." *Journal of Commonwealth and Comparative Politics* 24.

Resnick, Philip. 1982. "The Maturing of Canadian Capitalism." *Our Generation* 15(3).
———. 1989. "The Ideology of Neo-Conservatism." In McCullough 1989.
———. 1990. *The Masks of Proteus: Canadian Reflections on the State*. Montreal and
     Kingston: McGill-Queen's University Press.
Roberts, Wayne. 1977. "More on Naylor." *This Magazine* 11(3).
Robertson, David B., and Dennis R. Judd. 1989. *The Development of American Public
     Policy*. Glenview, Ill.: Scott, Foresman.
Robinson, Ian. 1993. "NAFTA, Democracy and Continental Economic Integration: Trade
     Policy as if Democracy Mattered." In Phillips 1993.
Rocher, François. 1991. "Canadian Business, Free Trade and the Rhetoric of Economic
     Continentalization." *Studies in Political Economy: A Socialist Review* 35 (Summer).
Rocher, Francois, and Christian Rouillard. 1997. "Using the Concept of Deconcentration
     to Overcome the Centralization/Decentralization Dichotomy: Thoughts on Recent
     Constitutional and Political Reform." In Fafard and Brown 1997.
Roxborough, Ian. 1981. *The Theories of Underdevelopment*. London: Macmillan.
Ruggeri, G.C. 1987. *The Canadian Economy: Problems and Policies*. Third edition.
     Toronto: Gage.
Ruggiero, Renato. 1996. "Beyond Borders: Managing a World of Free Trade and Deep
     Interdependence." Address by the Director General of the World Trade Organization
     to the Argentinian Council on Foreign Relations in Buenos Aires, World Trade
     Organization Press Release #55, 10 September.
Russell, Bob. 1987. "The Welfare State in the Aftermath of Keynes." Mimeo. Department
     of Sociology, University of Saskatchewan, Saskatoon.
———. 1990. *Back to Work? Labour, State and Industrial Relations in Canada*.
     Scarborough, Ont.: Nelson.
———. 1991a. "Assault without Defeat: Contemporary Industrial Relations and the
     Canadian Labour Movement." In Haiven, McBride and Shields 1991.
———. 1991b. "The Welfare State and the Politics of Constraint." In Bolaria 1991.
———. 1997. "Reinventing A Labour Movement?" In Carroll 1997.
Russell, Peter H., Rainer Knopff, and Ted Morton. 1989. *Federalism and the Charter:
     Leading Constitutional Decisions*. Ottawa: Carleton University Press.
Ryerson, Stanley B. 1973. *Unequal Union*. Toronto: Progress.
Sack, Goldblatt, Mitchell. 1996. "A Guide to the Labour Relations Act Amendment—Bill
     7." Toronto: Ontario Federation of Labour.
———. 1995. "Client Memorandum Re: Social Contract Act 1993 (Bill-48)." Mimeo.
     Toronto.
Safarian, A.E. 1974. *Canadian Federalism and Economic Integration*. Ottawa: Privy
     Council Office.
Salutin, Rick. 1997. "The Vision Thing." *This Magazine*, May/June.
Samuelson, Paul. 1983. "Sympathy from the Other Cambridge." *The Economist*, June 25.
Sanger, Matt. 1993. "A Tool to Dismantle the Public Sector." *Canadian Forum*, January-
     February.
Saunders, John. 1992. "NAFTA Signing 'Unlikely' before U.S. Elections: Hills." *The
     Globe and Mail*, July 29.
Savage, Stephen P., and Lynton Robins (eds.). 1990a. *Public Policy Under Thatcher*.
     London: Macmillan.
———. 1990b. "Introduction." In Savage and Robins 1990a.
Savoie, Donald J. 1992. *Regional Economic Development: Canada's Search for Solu-*

tions. Second edition. Toronto:University of Toronto Press.

Schultz, Richard. 1988. "Regulating Conservatively: The Mulroney Record, 1984–1988." In Gollner and Salée 1988.

Schott, Jeffrey J. 1995. "Paths to Hemispheric Integration." *Policy Options* 16(9).

Sherman, Howard. 1983. *Stagflation: An Introduction to Traditional and Radical Macroeconomics*. Second edition. New York: Harper and Row.

Shields, John. 1990. "Democracy Versus Leviathan: The State, Democracy and Neoconservatism." *Journal of History and Politics* 9.

———. 1991. "Building a New Hegemony in British Columbia: Can Neo-Conservative Industrial Relations Succeed?" In Haiven, McBride and Shields 1991.

———. 1996. "Flexible Work, Labour Market Polarization, and the Politics of Skills Training and Enhancement." In Dunk, McBride and Nelsen 1996.

Shields, John, and Bob Russell. 1994. "The Welfare State and the New Labour Market Relations: The Case of Part-Time Workers." In Johnson, McBride and Smith 1994.

Shniad, Sid. 1992. "GATT, the Canada–U.S. Free Trade Agreement and NAFTA: Economic Restructuring and the Corporate Game Plan." *Socialist Studies Bulletin* 29 (July-September).

Shragge, Eric (ed.). 1997. *Workfare: Ideology for a New Underclass*. Toronto: Garamond.

Shragge, Eric, and Marc-André Deniger. 1997. "Workfare in Québec." In Shragge 1997.

Siegel, Arthur. 1983. *Politics and the Media in Canada*. Toronto: McGraw-Hill Ryerson.

Silver, Susan. 1996. "The Struggle for National Standards: Lessons From the Federal Role in Health Care." In Pulkingham and Ternowetsky 1996.

Simeon, Richard. 1987a. "Inside the Macdonald Commission." *Studies in Political Economy: A Socialist Review* 22.

———. 1987b. "Federalism and Free Trade." In Henderson 1987.

———. 1988. "Meech Lake and Shifting Conceptions of Canadian Federalism." *Canadian Public Policy* 14 (Supplement).

———. 1989. "Parallelism in the Meech Lake Accord and the Free Trade Agreement." In Whyte and Peach 1989.

———. 1991. "Globalization and the Canadian Nation-State." In Doern and Purchase 1991a.

Simeon, Richard, and Ian Robinson. 1990. *State, Society, and the Development of Canadian Federalism*. Toronto: University of Toronto Press.

Simeon, Richard, and Mary Janigan (eds.). 1991. *Toolkits and Building Blocks: Constructing a New Canada*. Toronto: C.D. Howe Institute.

Simpson, Jeffrey. 1995. *The Globe and Mail*, January 27.

Simpson, Jeffrey. 1992. "Rude Awakening on Manpower Coming As We Doze through the Big Debate." *The Globe and Mail*, June 25.

Sinclair, Jim (ed.). 1992. *Crossing the Line: Canada and Free Trade with Mexico*. Vancouver: New Star.

Sinclair, Scott. 1993. "Shifting Power from the Provinces to Foreign Companies." *Canadian Forum*, January-February.

Smiley, Donald V. 1967. *The Canadian Political Nationality*. Toronto: Methuen.

———. 1975. "Canada and the Quest for a National Policy." *Canadian Journal of Political Science* 8(1).

———. 1988. "A Note on Canadian–American Free Trade and Canadian Political Autonomy." In Gold and Leyton-Brown 1988.

Spratt, Susan. 1992. "The Selfishness of 'Free' Trade." *Perception* 16(4).

Stanbury, William T. 1988. "Privatization and the Mulroney Government, 1984–1988."
    In Gollner and Salée 1988.
Stanford, J.O. 1990. *Stopping the Privatization of Petro-Canada: Redefining Public
    Ownership*. Ottawa: Canadian Centre for Policy Alternatives.
Stanford, Jim. 1995. "The Economics of Debt and the Remaking of Canada." *Studies in
    Political Economy* 48 (Autumn).
Stanford, Jim, Christine Elwell, and Scott Sinclair. 1993. *Social Dumping Under North
    American Free Trade*. Ottawa: Canadian Centre for Policy Alternatives.
Statistics Canada. 1984. *The Distribution of Wealth in Canada*. Catalogue 13–580.
    Ottawa: Statistics Canada.
———. 1992. *The Daily*. June 22. Ottawa: Statistics Canada.
———. 1993. "The Duration of Unemployment During Boom and Bust." *Canadian
    Economic Observer*, September.
Stevenson, Brian J.R. 1995. "Canada–Mexico Relations After NAFTA." *Policy Options*
    16(9).
Stevenson, Garth. 1977. "Federalism and the Political Economy of the Canadian State."
    In Panitch 1977.
———. 1981. "The Political Economy Tradition and Canadian Federalism." *Studies in
    Political Economy: A Socialist Review* 6 (Autumn).
———. 1988. "The Agreement and the Dynamics of Canadian Federalism." In Gold and
    Leyton-Brown 1988.
Stewart, Ian A. 1991. "How Much Government Is Good Government?" In Doern and
    Purchase 1991a.
———. 1992. "Global Transformation and Economic Policy." In Axworthy and Trudeau
    1992a.
Strick, John C. 1990. *The Economics of Government Regulation: Public Policy and Public
    Corporations in Canada*. Halifax: Institute for Research on Public Policy.
Struthers, James. 1983. *No Fault of Their Own: Unemployment and the Canadian Welfare
    State, 1914–1941*. Toronto: University of Toronto Press.
———. 1996. *Can Workfare Work? Reflections From History*. Ottawa: Caledon Institute
    of Social Policy.
Swimmer, Gene. 1987. "Changes to Public Service Labour Legislation: Revitalizing or
    Destroying Collective Bargaining." In Prince 1987a.
——— (ed.). 1997. *How Ottawa Spends 1997–98; Seeing Red: A Liberal Report Card*.
    Ottawa: Carleton University Press.
Taylor, Malcolm. 1987. "The Canadian Health Care System After Medicare." In Coburn
    1987.
Taylor, D. Wayne. 1991. *Business and Government Relations: Partners in the 1990s*.
    Toronto: Gage.
Teeple, Gary. 1995. *Globalization and the Decline of Social Reform*. Toronto: Garamond.
Teichman, Judith. 1993. "Dismantling the Mexican State and the Role of the Private
    Sector." In Grinspun and Cameron 1993.
Ternowetsky, Gordon W. 1987. "Controlling the Deficit and a Private Sector Led
    Recovery: Contemporary Themes of the Welfare State." In Ismael 1987.
Therborn, Goran. 1984. "Classes and States: Welfare State Developments, 1881–1981."
    Studies in Political Economy: A Socialist Review 14.
Thompson, Grahame. 1986. *The Conservatives' Economic Policy*. London: Croom Helm.
Trudeau, Pierre Elliot. 1989. "Who Speaks for Canada: Defining and Sustaining a

National Vision." In Behiels 1989.

Tupper, Allan. 1993. "Canada's National Policies: Reflections on 125 Years—A Commentary." *Canadian Public Policy* 19(3).

Tupper, Allan, and G. Bruce Doern (eds.). 1988. *Privatization, Public Policy and Public Corporations in Canada.* Halifax: Institute for Research on Public Policy.

United Electrical Workers. 1988. "Meech Lake Constitutional Item on the Corporate Agenda." *Canadian Dimension* 22(1).

Vickers, John, and George Yarrow. 1988. *Privatization: An Economic Analysis.* Cambridge, Mass.: MIT Press.

Vierhaus, Rudolf. 1973. "Conservatism." In Wiener 1973.

Walker, Michael. 1993. "Fewer Manufacturing Jobs Mean Greater Prosperity." *Issues of the Day: Canadian Speeches* 6(10).

Warnock, John W. 1988. *Free Trade and the New Right Agenda.* Vancouver: New Star.

———. 1993. "Buying Democracy." *Canadian Forum*, November.

Watkins, Mel. 1967. "A Staple Theory of Economic Growth." In Easterbrook and Watkins 1967.

———. 1980a. "The Staple Theory Revisited." In Grayson 1980.

———. 1980b. "A Staple Theory of Capitalist Growth." Paper presented at a Three Nations Conference—Dimensions of Dependency, Australia. November.

———. 1992. *Madness and Ruin: Politics and the Economy in the Neoconservative Age.* Toronto: Between the Lines.

———. 1997. "Canadian Capitalism in Transition." In Clement 1997.

Watts, Ronald L. 1991. "Canada's Constitutional Options: An Outline." In Watts and Brown 1991.

Watts, Ronald L., and Douglas M. Brown (eds.). 1991. *Options for a New Canada.* Toronto: University of Toronto Press.

Weaver, R. Kent (ed.). 1992. *The Collapse of Canada?* Washington: Brookings Institution.

Weller, Geoffrey R. 1996. "Strengthening Society I: Health Care." In Johnson and Stritch 1996a.

Whitaker, Reg. 1987. "Neo-Conservatism and the State." In Miliband Panitch and Saville 1987.

Whittington, Michael S., and Glen Williams (eds.). 1990. *Canadian Politics in the 1990s.* Third edition. Scarborough, Ont.: Nelson Canada.

———. 1995. *Canadian Politics in the 1990s.* Fourth edition. Toronto: Nelson Canada.

Whyte, John D., and Ian Peach (eds.). 1989. *Re-Forming Canada? The Meaning of the Meech Lake Accord and the Free Trade Agreement for the Canadian State.* Kingston: Institute of Intergovernmental Relations.

Wiener, Philip P. (ed.). 1973. *Dictionary of the History of Ideas: Studies of Selected Pivotal Ideas, Vol. 1.* New York: Charles Scribner's.

Wilkinson, Bruce W. 1996. "General Agreement on Tariffs and Trade." *The Canadian Encyclopedia Plus.* Toronto: McClelland and Stewart.

Williams, A. Paul. 1989. "Access and Accountability in the Canadian Welfare State: The Political Significance of Contacts Between State, Labour and Business Leaders." *Canadian Review of Sociology and Anthropology* 26.

Williams, Glen. 1979. "The National Policy Tariffs: Industrial Underdevelopment Through Import Substitution." *Canadian Journal of Political Science* 12(2).

———. 1988. "On Determining Canada's Location Within the International Political

Economy." *Studies in Political Economy: A Socialist Review* 25 (Spring).
———. 1994. *Not For Export: The International Competitiveness of Canadian Manufac-turing*. Third edition. Toronto: McClelland and Stewart.
Wilson, Michael. 1990. *Canada's Economic and Fiscal Performance and Prospects*. Ottawa: Department of Finance.
———. 1991. *The Budget*. Ottawa: Department of Finance.
Winsor, Hugh. 1992. "Mulroney Believes He Will Be Believed." *The Globe and Mail*, August 14.
Winham, Gilbert R. 1992. "Canada, GATT, and the Future of the World Trading System." In Hampson and Maule 1992.
Wolfe, Alan. 1981. "Sociology, Liberalism, and the Radical Right." *New Left Review* 128.
———. 1982. "The Crisis of Liberal Democracies—Part 1: The Crisis Unfolds." CBC Radio, January 4.
Wolfe, David A. 1984. "The Rise and Demise of the Keynesian Era in Canada: Economic Policy, 1930–1982." In Cross and Kealey 1984.
———. 1985. "The Politics of the Deficit." In Doern 1986.
———. 1992. "Technology and Trade: Finding the Right Mix." In Drache 1992.
Wood, Stephen (ed.). 1989a. *The Transformation of Work? Skill, Flexibility and the Labour Process*. London: Unwin Hyman.
———. 1989b. "The Transformation of Work?" In Wood 1989a.
Woods, H.D. 1968. *Canadian Industrial Relations: The Report of the Task Force on Labour Relations*. Ottawa: Information Canada.
———. 1973. *Labour Policy in Canada*. Second edition. Toronto: Macmillan.
Workman, Thom. 1996. *Banking on Deception: The Discourse of Fiscal Crisis*. Halifax: Fernwood.
World Bank. 1985. *World Development Report 1985*. New York: Oxford University Press.
World Trade Organization. n.d. "About the WTO." Available from World Trade Organi-zation (http://wto.org/about_wpf.html).
Wuthnow, Robert (ed.). 1983. *The New Christian Right*. New York: Aldine.
York, Geoffrey. 1992. "Defending the Definition of Poverty." *The Globe and Mail*, July 16.
Young, Robert A. 1991. "Effecting Change: Do We Have The Political System To Get Us Where We Want To Go?" In Doern and Purchase 1991a.
Zinser, Adolfo Aquilar. 1993. "Authoritarianism and North American Free Trade: The Debate in Mexico." In Grinspun and Cameron 1993.

Index